ERIC

ERIC

DORIS LUND

Perennial
An Imprint of HarperCollins*Publishers*

Note: Names of Ewing Eight patients who appear in this book have all been changed except for that of Eric's friend Michael.

Portions of this book have appeared in somewhat different form in *Good Housekeeping* ("Gift from a Son Who Died"), *Parents' Magazine* ("Growing Up Brave in Heart"), *Reader's Digest* ("Walk in the World for Me"), and *Swarthmore College Bulletin* ("Walk in the World for Me").

A hardcover edition of this book was published in 1974 by J. B. Lippincott Company.

HarperCollins books may be purchased for educational, business, or sales promotional use. For information please write: Special Markets Department, HarperCollins Publishers Inc., 10 East 53rd Street, New York, NY 10022.

First Perennial Library edition, 1989.
First Perennial edition published 2000.

Library of Congress Cataloging-in-Publication Data is available.

ISBN 0-06-095637-2

00 01 02 03 04 ❖/RRD 10 9 8 7 6 5 4 3 2 1

For Mary Lou and for Dr. D.—Monroe Dowling
—who stayed with it all the way.

Words on the blackboard in Eric's room
during his last year:

> *We are all in the same boat, in a stormy sea, and
> we owe each other a terrible loyalty.*

—G. K. CHESTERTON

CHAPTER 1

GOOD FRIENDS HAVE SAID, "But how did it begin? You must have seen it coming."

No one could have seen it coming. This had been a summer like many others. We live in a small Connecticut town in a house just a block from the beach, so our vacations are usually spent at home, swimming, picnicking, patching up small boats. And the front hall that September was, as usual, full of sand, mysterious towels that didn't belong to us, and an assortment of swimming fins, soccer balls, and basketballs. Like many mothers, I was half longing for school to start, half dreading it. Our twenty-year-old daughter, Meredith, had been married for two years and lived a thousand miles away. Now Eric, seventeen, was packed and ready to go off for his freshman year at the University of Connecticut. We would still have fourteen-year-old Mark and ten-year-old Lisa at home. With Eric gone, there would be fewer kicked-off shoes in the living room, fewer crumbs and Coke bottles scattered around. Yet now and then, a glimpse of him running past our bedroom door would start me feeling wistful.

One late afternoon as I went through the house watering the plants, I found Eric stretched out on the living room couch. I knew he'd been running earlier up at the high school track, yet there was something now in his languid sprawl that made me pause. It was rare to see Eric lying down.

"Mom," he said, "I don't feel right. I haven't got it when I run. And my head hurts a little."

Scarcely more than a week ago he'd had the complete physical for entering freshmen—blood tests, X-rays, the works—and he'd passed it all without a single hitch.

"Does your throat hurt? Or your stomach?"

"No. I've just got a headache."

Tension, I thought. Going to college is the big jump. Only two days away. He'd been a star in a small arena. Class officer, member of the special Key Club, the Drama Club, but more than all this a soccer hero. The game hadn't come easily for him, though. In our town, Greek and Hungarian boys dribble soccer balls as soon as they climb out of their cribs.

"That Phil Kydes," I remember Eric saying mournfully. "He's got about a twelve-year start on me. I could practice twenty-four hours a day and never catch up. What a player! When I'm on a field with Kydes and Sahnas and Marmanides, it feels so great. I have such respect for guys like that."

But Eric had studied the game and driven himself to the point where he, too, was respected at last. They called him "the blond Greek," and this made him proud. They were a good team. Three times they took the county title in a playoff against their traditional rivals in neighboring Westport. Usually they made it to the state finals, and once they won the championship for the whole state of Connecticut. The mayor of our town and the governor had attended the banquet that celebrated this event.

Now, as a college freshman, he'd be starting all over at the bottom. There would be more Greeks, more Hungarians, more talent from all over the state coming to the big university. There would certainly be a struggle for places on the team.

And there was something else. While soccer filled Eric's world at the moment, and he enjoyed dressing and acting the part of the casual jock, he knew there was more to come. College asks the big questions, or at least makes you ask them of yourself. His father had been a brilliant student, graduating from college with many honors. He was also a powerful six-foot-four-inch champion athlete. Eric had always been a thin little fellow until he started to train for sports. Although he'd shot up in the past two years, he surely wouldn't be taller than six-foot-one or -two. In many ways, Sidney was a hard man for Eric to follow.

I was thinking of these things as I poured the last drops of water on the jade plant. What I said was, "I think maybe you've been pushing yourself too hard, Eric. It's awfully hot and muggy anyway. Why don't you ease up? I'm sure you're going to make it at school."

He gave me the look that sons have given mothers for a thousand years. To avoid more conversation, he went out on the porch and lay down again to wait for supper.

The following afternoon Eric and I both wanted the car at the same moment. He wasn't languid now. He was dressed for action: soccer shorts, Adidas running shoes. "I've *got* to run at the track, Mom. I've only got two more days and I'm not in shape."

I was holding a sheaf of corrected type proofs Sidney had left for me to take to the printer. He was on a business trip. A few months before, he had been "reorganized" out of his job after seventeen years with the same firm in New York. Now I was trying to help him; we were both free-lancing—writing, drawing, doing everything we could to keep the boat afloat. Clearly work outranks sports, but Eric had his need.

"Look, you drive us to the field," I said. "Then I'll take the car and go to the printer's. I'll do a few other errands and pick you up later."

"Okay." He scowled to show me it was a compromise, got in, and started the car. The top was down and late summer sun poured warmth on our shoulders. I stole a look at Eric, thinking how I'd miss him when he was off at school. His hair, usually goldfish colored, was now a sun-bleached yellow. His eyebrows were almost white. And the hairs on his powerful legs gleamed gold against deep tan. Then I saw something on his leg—an ugly red sore, big and round as a silver dollar. There was another farther down. And another on his other leg.

"Eric! What have you got on your legs?"

"I dunno. Little infection, maybe." He shrugged.

"It doesn't look little to me. Impetigo is what it looks like. That's no joke. We'd better go to the doctor's right now."

"Mom! For God's sake!" He was furious.

"Listen, Eric, impetigo spreads like mad. They aren't even going to let you in the locker room with that on your legs, if that's what it is. We've got two days before you go away. Let's get the doctor to clear it up now."

"All right," he muttered. We drove straight past the high school playing field, the track where Eric loved to work out. He didn't even glance at it. He swung the car hard left at the traffic light. It was the first turn in the long road that lay ahead.

The sores on Eric's legs did not look like impetigo to our doctor. He told his nurse to call the hospital and to arrange to have Eric admitted for tests the next morning. "Be there at eight, Eric," she said.

Eric nodded and swung through the waiting room full of mothers and little children. He slammed the door as hard as he could.

I turned back to the doctor. "What tests? Everything was fine when he had his physical, wasn't it? That was just twelve days ago!"

"I want them to rerun some of the blood tests," said the doctor. "I've also ordered a bone marrow—"

I blanked out the words "bone marrow" instantly as if I'd never heard them before in my life, as if I'd never read a single book or magazine article or watched a single TV medical drama which spelled out in the plainest possible terms exactly what a doctor was looking for when he ordered a bone marrow. After all, there was that perfect physical exam only twelve days before . . .

Yet the next afternoon when the phone rang, my heart lurched as if I'd been shot. I'd been sitting right by the telephone, thinking of calling the doctor to ask about Eric's tests. Instead of dialing, however, I'd been drawing circles, spirals, on the little note pad on my bedside table. Now he was calling me. It rang. It rang. There was no way to undo this phone call.

I picked up the receiver. The doctor called me by my first name. He'd never done that before. There was a pause. Then I heard him say, "I'd like to talk to you and your husband together."

And I replied at once, "You don't have to. I already know. Eric has leukemia."

Once when I was nineteen and up at my family's summer house, we watched a huge thunderstorm come swiftly out of the mountains and march toward us across the lake. Bolt by bolt it seemed to be heading directly for our porch. I remember saying nervously, "They're getting the range!" With that the house was struck.

Now, many years later, sitting in my bedroom, still holding the telephone, that whole scene in the summer cottage, the same sensation, even the strange electrical smell returned at that moment. A tremendous flash split the world. The bolt entered the top of my skull as I got the message. Eric has leukemia. It was something happening right this minute in his bones. We'd been struck. It was ours.

I heard myself ask, "Do we have any time?"

"Oh, yes." The doctor's voice showed his relief that I was not, after all, being hysterical. "Six months. A year. Two years—"

Six months! Two years! Only yesterday he'd had forever, the immortality of being seventeen, when old age was something that happens to other people and you think your own summer will never end. The thought of his not living was so intolerable that I could almost feel my whole body leaping to defend against it. There must be some way out. How could we help him survive? If he had a tremendous goal to shoot for, wouldn't that make him fight to live? What did he love most? Surfing! The hot orange-pink poster of *The Endless Summer* had been on his door for months. I knew he'd seen the movie twice. Eric's dream was to catch the biggest, most perfect wave and ride it all the way to the beach.

"Can we take him someplace for Christmas vacation? I want him to have something wonderful. Can we go to Hawaii?"

"I think you can," said the doctor thoughtfully. "But first we have to get him in remission."

I was dazed, only half listening. I saw Eric in the sun, paddling out through the surf. Maybe Hawaii would make him well. Maybe it would be the endless summer after all. . . .

"—I've started him on massive doses of prednisone," the doctor was saying. "Also, I'm putting him on an antileukemic drug called mercaptopurine." There was a moment's pause. Then the doctor said, "Will you tell him? Or shall I?"

"Neither one," I said instantly. "Not yet." I was astonished to hear myself saying this, yet I was absolutely sure I was right.

The doctor demurred. "He's seventeen. He's bright. He's going to have to know."

"Of course he's going to have to know, but not now. Not yet."

There was no way to reach Sidney. I called two psychiatrists, both good friends, that afternoon and told them my news; I also told them what I'd decided to do. "Do you think this is right?" I asked. Both of them were so horrified to hear of Eric's illness that they could hardly speak to me. But both agreed I'd made the best decision. One said, "Let him come to the idea gradually. Let him get in remission first. If you tell him now, he might give up hope completely."

Hope! That was it. In a groping way I'd sensed I was on the right track. I wanted Eric to have hope, the ultimate wonder drug. It didn't make sense to give massive doses of cortisone or any other drug and give him total despair at the same time. Our first goal, then, was remission. I didn't know technically just what a remission was. But I'd read enough to know it was a good period of time, maybe lasting for weeks or months, when the disease was under control and retreated for a while. In remission you could live your life again.

"But what kind of leukemia does he have?" my friend was asking me.

"Kind? I didn't know there were different kinds. I don't know," I said. "But the doctor gave him six months to two years." That meant his leukemia was probably going to be fatal. I knew the scientists and doctors were working hard in their laboratories to come up with an answer. But in 1967 "six months to two years" was all they could promise us.

Sidney returned later that afternoon. We both remember the exact spot in the yard, the look of the trees, the strange pale color of the sky as I told him. All he said was, "Oh, really?" But I saw his face change. I think it changed forever in that moment. We turned and went into the house. Following him, staring at his scuffed briefcase, I thought absently, he really needs a new one. Then it hit me. My God, he doesn't have a real job! We don't have any Major Medical! And we're going to need lots of money. I'd been able to think of nothing but "Eric is ill." Suddenly I began to see the down-to-earth problems.

Eric spent the night following his tests in a local hospital twenty miles away. When we drove over the following evening to bring him home, we found three high school friends in his room visiting him. Two were going on to a hockey game somewhere. The other friend asked for a ride back with us. Our talk on the drive back was casual. But when we got home, Eric walked into the living room and sat down without turning on a light. Sidney disappeared into the kitchen. In the half-dark I could see two days of unopened mail spilling off the pine chest. None of us had picked up a single newspaper or magazine. There were coffee cups and Coke bottles here and there. An ashtray overflowed with butts and the curly peel of a tangerine. In the center of the room one of Eric's new suitcases lay open, its contents spilling out. I'd searched through it hurriedly the night before, trying to find his bathrobe and some clean pajamas to take to the hospital.

Eric sat in darkness in the wreckage and suddenly began to gasp with sobs. "I don't know what's happening. What's wrong with me? What have I got? Why can't I go to school?"

"You have anemia," I said at once. Sidney and I had agreed to tell him this for now. It would explain the necessity for blood tests twice a week, the visits to the doctor; even transfusions, if it came to that. "You know anemia is a blood disease. It makes you tired. That's why you've had headaches and trouble running. You can't go to school because the doctor has to check you every week, and also you have to take medication which may make you feel pretty sick for a while. But we've got a good doctor, and I'm sure we're going to get it under control."

Eric nodded and tried to stop gasping. In a few minutes he was calm enough to ask, "Can I go next term?"

"I certainly hope so." Goddammit, are we doing the right thing? I suddenly felt shaky, unsure.

"Let's take it a step at a time," I said. "And I've been thinking—it might help you to get back in shape if we all took a vacation at Christmas someplace warm where you could swim and surf. I've already asked the doctor about it. He thinks it's possible. I'm going to go over to the travel agent's tomorrow."

"That would be good." Eric spoke without feeling. His eyes had the look I'd seen in pictures of people who've somehow survived a giant earthquake or been blown clear of an explosion: How did this thing happen? What was I doing when I should have been watching out? His eyes asked these questions and many more. . . .

It was not going to be Christmas in Hawaii after all. Multiplying air fare times the five of us quickly brought us back to the beach of reality. The gaps between free-lance jobs had forced us to use some of our savings for everyday expenses. Still, I was hopeful that we could swing some sort of adventure for Eric. The Virgin Islands were nearer. I imagined crystal-clear waters, exotic fish. I saw Eric in the underwater sun, swimming like one of the fish.

Our graduation present to Eric had been a wet suit. He wore it on surfing trips to Rhode Island or some of the beaches out on Long Island. Once in a while when a storm managed to churn up passable waves on our own placid neighborhood beach, he'd put on his suit, get out his board, and try to ride. There were more spills than thrills. The best ride probably lasted forty feet, but it was good fun. The wet suit was really useful for spearfishing off our beach rocks, a sport he loved. He'd bought his own air tank but finally put it aside, thinking it unfair to the fish. It was a better game when he had to hold his breath, even if it meant he'd never get the big bass he wanted. Time and again a big striper faked him out, spinning off the point of his gun, escaping at the last minute.

I loved the beach, too, and was often able to watch the show from a distance. There was usually a pack of little boys trailing after Eric. When he was diving, they'd start clambering around the rocks or playing in shallow water, waiting to see him emerge, dripping, glistening, black as a seal, holding the wicked spear gun and sometimes a gaping fish.

"Eric! Eric! Whatcha got?"

"Just a blackfish."

Sometimes he chewed them out.

"Which one of you guys was paddling near me? Haven't I told you to stay clear when I'm diving? You saw me go in. Now look at the point on this gun. Peter! Tom! What if I mistook you for a fish and this thing went right in *here?*" He'd poke a finger sharply into a little brown chest. If he sounded fierce, it was because he cared. . . .

The travel agent was telling me now, however, that there was no way he could get us into the Virgin Islands at this late date.

"This late date? It's only the twelfth of September."

"I'm sorry." He explained. "Christmas is our biggest time. We've been sold out on air space since the first of August. And we've got quite a waiting list already."

I shook my head. I don't belong on this planet where people make reservations in June or July for a family Christmas several thousand miles away. How do they know the kids won't have chicken pox? How could we have known one of ours would have leukemia? That we would need reservations for an adventure?

"We ought to be able to go *somewhere.*"

"I can get you into the Dorado Hilton in Puerto Rico."

"All right." I felt let down. It sounded like Howard Johnson's. But at least it wouldn't have an orange roof. So we'd go to the whatever-it-is Hilton.

I'd forgotten that children see things differently. Ours had never been anywhere, really. Puerto Rico was foreign, and that was enough for them. They saw it poster fashion with brown-skinned natives, thatched huts, and lots of green jungly leaves. They spoke of catching monkeys and eating coconuts. In their innocence they dramatized, and I began to be happy. Even for Eric, who was watching the Pied Piper sweep all his friends away to school while he got left behind, the trip to Puerto Rico became the goal. If nothing more, it was swimming at Christmas. A time he would feel well again. And in September, he felt far from well.

My background had hardly prepared me to face the trials of Eric's illness with steadfast calm. I grew up with a thermometer in my mouth. In my family we never caught cold, we verged on pneumonia. The smallest blister was watched suspiciously for signs of blood poisoning. My father, who was a nervous humorist-cartoonist, had seventy-eight positively identified allergies (and another twenty-five or so which he was privately convinced of). He was even the author of a book entitled *The Happy Hypochondriac,* which featured on its cover a cartoon figure saying, "Mr. Herold, you look better." My cartoon father replies, "Well, I'm not."

It is possible that I married Sidney because he once told me that following his appendectomy (he was twenty-two at the time) he left the hospital on a ten-below-zero day and carried a heavy suitcase over bumpy, slippery ice about a mile back to his rooming house. Here was the invincible Viking I needed to father fearless children! Together we would turn the tide so that future generations might grow up ignorant of gargles, mustard plasters, and enema bags. I got exactly what I asked for, and I can hardly be sorry that my children turned out brave and confident. The only trouble was that now, when one of those children was struck by mortal illness, I was left with no one to commiserate with.

Sidney and I have always had very different conversational styles. I am more French than Nordic in temperament. (We even have a French ancestor in the family who wrote twenty-three French operas in the late 1770s, and Eric and I both looked very much like him.) I like everything out in the open—discussions, arguments, possibilities. With gestures. Sidney's Norwegian ancestry, engineering training, and Western upbringing all lead him naturally to understate. Where my family conjured up dangers and dragons, his had had to cope with real wilderness and real wild animals. His pioneer grandmother once spent a whole winter alone with a year-old baby (who was Sidney's mother), living in a cabin up on the Olympic Peninsula, miles from the nearest neighbors, in order to homestead a timber claim while her husband worked in a sawmill in town. Among her other tales of that winter was the time she had to set fire to her mop to chase a bear out of the cabin. Now, as Sidney and I faced disaster on our own doorstep, we found we had great difficulty talking about it.

One of our basic arguments has always been whether you can separate thoughts from feelings in ordinary husband-and-wife talking. I claim this is not only impossible, the very idea infuriates me. Sidney protests that this is exactly why he doesn't know what I'm talking about a lot of the time. If I said something about Eric's illness, he might ask if I spoke from fact or fear. And I might reply tearfully, irrationally, "What in God's name does it matter? Comfort me!" Leukemia, with all its unknowns, was a conversational bog for both of us. We made our way through it painfully day by day.

Eric played the edge coolly almost from the first. I think it helped keep him sane, though at first it almost drove me mad. I know it helped him stay physically and emotionally strong, but it often left me weak with worry. There was much that I didn't know. But from being an avid reader, and from having watched three friends lose relatives to leukemia, I knew a great deal about his real peril. I'd also been told that the full name of Eric's disease was acute lymphocytic leukemia, a type usually seen in small children. Leukemia, or cancer of the blood, can be acute or chronic. More typically, chronic leukemia is a disease of older people. In children under twelve the disease is usually acute, but it is these younger patients today who are getting the longer and longer remissions from modern drugs. Eric, at seventeen, had a poorer prognosis. And in Eric's case, "acute" was really an understatement. In the twelve short days between his perfect physical exam and our discovery of the sores on his legs, the disease had progressed so rapidly that the specialist who performed the bone marrow examination, sinking the long hollow needle into Eric's sternum, had a hard time finding sufficient marrow to examine. "I knew there was something terribly wrong," he told our doctor later, "before I even looked at the slides. It just didn't feel right. I wasn't getting anything."

Most bone marrow examinations, in fact about 99 percent, are performed in the hipbone. But in cases where speed of diagnosis is important, the sternum, or breastbone, is the preferred site. Such a procedure is much more dangerous, as a slip of the needle could puncture a lung. But the quality of marrow obtained is thought to be more indicative of the patient's true condition. Our own doctor said he suspected Eric had acute leukemia the minute he saw the multiple staphylococcus sores on his legs. The wild, immature white cells had crowded out the good cells, leaving him no defense. Infection had thus begun to spread rapidly through Eric's body. So, in addition to the prednisone and the antileukemic drug mercap-topurine, he had also been given an antibiotic to clear up the staph. The legs had healed quickly. But the doctor had told me a simple cold or passing virus could easily bring him down again. I'd also been cautioned to watch out for bruises, nosebleeds, or cuts or wounds of any sort that failed to stop bleeding. What an order for the parent of an athlete! Sidney understandably didn't want me to overprotect Eric. Eric, himself, hated coddling. So while I tried never to leave him alone in the house, at the same time I didn't want him to be aware of my hovering. When we went somewhere in the car together I had bath towels hidden in the trunk in case of severe nosebleeds. We all fumbled and struggled our way through hard days those first few weeks, as he got adjusted to the drugs and his new lonely situation.

There were times when he could hardly get out of bed, but he always managed to get downstairs once or twice to let Sancho, our little black dog, out to run. "Go on, Sancho! Run like hell, boy!"

Sancho would linger mournfully for a second or two just over the threshold, wagging his tail urgently, looking up at Eric with puzzled black eyes. They had always run together.

"Go on, dammit. *Run,* Sancho!"

Sancho then took off like a rocket, leaping hedges, roaring through Mrs. Bergamini's flowerbeds, flying after the Fays' cats who scattered into the treetops; and finally, with a last imploring circle around our driveway, Sancho streaked away, headed for the beach. Dogs are forbidden on our beach. Dogs, for that matter, are forbidden anywhere in our community off a leash.

"Eric, you know Sancho isn't supposed to run around alone. Why do you keep letting him out?"

"Somebody around here ought to run," he growled.

"Listen, he's already spent one weekend in the pound. He's a Wanted Dog! Do you realize there's a twenty-five-dollar fine for second offenders?"

"I'll pay it myself!" Eric glared at me. "You can't keep a dog like Sancho cooped up in the house." He stumbled back to bed. I sighed, knowing too well what he really meant.

Then along would come a day when Eric, surprisingly, would suddenly feel well. Then, like Sancho, he too escaped from the house as fast as possible and ran out into the world looking for life. Sometimes this change from illness to apparent good health came too swiftly for me. I remember one time when he'd been struggling with a vicious bout of nausea (one of the common side effects of the drugs). I started up the stairs to bring him a cup of weak tea. He passed me on the way down, wearing swim trunks, carrying his spear gun. Ignoring the tea, he said, "Maybe I'll get you a fish for supper."

There were other times during those first two months when I watched him go out to play pickup soccer, or basketball in a local evening league, knowing that he had a hemoglobin of only 5 or 6, a count so low that some patients begin to gasp for breath or feel faint. His basketball teammates were considerate; as they went galloping after the ball at the other end of the gym, they'd shout, "Stay there, Eric! We'll be right back." They didn't know what was wrong with him, then, although they knew he was ill.

There were times, too, when I regretted our decision not to tell Eric the whole truth. The mail was a problem; I tried to get to it before he might see it. Although I'd had quite a few long conversations with various officials at the University of Connecticut, explaining why Eric could not go to school, asking if we could get our tuition back, asking if he could go to college when he was well enough, and explaining that he did not know the true nature of his disease, I was afraid that some unfortunate letter might arrive, addressed to Eric Lund, which would baldly discuss the whole problem. The people I talked to were always very understanding, but a university is a big place. There was a chance that someone uninformed would write the wrong letter.

Something else worried me. Our town is very small, smaller than the usual commuter town. Neighbors can be friendly, good-hearted, curious, concerned; some of them are also just plain nosy. People stopped me in the market or the post office. "I see Eric's still at home—" "Has Eric decided not to go to college?" "Is Eric looking for some sort of job?" "Is Eric all right?"

Eric's face was, by this time, swollen with cortisone. His friends kidded him about putting on weight. He took their joshing pretty well. "You guys are just starving to death. You get the neck of the chicken, right? I get steak every night, hashed browns, the works." (This was partly true. In those days I cooked for Eric as if he were a visiting oil sheik. I served him steak—when he could eat—so often I was afraid he'd grow suspicious.) One evening he came in angry, however. "Some bastard just told me I look *better* fat. Now that's an insult!"

What worried me most was that some older busybody would guess the reason for his changed appearance and start some gossip that might get back to Eric. One day I ran into a former nurse I'd known slightly. We were in the library, and she zeroed in on me immediately. No escape. "My goodness, I saw Eric yesterday! What on earth's the matter with him? I was wondering—" Her voice boomed all over the quiet room.

I put a finger to my lips, shushing her, indicating the people around us trying to read. "Just a little problem; it's being taken care of," I whispered and fled. Well, I thought grimly as I got in the car, you wanted to lie. Now you've got to live it out.

The relief came a few days later. It had been eight weeks since we'd discovered Eric was ill. The phone rang at eleven thirty on a Thursday morning. Normally our doctor is a quiet-spoken, serious man. That morning he could not keep the jubilance out of his voice. "I've called to tell you Eric is in good remission," he said. We had achieved our first goal.

Since Sidney and I can't discuss trouble, neither can we shout for joy in the same breath. To him I seem flamboyant. To me he seems taciturn. On this good day, however, we went out to lunch at our favorite restaurant on the water. It was a quiet celebration. I remember saying, "I don't think we ought to tell Eric yet, though, do you? I mean—let *him* have some of the good time, too."

Sidney nodded. We touched glasses, silently toasting the future, daring to hope. Maybe Eric's remission will just last and last, I thought. Maybe he'll never have to know. . . .

A pair of mallards swam slowly by, their funny feet pushing backward, leaving ripples on the placid water. How comforting! We must have seen them like that hundreds of times—the showy male in front, the dowdy brown female paddling meekly behind as usual. Watching them, I began to unwind. The world steadied and grew beautiful again. Yellow marsh grass, calm high tide, pale November sky. They were there as they'd always been. And the tide would come in again tomorrow. All might still be well.

If we'd expected remission to end our problems, we were in for a quick awakening. The cortisone was carefully withdrawn, and I was happy to see the sharp features of Eric's real face returning. The mercaptopurine was continued, however. Soon we were faced with the built-in problems of what was then the conventional leukemia treatment. When you use drugs to destroy the bad cells, you also destroy the good ones, but not, you hope, as quickly. The better drugs, like the better TV Westerns, are less violent, and most of the time they allow the good guys to outnumber the bad guys. At least for a while. But even during a period of remission, when the bone marrow is once again producing substantial numbers of good cells in the blood, and the patient is not in such critical danger, he may develop problems as his resistance to the drug increases. It wasn't long before Eric's weekly blood check showed that his good white cells and hemoglobin were once again too low. This time he was sent to the hospital for transfusions: two pints of whole blood. It was my first experience with the swaying apparatus, the plastic sacks, the tubes, the needles. Eric bore it with calm indifference. In a matter of hours, his pale face had a marvelous glow. You could see the life pouring into him, and you could certainly see his impatience to be up and out. When the doctors finally said he could go, he ran ahead of me down the hospital steps, swinging his duffel bag as if he'd just returned from a great weekend. I handed him the car keys and went around to the other side. We didn't talk all the way home. I was still trying to take it all in; he was trying to shut it out.

The following week he came down with bronchitis. "Just a little cough," he said, brushing off my suggestions to take care, to call the doctor. The doctor, looking him over the next day during his regular weekly blood check, spotted the trouble anyway and started him on a new round of antibiotics. Sidney's apparent detachment was comfortable for Eric, but all this while a silent battle had been building between mother and son. Most of the time I was controlled enough not to fret over him out loud, but he saw my eyes, he read my concern in gestures, in a thousand small ways, and he rejected every shred of what he considered babying.

Probably the critical moment of combat between Eric and me occurred one day in November when a friend offered him a ticket to the Jets-Giants game in Yankee Stadium. It was freezing, windy, beginning to snow. The bronchitis was fairly well licked but he was still coughing, still on antibiotics. When he announced he was about to take off for Yankee Stadium, I almost shrieked in protest. Sidney, who doesn't mind cold weather and who trusted Eric to take care of himself, thought it was all right for him to go. But I managed to say, "I still think you'd better check with the doctor, Eric." No doctor in the world would let him go. I was sure of it.

Sidney went back to his typing. Eric angrily dialed the doctor on the kitchen phone as I stood nearby, trying to calm down, stirring a pot of lentil soup. The doctor not only told him he could go, he congratulated him on the free ticket and said he wished he could go along.

So off went Eric with antibiotic pills in one pocket of his black loden coat and leukemia pills in the other. He was hatless, gloveless—and very happy. I watched him go by the front window and down the path. He should be wearing *two* pairs of socks, I thought, and his muffler isn't tied tight enough—it gave me almost physical pain to see it trailing carelessly over one shoulder. The first snowflakes settled on his hair, his blond eyebrows. I watched helplessly. There was nothing I could do.

I watched, and I was changed. In that moment I began to understand. Now might be all he would ever have. He had to live his life. And living meant running risks. There was no way to wrap him in cotton. He had to run free to be a whole man. I wanted that. I discovered I wanted it more than my own peace of mind or my need to mother him and be sure I'd done all I could. There was no longer any "sure." I accepted the terrible precariousness of his life from that moment. I let go and said, "Eric—*live!*"

CHAPTER 2

THE SNOWFLAKES AND THE COLD, the long hours in the open stadium, did Eric no harm at all. He came home from the game exhilarated and determined to have more, not fewer, adventures. The next day he asked me not to cook any more meals for him. "Just have some stuff in the icebox I can throw together when I want it. I'm going to be out a lot. I don't want to have to tell everybody my plans all the time."

He had some other requests: "Don't do my laundry, please. I'll do it. Don't clean my room, I'll take care of it. Just pretend I'm off at school or working somewhere. You wouldn't be following me around taking care of me, would you?

"And another thing." He seemed fairly fierce about this one. "I don't want you calling the doctor any more. I can handle this myself. No sweat. It's *my* problem. I've almost got it licked anyway. I'll let you know if there's anything you need to know."

Well. I thought of saying, "Do drop me a postcard from time to time and let us know how you're getting along." I considered bringing up all the other mothers who would have driven him mad with their fussing. I also considered asking for my medals right then and there: for tact, for patience, for endurance and a dozen other things. But what I said was, "Okay."

After all, he had no way of knowing about the private battle I'd won with myself by the front window as he went off to Yankee Stadium. I still looked exactly like the mother he'd always had. Also, as a very little boy, he'd been subject to many illnesses, some of them serious, and I'd had to spend a lot of time with him. We'd both enjoyed it: lots of reading, singing, rocking, hugging; lots of walks when he'd held my hand, when he was too shy to play with other children. We'd been very close, but by the time he was nine he was off in the boy world playing ball, climbing fences, getting chased, or trying to stay underwater longer than the other guys. These were the days when I'd occasionally see him practicing his father's heavy-eyebrowed squint in the mirror. "I wish I didn't look like you," he said. "Do you think maybe I'm beginning to look more like Daddy?"

The victory by the window was real, I could tell, for along with the mild hurt I felt at being suddenly dismissed from all my jobs, and more or less stripped of my epaulets, I felt a surge of joy. Independence, strength, courage—how wonderful to see these things in a son! Eric was going to need them all, for he still didn't know how ill he was. He was not quite eighteen. He was not yet a man, but he was getting there.

The travel agent called to confirm our Puerto Rican hotel reservations for the Christmas holidays. He also asked for a $400 deposit to hold the rooms.

"What happens if we can't go, for some reason, at the last minute?"

"I'm afraid you have to forfeit the deposit," he said. "You see, the hotel has to protect itself. They might not be able to rent the rooms at that time, and—"

"I see. Well, no problem. I'll bring you a check this afternoon." Never mind, I thought. We're not going to cancel out at the last minute. Eric was in remission and feeling so well he was thinking of looking for a job. He'd found a few new friends and they often ran in to New York together, on the spur of the moment, to explore the Village or go to Chinatown or poke around the record shops on Lexington Avenue. He needed money to finance these small adventures, and he didn't like taking it from me or his father. But Sidney found a way around that problem that helped for the time being. One day, as he gave Eric $10, I heard him say, "Some day I may need money, too. I know you won't even ask me the reason. You'll just give it to me."

Earlier I might have fretted over Eric's trips to the big city, thinking, "Will he catch flu? Will he get food poisoning?" But now, by accepting danger, I seemed to have slain the fear that had followed me around most of my life. Besides, I was too happy and busy getting ready for our trip to worry about possibilities. I got down suitcases, pulled out summer clothes and swimsuits, made a reservation for Sancho at the local boarding kennels. This last item turned out to be almost as difficult as getting our own airplane reservations to the Caribbean. All those people who were going to Hawaii or the Virgin Islands, all those more fortunate souls who had forced us into the Dorado Hilton, had booked their poodles and boxers and German shepherds into the kennels for Christmas with down payments made last July. I put Sancho on a waiting list and spent three days shopping around for kennels in nearby towns. Fate smiled on us, however; somebody's poodle canceled out for reasons of ill health. Sancho was in. All that was left to do was pack and compose a note to the milkman.

Four days before we were scheduled to fly away, the doctor

called. (In honor of Eric's wishes, I hadn't been calling him regularly.) "I don't want to alarm you," he said, "but Eric's counts are way down. I think we may be about at the end of the usefulness of this drug. In any case, we've decided to transfuse him right away. There's a bed available at the hospital. I want him there this afternoon."

"All right. I'll bring him over."

We'd worked hard to make this trip possible, and I refused to believe anything could stop it. Somehow we'd get there. Even the bottles and tubes didn't seem quite so frightening the second time around. I looked at the sack of blood swaying above Eric's bed, and for the first time it was beautiful. The deep red of precious life! Thank you, unknown someone, who gave that. Thank you for the color that will soon flood his cheeks, the good cells that will restore him to the world once more. Do your work, and then let us be off—

But the doctor called again the following morning. "He's not responding as we'd hoped. His counts aren't coming around, even though he's had four transfusions so far. Transfusions, you know, aren't always routine. There can be complications—"

"What complications?" I said.

"Some unknown factor. For one reason or another, the patient's body refuses the blood. Other things, too. We have to watch out for allergic responses."

"What's happening with Eric?"

"We don't know. He's running a fever. It may be that he has an infection. I've asked for a consultation."

Puerto Rico. Two days to go, and holding.

"Do you think we can go on our vacation?" I'd already discussed our plans with the doctor. We were to be away three weeks. I'd wondered about blood checks and medication. At that time he thought it would all work out.

"I just can't answer that. We'll have to play it a day at a time. But"—he waited a moment—"I do think we have to tell him what his illness is now."

Yes, now. No way out now.

"I agree. I'll do it. I *want* to do it," I said quickly.

Once again Sidney was away on a business trip, but he was expected back around suppertime. I walked into Eric's hospital room about three in the afternoon. He looked pale, he seemed restless, but his arms were free of tubes.

"No needles?"

"Not for a while," he said. "Something isn't going quite right. The laboratory's checking it out. I'm supposed to get another pack or so tonight, though. Red cells."

"Eric. Do you know what's wrong with you?"

"No." His voice was innocent, young, curious. At that moment his defenses were down. He sounded more child than man.

"You haven't had any ideas about it?"

"No." He shook his head again. "Why, what is it?"

"You've got leukemia."

He heard it. "Excuse me," he said, jumping out of bed, running for the bathroom. He was very sick for a minute.

"I'm sorry," he said, going past me back to bed.

I waited. It seemed to me all the vital processes of my body came to a stop as I waited. Eric looked off into the distance but he saw nothing. His eyes were wide, looking inward. He seemed to be listening for something.

"You know," he said at last, with a little smile, "I'm not scared. It's funny but I'm really not scared. I can handle it, Mom. It's going to be all right. I know I can beat it."

"I know you can, too."

Then he leaned back on the pillows and gave a deep sigh. "I'm so glad it's not Mark. I know how I'd feel if this happened to Mark—"

This was a sudden unexpected test for me. I'd not yet fully thought about how it would be for *Mark* to lose Eric! Two brothers who'd loved each other from the first day. I'd expected brothers to fight at least half the time. When we built our house we'd carefully planned a separate room for each. But Eric wouldn't have it. "Put his crib in with me. I want him right here when I wake up."

Tears rushed to my eyes. I got up and looked out the window, my back to Eric. "Do you want me to tell Mark?"

"No," he said. "I want to do it."

A nurse came in to give Eric some medication. She said the technician would be up soon to do another blood check before tonight's transfusion. Time for me to go. As she left, I stood up.

"Eric, tell those cells of yours to concentrate. Let's make this transfusion good. Think Puerto Rico! I'm betting we can still make it."

It was a stupid thing to say. Even corny. It was all I could think of.

"Yeah, I'll try. And thanks for telling me everything, Mom." He looked tired. "Bring me something to read when you and Dad come back tonight?"

"Sure. What do you want?"

"Anything."

• • •

Walking down the hall, I was surprised I could walk and breathe. What's the matter with me? I should be shrieking, falling on the floor.

I drove home on the turnpike. Look at me, I'm driving. Trucks. Darty little sports cars all around me. Big-shouldered Oldsmobiles. Traffic, traffic. I just told my son he has a disease that kills. But I'm driving. I even remember to push the right-turn signal. I slow down and make a beautiful turn at Exit Fourteen. Passing the cleaners, I remembered —Oh! Our clothes for the trip. There was a generous parking space, for once, and I wheeled into it.

"Nice day, Mrs. Lund."

"Yes, it is. A little cold, though."

He handed me the clothes wrapped in plastic bags. Pink dress, yellow slacks, Eric's pale blue blazer, Sidney's white linen jacket. I paid for them, went out, and put the clothes carefully on the front seat beside me. One more stop on the next street. The corner news store was a popular hangout for the popsicle and comic crowd; the older run-out-of-milk-or-cigarettes crowd came there, too. Right now it seemed to be empty. I was glad.

"Do you know if Eric's had this one?"

I'd been in buying magazines several times in the last two days. Pop, behind the counter, knows Eric's in the hospital, doesn't know why, doesn't ask.

"No, that just came in. You took him the *Illustrated* last night, remember? But I'm sure Eric hasn't seen that one."

"Good." I started to fish in my purse for money. There was a tall partition, dividing the store, which was strung all over with plastic toys and kiddy favors for birthday parties. Beyond it was the frozen food cabinet. Someone was there. Someone had been there all along. Now she came toward me, someone I knew. The last person I wanted to see. The local hot line.

"Hi!" Big smile, searching glance. "Trouble at home? Something wrong?"

"Yes. Something's wrong."

"Oh! Nothing serious, I hope."

"Yes, it's serious. Eric has leukemia."

To me it sounded like a shout; it was only a whisper. Now the news would spread. All right, let it spread. Let everybody know!

The woman flinched as if I'd struck her.

I crossed the street and walked unsteadily back to my car. I knew I was very angry. But there was another feeling. Guilt. This was the first time I experienced the guilt that came from telling someone that Eric had leukemia, which translated meant that Eric, barring some miracle, was probably going to die. People hardly want to hear such news. Their eyes tend to slide away. Dying is un-American. My college roommate, a friend of twenty years, said, when I told her, "Don't tell me any more." (Much later, Eric spoke of this problem, too. "I wish I never had to tell *anybody*. But there's no way; it just isn't practical. But when I have to explain my situation, the funny thing is, I feel guilty. Like I was using it or trading on it for some advantage." In fact, he did the opposite. In most situations, he asked more of himself, forgave himself less or not at all.)

I tossed the magazine in the back seat. And as I started the car, I thought, "Take it easy. You're not exactly in great shape to drive. So drive very slowly."

Habit would have protected me better than caution. If I'd been going my usual 25 to 30 miles an hour, I'd never have attempted the impossible. But as it was, going a slow 10 to 15, when the bright clean clothes in slippery plastic wrappers—the clothes for our vacation!—started to slide off the front seat onto the dirty floor, I made a dive for them. *Crack! Flash!* (The lightning again!) My head smashed against the windshield. I looked up amazed. Not hurt. No blood. But I had managed to run into the telephone pole by the boatyard, half a mile from my own house, going 15 miles an hour.

Men ran out from the boatyard, waving their arms, signaling me not to move. They quickly set up sawhorses. They directed traffic around the broken pole. The fender of my Falcon was jammed up against it. The pole itself, while cracked and leaning, was not broken clear through; it hung crazily by its wires. One broken wire trailed in the street. That accounted for the flash. Little boys were collecting; men were sternly waving them away.

A man who seemed to have appointed himself Chief of Operations finally put his head up close to the car window. "Back up slowly!" he yelled. "Back up if you can. I'll tell you what to do next."

I backed up slowly. The crumpled fender made a protesting, croaking noise as it rubbed against the tire. But I could move. The pole held, supported by its own wires. I drove a hundred or so feet away, parked, and got out. Now I had to wait for the Law.

The Law arrived a few minutes later, red light flashing but no siren. (I was glad about the no siren.) I expected the Law to say, "Well, lady, what's going on here? Where's the fire?"

Instead he took my arm gently and inquired, "Are you all right?"

"Yes. Fine. I'm all right. I bumped my head but I'm not really hurt."

"You're sure?" He took his time.

"I'm sure. I'm awfully sorry. It was a very stupid thing to do." I explained about trying to pick up the clothes. "If I'd been going my usual speed I'd never have tried it. I was only going fifteen miles an hour."

The young policeman smiled. "You'd be surprised how many people make that same mistake. Now, let's get in my car and sit down."

We sat down and he pulled out some forms.

"Tell me," he said. "What happened today? Why were you only going fifteen miles an hour?"

I was caught off guard by his perceptiveness. I didn't cry but I was gasping a bit, almost out of breath, as I told the story. I told him everything.

He was still for a minute. He gave me a long look, then he shook his head. "Life and death," he said. "This morning my wife gave birth to twin baby girls in that same hospital."

"Are they all right?"

"They're beautiful."

We stared at each other.

"I know who your son is," he said. "I'm a soccer fan and I've seen him play."

A small crowd was gathering, looking at my car, glancing at me in the clutches of the Law, pointing at the pole.

"You know, I'm terribly sorry but I've got to arrest you. There's no way out. You'll have to appear in court."

"I know. Could you arrest me after the first week in January? You see, if Eric makes it, if he turns the corner tomorrow, we're hoping to go to Puerto Rico the next day, to give him a vacation in the sun. That's why I stopped at the cleaners, to get our clothes for the trip."

"How about January twelfth?"

"That's fine. Wonderful!" This is idiotic. I sound as if I were accepting an invitation to dinner. What a nice policeman!

He continued to write out my summons, getting the vital statistics, when suddenly a blond acquaintance of mine, a neighbor of many years, poked her head in the patrol car. I thought she might be going to inquire after my health or ask if I needed help getting home. She hardly gave me a look. I was the prisoner. Instead, she addressed the patrolman vigorously. "I want to know when that pole's going to be fixed. I've got company coming for dinner, and my oven won't go on—"

The young patrolman barely glanced her way. "Madam, I wouldn't know. Call up Connecticut Light and Power."

She vanished. He shook his head.

I began to laugh. "Would you believe she's a neighbor of mine? She's lived down the street for at least ten years!"

The policeman had stopped writing. Now he suddenly tore up the summons. "I can't arrest you. I can't, that's all. But I'm going to give you a one-point warning. It goes on your driving record. Just make sure you drive carefully from here on."

"I will. I promise. What are your twins' names?"

He told me.

"Those are lovely names."

"I hope Eric makes it," he said. "I want you to go on that vacation."

"Thank you for everything!" I was filled with happiness, just to be in the same world with this policeman. I got out, waved good-bye, and started off toward my car.

"Hey! Just a minute." He followed me and inspected the damage carefully. "I want to be sure you can drive home safely. Start it up now."

I did. He listened to the tire croaking against the bent fender as I moved a few feet.

"I only live a few streets away."

"Okay. Take it easy. Good luck, now!"

"Good luck to you, too! And to your wife and babies!"

I never saw him again. I hope he's had that good luck.

When I turned into my driveway, I could see that my notoriety had preceded me. Lisa stood on the front stone steps, swollen with dignity and resentment. Little boys were prancing around her, giggling.

"Hey!" a little boy screeched. "Here she comes! Lisa Lund's mother! She took down a pole. *Look* at that car!"

Lisa burst into tears and rushed into the house. I followed and she whirled around. "They chased me all the way home shouting, 'Yah, yah! Lund's mother took down a pole!' I'm not going to school tomorrow. You're too famous."

"You're too easy to tease."

We went on into the kitchen where Mark was stirring a pan full of canned ravioli for the simple snack he usually makes fifteen minutes before dinner because he can't wait. "Nice eye, Mom! You took out the main transformer. Nobody in the whole south end of town has any electricity. That's my mom!"

"What do you mean nobody has any electricity? You're cooking ravioli. And the usual twenty-four lights are on all over the downstairs."

"*We've* got power, yeah. And a few other houses down the block. But we're on another line. Everybody else from Pine Street up to the middle of town is out."

"Beautiful!" I said. "That's really batting a thousand. I picked the right pole."

Sidney arrived at that moment, briefcase still in hand, looking confused and upset.

"You missed the overture," I said.

"What's going on? I *saw* the car. Are you all right?"

"I'm fine. I'm awfully sorry about the car. I just hit a pole going fifteen miles an hour. It could have been worse. That pole was about to go anyhow. I looked at it after I hit it. It was old and rotten and full of holes. I'll tell you the whole story later. Let's have a drink."

I told him what had happened as we drove to the hospital that night. All the houses were dark along the way as we started out. Here and there we could catch a glimpse of families eating dinner by candlelight.

"Guess who's the big subject of dinner-table conversation tonight?" said Sidney.

"Me."

As we turned the corner by the boatyard, we could see a huge CL&P truck maneuvering a crane, trying to brace up my pole (yes, *my* pole) with a heavy new black one. There were floodlights, sparks, men in hard hats clambering up and down.

"Wow!"

"Well, I told you that pole was no good."

At the hospital we found two doctors checking Eric as he finished the second of two transfusions. Eric was sitting up, alert, flushed as if he'd been running.

Our doctor looked pleased. "He's doing fine. We're going to watch him. But his fever's down, his other signs are stable. I'm pretty sure his blood counts will be up tomorrow. I think we're out of the woods this time."

When we drove home an hour and a half later, the CL&P

truck crew was still at it, working under floodlights. The old pole was almost lashed into place with heavy wire wrapped around the new one to hold it up. The night was cold and there was a bitter wind blowing off the river. I looked at the men and felt sorry. But I also thought—Puerto Rico!

CHAPTER 3

THE DORADO HILTON WAS the Dorado Hilton. Just as I'd thought. But the children spread out their towels and lay down happily in the expensive sunshine. They learned how to order expensive club sandwiches and seventy-five-cent Cokes and charge them to their room numbers, which is a lesson in a certain kind of sophistication if not economy. Eric and Mark played eighteen holes of expensive golf for the first time in their lives on a championship course overlooking the ocean. Their golf was terrible. Their golf manners left something to be desired. (Once Mark drove his golf cart too close to one of the velvet broadloom greens and nearly got shot by a firing squad.) The view from every fairway, however, was breathtaking. Fat clouds, like a layer of pink whipped cream, floated on the horizon beyond the sea. They never seemed to be going anywhere. Never once did I see them bustle across the top of the sky, New England fashion.

The boys found a free coconut lying on the beach and succeeded in bashing it open against the wrought-iron fence of their balcony. They sat in swim trunks, feet up on the railing, breaking off chunks of the sweet white meat, drinking the milk clumsily and laughing when it ran down their chins and brown arms.

Lisa attended all the turtle races, Bingo games, and other jivey activities which the hotel's social director was forced to invent every day. Lisa was the perfect age for the Dorado Hilton. She loved going up and down in the self-service elevators. She loved the enormous menus with tassels, even if what she always wanted was a hamburger, priced outrageously. But her favorite pastime was sitting on the edge of the pool, dabbling her legs in the water, while she scribbled down her address in lavender ink on the backs of paper napkins and finally exchanged them for other scribbles from other little girls. (For years afterward she would receive a letter now and then from Leonia, New Jersey, which invariably began, "Hiya, Lisa! Whatcha been doing? Long time no write, huh?") It is easy to find lifelong pen pals in kidney-shaped hotel swimming pools when you are ten years old. The pool was too full of shrieking small fry but Eric enjoyed it anyway, practicing his dives at the deep end off the high board. "This is good for my arms," he said once, coming up to drip beside me. "The needle marks and bruises are going away."

It was the beach that was the biggest disappointment. The minute we'd arrived and our bags were only half unpacked, we'd pulled on our suits and rushed down, ready to plunge in the blue water you always see on postcards. It wasn't very blue. There was no surf. The water, in fact, overshadowed by too many heavy, leaning palms, had the look of a grumpy lake. In the middle of the disappointing small strip of sand was a large sign which said POSITIVELY NO SWIMMING ALLOWED ON THE BEACH.

Sidney ignored the sign and marched into the water. The boys followed. I yelled after them, "Didn't you read the sign?" Lisa, who is wise in matters of danger (never risking artichokes, for instance, since she's never eaten them before), retreated to the pool.

It's one thing to play the cool mother; it's another to play the fool. (While I sometimes can't resist touching WET PAINT, I rarely touch a high-tension wire just to see if the sign painter knew what he was doing when he wrote DANGER! 13,000 VOLTS.) We shouted a few abusive remarks to each other across the water. But soon several other would-be swimmers, encouraged by the sight of my family paddling out to sea, also began wading in. I retreated to sulk on the sand. Someone at the far end of the beach blew a piercing police whistle and started running in my direction. He was wearing the usual lifeguard suit: shoulders, biceps, bulging calves, white hat, white zinc nose, and white trunks.

"Can'tcha read the sign, lady?"

"Yes, I can read." If I was annoyed before, now I was furious. "But I'm not responsible for all the idiot males in the world. Why don't you allow people to swim on the beach anyway?"

"Sea urchins. They get you in the foot, cause you a lotta trouble. They're poisonous."

He blew his whistle several times more, making vigorous "Come in! Come in!" gestures at the swimmers. Jesus Christ! We have spent maybe a thousand bucks and flown over a thousand miles so Eric can come down here and step on a sea urchin! Justice might have arranged for Sidney to step on one, but Justice, in my experience, is not to be relied on. I only wanted all my family back on dry land immediately. I added my own urgent waves to the lifeguard's.

By the time Sidney, Eric, and Mark reached the shore they were highly irritated. As the lifeguard was explaining the dangers of sea urchins, one of the other swimmers, now returning, gave a yell. He'd been stung, bitten, or whatever it is that a sea urchin does. Aided by his companions, he hopped ashore and went off to seek medical help.

You might think this would have vindicated me in the eyes of my loved ones. Hardly. They reacted as if I had planted the sea urchin myself to prove the need for the sign. Immediately they went off by themselves, leaving the hotel's protective wire-fenced embrace, to look for a better beach. I went back to the room. They returned triumphant, an hour later, having found a beach only a quarter of a mile away. Beautiful, sparkling, public. No signs anywhere about sea urchins or other underwater monsters.

I was never able to enjoy it with them. I was too mad, too strung out from the weeks before, and I came down the next day with a sore throat and fever. I spent the whole first week in bed sampling the room service, fiddling with the TV to make it hold still, and trying to turn off the air conditioning. Occasionally Lisa came to stand in my doorway, gaze at me sadly, and blow me a kiss. Sidney was brisk, busy, athletic. The boys stuck their heads in now and then.

"Hi, Mom. Sorry you're sick."

"Hi! I'd love to see you but don't come any closer—"

The two were together every minute, plotting what they'd do next, laughing the same old conspiratorial laughs. I had time to wonder if Eric had told Mark that he had leukemia. They seemed exactly as they'd always been, close, happy, self-sufficient. I looked for changes or strain in Mark and found none. If things had worried him in the past, I realized he'd probably always talked them over with Eric. Eric, more than I, perhaps more than Sidney, too, had brought him up. I never did find out when Mark learned that his brother had a fatal illness.

At the end of that first week I was left with a heavy cold, so I tried to stay away from the children. They seemed to be having fun, though it wasn't the exotic, adventurous, travel-poster vacation we'd wanted for Eric. But he swam every day, he got the impressive tan which passes for good health, and he played lots of basketball with his brother, shooting for hoops which the hotel had installed in various palm trees. One afternoon he and Mark explored a nearby village to see how the "natives" lived. Except for the flaking, Spanish-arched houses, they might have been exploring some sections of Newark, New Jersey, or Bridgeport, Connecticut. They saw an over-abundance of children, TV antennas, slightly dented cars—with car parts strewn about the yards—rusty porch furniture, leafy plants climbing from tin cans, and very little living space. They walked back to the hotel feeling slightly depressed. On the way they passed an old man who raised a gentle hand. *"¡Feliz navidad!"*

"*Feliz navidad* to you, too!" they said to him. At last they had used their high school Spanish. The outing was a success.

One night Eric had a small adventure all his own. He was wearing the pale blue blazer (dinner was served rather formally so we usually got dressed up), he was bored, and it was only 10 P.M., too early for bed. Mark was watching a TV drama of cops and robbers in Spanish. Eric wanted something more. Without telling anyone, he went downstairs and pushed open the heavy carved doors of the hotel's gambling casino. He was immediately challenged by the suave, cold-eyed manager. "Are you over eighteen?"

Eric was eleven days short of eighteen, a fact which his driver's license would have revealed at once if he'd been challenged further. But he drew his eyebrows together in his father's frown and glared back, demanding, "What do you think?"

He played roulette and won eleven dollars. The next day he was as elated as if he'd won eleven hundred.

Perhaps the best thing about the trip was that it put some

physical distance between Eric and the annoying realities of his illness: lab tests, doctor visits, hospital trips. He began to relax. Soon he began to have dreams. He told me, "They're almost the same every night. I dream I'm somewhere up at college. I'm supposed to be taking exams. But I've never been to any of my classes. I keep looking all over hell for them, but I just don't know my way around. There are a bunch of clocks on the walls and I can see it's getting late and the exams are about to start. I'm frantic because I haven't done any work, but I get more and more lost. Man, it's an awful feeling! I'm so glad to wake up and be here and see the sun outside."

These dreams of frustration were the first signs of Eric's growing desire to study. In an era when half the kids in the country were protesting the irrelevance of education, the narrow-mindedness of their dumb professors, and the futility of their own lives—and dropping out by the thousands to prove it—Eric could hardly wait to get back in. The illness which had prevented him from taking the big jump was beginning to be a spur.

"Do you think I can go to school the second term when we get back?"

"We'll see." (That terrible phrase which parents have used since time began: "Can I have an ice cream cone?" "A bike for my birthday?" "New shoes for the dance?" . . . "We'll see.") The doctor had told me he was thinking about a change in drugs. There were indications that mercaptopurine was no longer fully effective. Eric was out on parole, but he'd have to check in when we got back. I wanted to promise him the world. There was nothing I could promise him at all but "We'll see."

• • •

Getting back from the moon is somewhat easier than getting back from Kennedy Airport after Christmas. We got stacked, and it was easy to imagine the air filled with hundreds of airplanes all around us. We couldn't see anything, however, for New York was having a snow and ice storm that would have made excellent stage effects for the last act of *King Lear*. By the time we finally landed, got our car out of the long-term parking lot, and drove home to Connecticut, it was 1 A.M. and we were wrung out. I looked at the children and thought, "My God! They've lost their tans already!"

Our house did not look inviting. It sits well back from the road, and it was surrounded on all sides and up to the windows by several feet of drifted snow. Naturally the driveway had not been shoveled. We finally parked the car, with all of our luggage, near the middle of the road about seventy feet from the front door. "I think the snowplow will run into it," I said to Sidney.

"Never mind," he said. "This is the last road in town to get plowed."

We hacked our way into the house, snow filling our shoes, gratefully shut the front door, and found no improvement in the temperature. Our breath was frosty and visible in front of our faces. I looked around the living room and suddenly got the message. Every plant in the room was dead. Stone cold, permanently dead. "The furnace must have blown!"

The neighbor who had kindly offered to water the plants during our vacation told me the next day she began to suspect something was wrong as the plants shriveled all at once. But she didn't know what to do. It was a miracle that every pipe in the house didn't burst. This may have been because our children never mastered the art of turning off water faucets. We went around inspecting the other damage.

Perhaps the saddest sight of all was Mark standing in his room, a room that had once been alive and beautiful with eight fish tanks, dropping all his dead tropical fish one by one, into an old wastebasket.

"Oh, Mark! I'll get you some more!"

There went his prize angelfish. He'd nursed that fellow along carefully for over three years. Now he was just a dead giant.

"It's all right. It's all right." Mark wouldn't look at me. "I'll just have to start over."

It was Eric who finally put things back in immediate perspective. "Gee, but I'm cold," he said.

He was, in fact, having a chill. What were plants, what were fish? We dropped everything and built fires. There are three fireplaces in our house and we fed them furiously, like stokers down in the bowels of some old ship. Sidney replaced the furnace fuse, but very soon it blew again. He called the oil company's emergency number. It was going on 2 A.M. but he called anyway. I found an electric pad and put it in Eric's bed. At least the power hadn't gone out. Wool socks. Extra sweater. He didn't protest (which worried me most of all). I made hot cocoa. Lisa and Mark drank it in front of the fire and began to feel better. Eric drank his in bed and began to feel better. "I'd like another quilt. Then I'll go to sleep. I'm tired."

Houses get warm again. Plants can be replaced. Sidney went to a greenhouse on my birthday and brought home fifteen little pots of different growing things. Eventually Mark's fish tanks glowed again with little swordtails and neon tetras darting about in a new water world. (We didn't replace the angelfish, though. We were still mourning him.) It was nice to have Mark's room *sounding* normal again, too. When all eight tanks were going at once, the whole upstairs sounded like a coffeepot bubbling gently on the back burner. All was well—except that Eric was coming out of remission, and so nothing was well.

He'd survived his chill, but it was an indication, as I'd feared, that his blood counts were getting low. So he was not going to college, he was going back to the hospital. This time he knew what it was all about; there was no way to pretend it wasn't serious. Yet that is exactly what my instinct told me to do.

"Why don't you commute to some college around here when you get out of the hospital?" I said, a day or so before he was scheduled for transfusions (as if transfusions were, after all, only a minor inconvenience).

"I've been thinking of that. But then I'd need a car. I couldn't tie up yours all day."

I'd been thinking of that, too. Sidney and I had looked at our savings. They were going down, all right, but we figured we could just manage $1,500.

"After all," I said to Sidney, "this may be the only car he'll ever have. I don't want it to be some heap. Let's make it good. With fifteen hundred bucks he can get something pretty nice in the secondhand market." So we went to the savings bank and got a check made out to Eric.

Now I tossed the check at him. "Go pick out something jazzy. See what you can get with this."

"Wow!" said Eric. "Just like that!"

"Why not? When you find something you like, get your father to take a look at it. Then when you get out of the hospital, we'll go get it right away."

Eric spent that evening poring over automobile ads in the newspaper. The next morning he set off happily to prowl through the car lots of several nearby towns. By four thirty that afternoon he was back home with a gleam in his eye. He was in love with a second-hand Mustang.

"It's a beauty! Silvery blue-green. Two-door. *Good* tires. I think the motor's okay. They let me drive it. But will you go take a look, Dad?"

"Sure, I'll do it tomorrow."

Three days and seven transfusions later, I went to the hospital to pick up Eric. He had already begun taking some new drug that would, we hoped, put him in remission. He looked—not great, but all right. The seven transfusions had done their work for the moment. As usual he ran ahead of me to our car. I tossed him the keys—it was now part of our routine—then I went around to my side. Eric gunned the engine a moment, wheeled around in the parking lot, and turned out into the main street. "Now," he said, "let's go get my horse-car, my Mustang."

Eric had enrolled in the University of Bridgeport, about twenty miles away, before doing his time in the hospital. The second term was not due to start, however, for several weeks. In the meantime, he was careful to be seen at least six or eight times a day, driving his blue-green Mustang with its white-wall tires and silver wheel covers slowly through the main streets of our town. He wanted maximum exposure. When he was not driving his car, he was polishing it, vacuuming it, checking the tires or the oil, or just peering seriously under the hood. In a short time, he learned a great deal about what went on under there. He talked knowledgeably to Sidney about pistons, spark plugs, carburetors, and other stuff. Owning a beautiful car, even a secondhand one, can help make a man or a wild fool of a boy. For Eric, at just eighteen, it was a great leap in growing up. He'd thirsted for responsibility. Now he drank it down with joy.

I felt joy for him, too. I stopped working and backed away from my typewriter to watch out the window every time he pulled in or out of the driveway. But my joy was flawed. The doctor had called shortly after the second drug was begun, to tell us that Eric was not responding to it the way he'd hoped he would. If the marrow didn't show some improvement by the end of the week, the doctor would have to start him on something else.

We'd been going down this road for only four months. Yet already it seemed we were running through or using up some of the best drugs available.

One evening later that week my eye was suddenly caught by a news item in the paper. The headline read something like this: "New Drug Offers Best Hope for Control of Leukemia." I read on; it was the first time I'd heard about asparaginase. It's hard not to be carried away by a news item that you know is also a PR release. It's harder still to keep your heart from pounding in some excitement when you read that "scientists cautiously predict that the new drug, which works on a completely different principle from the usual antileukemic drugs, offers new hope not only for control of the disease, but possibly for an eventual complete cure."

I kept on reading. "Experiments are not yet fully complete," etc. Then I read the catch: "Unfortunately supplies of the new drug, asparaginase, are greatly limited at this time. The drug is extremely difficult to produce in quantity. Also, at the present moment, asparaginase costs approximately upwards of $300,000 per patient treatment. . . ."

Limited? Difficult to produce? $300,000 per patient? Who cares! This could be survival! Sidney and I determined that night that Eric would be one of the fortunate few who would get his chance at asparaginase when the time came. There was no way of knowing when that moment would be upon us, but we wanted to be ready.

The next morning I called our doctor. We talked at some length. He was not only a friend but a neighbor of Dr. Joseph Burchenal, Director of Clinical Investigation at Sloan-Kettering Institute. I learned that the line of patients hoping for a chance at asparaginase formed on the right, just outside Dr. Burchenal's door.

Several times in my life, during years past, some errand in New York had taken me down 68th Street between First and York avenues. I had glanced up at the huge red-brick slab of a building, not unlike a jail, with the stainless steel letters on one side— Memorial Hospital for Cancer and Allied Diseases. That building meant death. You looked at those words and you said, "Not me!" You thought, "How lucky am I to be running free in the world on this day." And you walked a little faster.

Now Eric and I were walking down the same street, heading for the Sloan-Kettering Institute, which is directly across the street from Memorial. Once again I was glancing up at the letters spelled out in steel on the side of the hospital. Strangely, this time they held comfort for me. They had been shining there a long time, testifying to the endurance of men and women who can deal with Cancer and Allied Diseases every day of the year. We were going to need their help. We could be thankful they did not desert. We could only hope that their work would be done in the laboratories in time for Eric to survive.

Soon we were sitting on straight chairs in a small office on the second floor of Sloan-Kettering. Across from us, Dr. Burchenal, who had been talking to us for just a few minutes, suddenly picked up a small bottle from his desk. "This is our total supply of asparaginase at the moment," he said. "About three hundred thousand dollars' worth."

It looked hardly more significant than the 49-cent bottle of aspirin you find in any medicine cabinet. But it was hope in a small bottle, only eighteen inches away.

Eric was staring at it.

"You don't need asparaginase yet, Eric," Dr. Burchenal said, reading him. "We can hold you off with drugs that are more available, that we know more about. And," he went on, "this afternoon I have to make a decision. There are six patients who ought to be getting asparaginase right now. I think we have enough in that bottle for two."

He confirmed the news report that asparaginase was scarce and hard to make. He also told us that there was hope soon of speeding up production and improving the difficult purification methods. There were drug firms working on it for the first time in Europe as well as the United States.

I thought the interview must be about at an end, but Dr. Burchenal suddenly leaned back in his chair and began what seemed, at first, a rambling story for a man with such a busy schedule.

"When I was just getting into medicine, I studied with a very fine man, an older doctor. He'd had diabetes many years before, for a long time, but he'd managed to keep himself alive by staying on a very strict diet. He lived to see the discovery of insulin, which saved him, of course. Well, at the time I knew him, he was interested in pernicious anemia, which was then a mysterious and hopeless disease. The only way we could keep patients alive at all was with constant transfusions, and some people just got to the place where they didn't want any more; they wanted to die. But this doctor was very stern with them, kept after them, wouldn't let them give up, and of course he was working and experimenting all the time. Well, finally he discovered that his patients started to get well—he even began curing them—if he could get them to eat a pound of raw liver a day!"

Eric grimaced slightly. I laughed, knowing how he hated liver. "We can be thankful you don't have to do *that* anyway."

"It was the B vitamins in liver that worked against the anemia, of course," Dr. Burchenal went on briskly. "And what I'm asking you to do right now, Eric, is just to put up with the discomforts of this thing until we've got it licked. We know we can cure mice. But leukemia is a nasty disease. And the most effective drugs we have for people make them awfully sick. . . ."

Eric waved off the discomforts. "All I want to know is, can I do anything I feel I can do? Like play soccer?"

Dr. Burchenal smiled. "We've got a jockey who rides the race tracks on Long Island. He's a leukemia patient of ours. Then there's a football player—I think he's with the Cleveland Browns."

This was what Eric had come to hear. He asked no more.

Walking back to our car, I thought how skillfully Dr. Burchenal had presented the problem. And he'd not wasted his time giving the challenge to Eric. Here was a runner who might go the distance.

As we approached our car on a nearby street, I saw it had a parking ticket. For three days parking rules had been suspended in New York because of a garage strike. We'd checked the radio before leaving home, and the strike was still on at 8 A.M. But apparently it had been settled while we talked of life and death in Dr. Burchenal's office. The police, wasting no time, had nabbed us.

A watchman from a warehouse bustled out, yelling, "You shoulda known better, lady! The towaway squad was just here. If they coulda got your car out, it wouldn't be sittin' here now."

We were jammed in, all right. When we'd parked several hours ago, there'd been no one behind us. In the meantime a heavy truck had pushed his nose up against our back bumper.

"Don't worry, I'll get it out, Mom," Eric said. He got in, slammed the door, started the motor, and began to inch the car back and forth. It looked impossible but he was doing it, working calmly, skillfully. I stood on the sidewalk watching. Suddenly I burst into tears of rage and frustration.

The watchman looked at me uneasily. "So it's twenty-five bucks. It coulda been fifty! And they'da towed your car away to God knows where. Don'tcha know you're lucky, lady?"

CHAPTER 4

THE SECOND SEMESTER at the University of Bridgeport was due to begin in another week. Eric wasn't entering as a freshman for several reasons: he wasn't yet ready to carry a full schedule, and he'd never abandoned his original dream of playing freshman soccer, and eventually varsity soccer, at the University of Connecticut. So he'd chosen several courses in English, History, Art, and Mechanical Drawing, all subjects he enjoyed and for which he might eventually get credit. The subject which interested him most passionately, however, was getting out of the house and into a classroom. Any classroom! My own interest in this last subject was growing keener every day. We'd been cellmates long enough. No matter how much we tried to stay out of each other's way, to be polite, to make allowances, we were each grittily aware of the other's presence. Now we were both hanging on the bars, longing to be sprung.

Since our visit to Dr. Burchenal, I'd been feeling more secure. We were connected now to the center where the problem was being fought at every level with the strongest, most effective weapons in the world. We didn't have asparaginase yet. But we had something else. After a conference with Dr. Burchenal, our doctor had prescribed a different antileukemic drug for Eric which was said to be very effective. Its name was methotrexate.

Eric kept the bottle on the kitchen table. No one had to remind him to take the pills. He was, as he'd wanted to be, in charge. A day or so after he brought the methotrexate home from the pharmacy, I happened to notice the box, in which the drug had been packaged, in the kitchen wastebasket. Out of curiosity, I fished it out and began to read the little folder which was stuffed inside. It was hard to read, the tiniest type, but it described the many possible side effects of the drug. I read the list and my heart began to pound. This was a rough game we were in.

Had Eric read the list? I didn't know, but I tore the folder into shreds. No matter. Within a few days he developed the first side effect described—an ulcerated mouth. I looked at him as he set off for the first day as a commuting student to the university. His lips were bloody, swollen twice their size. He couldn't talk. He couldn't really eat. He was wearing an old faded denim jacket and some new skintight pale jeans and carrying a notebook under one arm. He couldn't smile but he gave me a wave, jumped into his Mustang, and was gone.

I went to the supermarket and bought plastic straws. Lots of different canned fruit juices (fresh orange juice hurt his mouth). Chocolate powder for making milkshakes. Ice cream, Jell-O and some extra eggs. He couldn't manage meat.

A bone marrow and some blood tests taken the following week showed that methotrexate was doing the job. Eric was once again almost in remission. But the ulcers were not improving. Reluctantly, our doctor took him off the drug. He called to tell me what was in store.

"We're going to have to leave him alone for a month until this thing clears up."

"You mean no drugs. At all?"

"I'm afraid so. We can't start him on anything else until this drug is out of his system."

So it was going to be the high-wire act without the net. Could he hold on, or would we lose him? The month of March—the longest month in the year, I've always thought—stretched ahead of us, forbidding, drizzly, gray. Every one of those thirty-one days seemed to loom ahead like a separate razor-edged hurdle for a tired runner.

Eric took the first few weeks in stride. He never missed a class. When I asked if he was enjoying his work, he nodded. His mouth was improving, but slowly. It turned out that I was the runner who was tired. Suddenly I had to get out. Sidney was agreeable. He can cook and cope and sometimes likes to run the show. I did four loads of laundry, stocked the freezer and the icebox, and bought a plane ticket to Florida where my mother and sister live.

I lay on a hot beach and stared at grains of sand. I floated in the green water beyond the surf and watched the gulls float above me, riding out the last breath of a breeze. I did these things over and over until my head was empty, until I was sundrugged and melted down like one of the jellyfish left behind by an ebbing tide. It was one thing to have accepted the dangers in Eric's life and to let him run his risks. It was another to watch him doing it day after day. Sidney's defenses let him tune out on the daily struggle more successfully than I. It's not that he lacks concern, but he takes a longer-range point of view. I'd never been able to do this. Now, for the first time, I acknowledged my own need to survive. Lose Eric I might. To lose myself along the way would be a senseless waste. We were runners in a marathon with no foreseeable end. To stay in the race I would have to learn something about the first essential of good running: pace.

Spring was making a cautious comeback when I returned the first week in April. The overgrown willow was streaming gold branches all over the yard, reminding us it should have been cut down last year. (Lisa had begged us to spare it; she was not quite through climbing trees.) The maple was waving tiny clenched fists of new leaves. Onion grass and clover seemed to be running well ahead of the crabgrass. And little children, taking the short-cut through our backyard, were stopping as they always did, to pat the new pussy willows.

I walked around the yard, that first day home, feeling comforted. Eric had lived through the long month. His mouth was completely healed. He looked healthy, even happy, in the glimpse I'd had of him. It came as a shock that evening as I was cleaning up the kitchen after dinner when I saw him once again uncapping the methotrexate bottle and gulping down a pill.

"Eric! What are you doing? I thought you were off that stuff."

Eric was already on his way out of the kitchen. "Call the doctor if you want to, Mom. He'll explain it to you. I have to get to work. I have an exam tomorrow."

His tone wasn't rude. It was brisk, unemotional. Probably he, too, had to put down a few fears of his own before he could swallow that pill. Sidney had already gone off to a meeting. I didn't often phone our doctor in the evening. But suddenly I was nervous and impatient; I felt this couldn't wait. Besides, Eric didn't often give me an invitation like that.

"Yes, we've put him back on methotrexate," the doctor said when I reached him. "At a quarter of the dose he had before."

"But why?"

"Well, except for the mouth ulcers, he showed a very good

response. His marrow was much improved in a relatively short time. His good cells held their own, too."

"I know, but 'except-for-the-mouth-ulcers' is a pretty big 'except,' isn't it? Won't he just get that awful mouth all over again?" I felt childishly exasperated, close to tears.

"Not necessarily." The doctor went to some pains to reassure me and to explain the reasoning behind this new move. "When we started Eric on methotrexate, we gave him the dose that's considered right for his age and weight. But it was much too strong for him. He seems to be unusually sensitive to drugs. Now we're hoping that he'll be able to tolerate this smaller dose and still get in remission."

"He's not in remission, then?"

"No. But we should know how he's doing by the end of the week. I'll make it a point to call you and tell you exactly where we stand."

The news was good. Remission. The mouth ulcers did not return. The news continued good month after month. No other side effects developed. The routine blood tests every week and the bone marrow examination every six weeks confirmed our best hope. The second remission was holding. Miraculously, it seemed that a perfect balance had been achieved at last.

Eric had the strength of ten that summer. After the long winter of illness and frustration, he shot back into life like a team of greyhounds suddenly released at the starting gate. He seemed to be everywhere at once: swimming, spearfishing, surfing, water-skiing, running. Especially running. If he had wanted to make the freshman soccer team before, now he was possessed. Every few weeks he called up the freshman coach at the University of Connecticut to reassure him that he was in great shape, that he was working out, that nothing was going to keep him from being a freshman this year, and that if they had ever counted him out as a possibility, they'd better do their counting over. When he wasn't running he was practicing kicks, dribbles, running sweeps at the ball. He and I exchanged a few words when I caught him demonstrating his ability to juggle the ball in place, kicking it from one foot to the other, in the living room.

"It's raining," Eric protested. "I just got the hang of this and I don't want to lose it."

"I don't care if it rains forty days and forty nights. Kindly remember this is the living room."

Eric picked up his soccer ball and went by me with a disgusted look. "Then what about live and let live?"

This was also the summer that Eric started working for Manpower, Inc., an outfit that recruits people for temporary jobs. The jobs usually changed every two or three days. He liked that. There was variety, less boredom, more challenge. Once he spent three days unloading freight cars at a railroad siding.

"I'm glad this one's over," he told us, standing at the kitchen sink, covered with sweat, drinking glass after glass of cold water. "That job saved me six months of bumming around the railroads. Railroads are supposed to be very romantic. Big deal. If I never see another freight car it's okay with me."

From railroading he went to Fit-Rite Sportswear and shoved boxes around. Then came a job with a local nursery, digging up bushes, balling the roots, loading them into a delivery truck. Doing the laundry, I could usually tell when he'd changed jobs; the stains on his jeans switched from factory dust to garden dirt, or from grease to grass.

One evening he walked in looking cleaner than usual, but he had a glowing sunburn.

"You got a nice color today, Eric."

"Yeah. I worked at Fox's Funeral Home."

He's putting me on, I thought. My eyebrows lifted skeptically.

"Outside. Not inside." He smiled. Then he sat down. "I'll admit it threw me a bit when Manpower told me to go over to this funeral home this morning. Then I thought, 'What the hell. Don't walk away. Walk up and take a look. See what it's all about.'"

"Well?"

"It's an okay job. Really nice. Beautiful grounds! You should see their grass. I worked on hedges today, though, and they've got miles of hedges. This job really builds the arms!"

I waited to see if he wanted to say more.

"I haven't been inside yet. I don't know about that."

As it turned out, Eric kept his job at Fox's Funeral Home the rest of the summer. One day I asked him where the place was.

"Way out U.S. One. Past the new shopping center on the left."

"Really? I have to go shopping there today. There's a good store for curtains and bedspreads."

"Hey, Mom," said Eric. "Take a look at my hedges as you go by. They really look nice."

Several times after that I drove past and managed to catch a glimpse of Eric at work. Once he was holding the electric hedge clippers high, trimming the long stretch of privet. Another time he was edging the grass by the driveway. He kept that grass silky and immaculate, mowed, weeded, and unflawed by the common dandelions and bald spots from ball playing which ornamented our yard at home. Was he taking such care, I wondered, in order to propitiate the gods? Was he proving something every day? "Look at me, I'm alive, I'm on the outside—not like those guys in the boxes inside." Or was he just doing his usual good job? There was no way to know.

I was surprised, however, when he began to work evenings at the funeral home. He dressed very carefully: dark jacket, shined black loafers, dark striped tie.

I dared to tease him. "Are you in the receiving line?"

"Sort of." His smile was shy. "I park cars and help the old ladies out."

One night he came back from work wide-eyed. "I don't know," he marveled, "but I think our customer tonight musta been some big cat in the Mafia. You never saw so many black Cadillacs all full of guys in sharp black suits. The whole parking lot was wall-to-wall Cadillacs! You can bet I was careful parking those babies!"

In the beginning Eric just took a day off when it rained. After a while I noticed he was going to work no matter how wet it was outside.

"What do you do at Fox's when it rains?"

"I work inside. Vacuuming the whole place, up and down the stairs. I arrange flowers, too."

"You arrange flowers!" This was too much.

"Not in vases. Not like you mean. They mostly come arranged already. I mean I have to decide where they ought to go—at the head or the feet. Or around in back. Or someplace else."

"Well, that's a problem, I'll admit."

Eric took a handful of cookies out of the cookie jar and sat down on the kitchen stool.

"You know, John, the embalmer, is a nice guy. We sit out on the back steps and eat our lunch together."

He ate cookies for a minute; then he went on.

"John's got his problems. Like this four-hundred-pound guy wouldn't go in his casket. If he tried to get the arms in, then the belly would come up."

He looked at me and gave half a laugh.

"Mmmmmm." I nodded. I can take it if you can, I thought. You really are taking a good look, aren't you? You want to know what this is all about. How do we treat our dead anyway?

"Ask me anything about caskets," Eric said. "I'm an expert. I can tell the cheap ones from the two-thousand-dollar jobs in one look now."

"I never cared much for them myself," I said.

"Me, either," Eric said. "I'm an outside man myself. I'll go inside once in a while. But not downstairs. No way."

He looked off in space a moment. I'd seen that look before, the afternoon in the hospital when I'd told him what was wrong with him. He swung off the stool and turned around.

"That John's a real nice guy, though," he said, grabbing an apple and walking out the back door.

Friends didn't want to hear that Eric was working in a funeral home. Their eyes said, "Macabre." Their eyes said, "Sick."

You're wrong, I thought. It's strong, it's good. He didn't run away. He's learning to live with it, even laugh with it sometimes.

Then one day as summer was ending, and the job, too, was about to end since college was starting soon, Eric came home and I could see right away he was shook.

"You'll never believe this," he said with a wondering look. "But let me tell you about it anyhow. . . ."

He took a deep breath.

"I ran over the long hose with the power mower today. It was a dumb thing to do and I had to splice it. Well, the hose is attached to a faucet inside the big garage. I guess that's so they can roll it up and store it there and lock the door. Anyway, I'm working on this splice on the hose inside the garage and it looks pretty good. So I decide to test it—"

He began to laugh. He laughed until he cracked up and couldn't go on. I waited.

"Okay," he gasped, trying to stop. "Well—I turned on the faucet, see, and nothing happened. So I turned it on harder. Still no go. I figure then the hose is kinked up. I'm looking for the kink when all of a sudden, *wow!* All that water, all that power starts to go. The hose flips out of my hand and right into the front window of the hearse, spraying water all over hell. I ran up and tried to pull it out when, Jesus, this terrible loud wailing sound comes out of the hearse! I can't move. I mean I'm really totaled, paralyzed. People start running out from the funeral parlor. And you know what it was?"

I am somewhat paralyzed myself now but manage to shake my head, no.

"The water short-circuited the horn! God, what a spooky sound. It wasn't human. But then again it wasn't like any horn I ever heard either. And after all this was a *hearse*. It took John about five minutes to get at the trouble and cut it off."

We looked at each other for a minute.

"I don't believe in ghosts or spirits or any of that junk," Eric said finally. "Just the same, I was damn glad to get out of there today."

• • •

It was the anniversary of our discovery of Eric's illness, not a day we were likely to forget. Once again Eric was packed and ready to go off to college. This time there was a difference. He was no longer the eager, bright, but uncertain seventeen-year-old. His eyes had lost their innocence; they were not hard but they held a man's look of determination.

It was impressive to watch him pack, get organized to leave. At no one's urging, he put an ad in the paper to sell his Mustang. He made sure it was polished and tuned up when a buyer finally came around. After the sale, he kept some of the money for personal expenses, gave the rest to his father to help with college. "I can't afford to keep a car up there," he said briefly.

I remembered the doctor's words of a year ago: "Six months. One year. Two years." We were one year down but going strong. His second remission was now almost six months old and still solid gold. You looked at him and you couldn't help thinking, "He's got it made." The hard physical work of his summer jobs, the long hours in the sun had done their work. His slim body was brown, powerful, the body of an athlete in top form.

We knew he would still have to have blood tests every week. Our doctor had arranged to have these done in the university infirmary, with a telephoned report to him to follow immediately. Eric also would have to make the journey into Memorial's outpatient clinic every sixth week for the usual bone marrow evaluation. But these things were routine, after all. We had all grown used to them, and they no longer seemed so threatening.

Sidney and I were not the only ones beguiled and convinced

by Eric's strong comeback and healthy good looks. Our doctor told me, "I'm not worried about Eric any longer. We can hold him with methotrexate for years if necessary."

It was with this blessing tucked comfortably in the backs of our minds that we set out one September morning to drive our son, and about one thousand pounds of his personal belongings, up to the tiny dormitory room he would share with some unknown classmate for the following year.

CHAPTER 5

DRIVING HOME FROM the university, I felt empty, curiously let down—and I knew why. When they hand you that small bundle in the hospital, you feel the baby is yours forever. I have made this mistake four times in my life and I'm sure I'd make it again, in joy and foolishness, if I were still in the baby business. There's no help for it. Nature hooks the parent, and all the while she's prodding the impatient offspring to be up and gone.

The first time Eric tried to leave home he was six and he'd just learned to read and write. No doubt he felt a dramatic necessity to show off these new skills. He disappeared one afternoon, leaving the following note:

Dear Mommy and Daddy,

I will be back in 20 years. I have gone to sea do not worrye I have 300 cookies with me

love youe son
Eric

We kept our cool, guessing he'd probably return home once the cookies gave out. It was nice to see him in his accustomed place that night at the dinner table when I started to serve fried chicken.

The next time Eric ran away he was nine and furiously angry. He made a great deal of obvious noise, thumping and banging, as he got a big suitcase down from the attic. He packed it heavily with important belongings, struggled downstairs, got the front door open, and announced in a loud voice that he was going to South America. Forever. *Slam!*

"Forever" turned out, once again, to be until dinnertime. But nobody laughed at him. Instead, his father suggested that getting to South America, which was thousands of miles away, might take a little practice. "Why don't you try South Norwalk tomorrow for a start, Eric? Here's a stake for you."

Sidney pulled out his wallet, laid a dollar on the table, then found some change in his pocket. Eric's blue eyes opened wide in astonishment, delight, and just a touch of apprehension.

"You can get the bus up at the corner by the gas station. Come back when you feel like it." Sidney put down his coffee cup, got up to look for the evening paper, and made no further suggestions.

Next morning I saw Eric, who suddenly looked very small, standing on the corner by the bus stop as I drove uptown to get a few groceries. Forty minutes later I drove back. He was still there. The bus hadn't come. There was no way I could honorably give him a lift to South Norwalk. You can't have your mother providing the transportation when you run away. I thought of driving past him, casually, with the window down, saying something like, "Say, how's your running away coming along?" Awful. Worse than awful, insulting. So I went on home.

Eric returned home late that afternoon as triumphant as if he'd just opened up the Northwest Passage. He'd explored the harbor, the bridge, the docks, chatted with a policeman while he lunched in a diner, bought a 39-cent ballpoint pen in Woolworth's, and then, just as his funds were running low at the end of the trip, he'd found a new supermarket which was giving away balloons and free orange drink to celebrate its opening. He had 7 cents left over after paying his bus fare home.

In the years that followed, Eric took many brave whacks at the parental ties. But we were all just as unprepared, as parents and children usually are, for the big cut that comes with college. There were still many strands of necessity and irritation binding us together. There were strands of affection, too. But when we said good-bye to Eric at his college dorm, we all knew that the long good-bye of growing away had begun.

Three days after we parted, we got our first letter.

Dear Mom, Dad, Mark and Lisa,

Hope you're all well, I'm fine. Classes started today. English looks good, International Relations, too. So far I've spent money for the following: Lamp $2.97 Books $33.96 Food $1.70 Laundry 25¢ Stamps 60¢ I'd appreciate mail from home and brownies, also the DEAD END sign from my room.

Love,
Eric

What college freshman has not written letters home like this? It was skimpy, it was ordinary, and we rejoiced in every word. Now we were back on the track with other mothers and fathers, other healthy sons. We could hardly wait for the mailman to rattle our box each day, and when there was a letter from Eric, we read survival in every line. Soon the pages began to be full of soccer talk.

"Soccer practice was O.K. I really felt strong. Chris Todd and I both did pretty well. There is a guy from Swaziland, one from Korea, one from Israel and some others. We did sprints up the stadium steps. . . ."

By late October 1968 Eric was co-captain of his university freshman team. He'd played in most of the games, racked up several goals and assists, acquired an impressive black eye during one match in a collision with somebody's head, and narrowly escaped a fight with an upset cadet when the University of Connecticut beat the Coast Guard Academy four to nothing.

We drove up to the university at Storrs several times to see him play, and once we journeyed as far as Boston when Connecticut was scheduled to meet Harvard's freshman soccer team. It turned out to be a hard-fought game. Connecticut finally lost but Eric scored a smashing goal. He wrote home a few days later, "It really felt good to score with you there."

Soccer season drew to a close. Christmas vacation came and went. Eric's remission was holding. His bone marrows, taken every six weeks, remained good. His blood counts were still high. But as January got down to the serious business of winter, students began to get sick.

I could still see the Eric of a year ago, going off bareheaded in a swirl of snowflakes to that game in Yankee Stadium. In spite of my year-long resolve, I began to feel the old itch of worry. But Eric wrote us:

> *Everyone comes by and asks me for Vitamin C.*
> *There's a never-ceasing cold which is rampant in this*
> *place. I can't catch it because I own all the Vitamin C.*

If I survived last week up here (which I did), I can survive ANYTHING!

> *Love,*
> *Eric*

The capitalization and underlining of "anything" were the first indications in months that Eric wondered, as he surely must have, whether his remission would continue to hold. In his next letter he wrote:

> *Here's a psychological observation: Fewer people are sick since they stopped talking about the flu. . . . I've got another black eye, though. You see there was this hill completely frozen over and I was pretending I was Jean-Claude Killy. I should have taken my hands out of my pockets.*

Occasionally Eric wrote just to Sidney or just to me. In the middle of February I got a letter that let me in a little.

> *I've been perfectly healthy now for about a year and in my own mind I know I've licked what I had. Whether or not I want to admit it, being sick was exciting. However, to say I've changed because of it, and now I have some great insight into life, would be to admit that I thought at one point I was going to die. I never did.*
>
> *However, I can't tell what's been going on in my subconscious. Maybe I've repressed something I felt. Before, my goal was to get better and to come to school.*

Now I've done that and I need new goals. I don't have
any really, I'm still searching. But I'm glad I feel I can
write to you. I think you'll understand what I'm trying
to express. . . .

In May we passed the one-year anniversary of Eric's second remission. It was easy to recall the doctor's words: "we can keep him on methotrexate for years." Things seemed stable enough for me to attend to business once again. At my father's death, three years before, I'd taken over a small advertising service, drawing cartoons and writing copy for several of his customers in Florida. It was easy, pleasant work; more than this, it was a modest monthly anchor to windward that we could count on to hold through the choppy seas of free-lancing. But to serve my clients, I had to visit them once in a while. Now I was ready.

Sidney gave me his blessing and said, business and finances permitting, he might be able to join me later for a weekend in the sun. For him three days of hard swimming was as relaxing as a two- or three-week vacation. He liked to go way out past the breakers and do half a mile or more each morning and afternoon. I was used to trudging up the beach, covering the same distance on foot, while all the disapproving surf fishermen along the way warned me that "that man out there" was certainly going to be eaten by sharks.

Sidney didn't get his swim that season, however. I'd been away just a week, things were going well, I even had a new client, when I was called to the hotel phone one morning. "Long distance," said the girl at the switchboard. It was Sidney. He said, "Eric's out of remission. He came out very fast. They're giving him some drugs—I don't know which ones—to hold him until the term ends in about another week. But when school's over, they want him to get started on asparaginase right away."

"I'll be there by then," I said.

During that next week I bought a plane ticket for New York and tried to finish up my business quickly. I gathered my stuff together for the trip. And I got two letters from Eric at college, both written after his relapse. He told me the score casually. "Dr. Burchenal and his boys run a tight ship. I've had a shot of vincristine and I'm again taking prednisone, four tablets three times a day, with, as yet, no ill effects."

But there was a new what-the-hell craziness in those letters, a freaky humor and a wild busting out of rebellious energy. Come take me if you can, he seemed to be saying. I'm alive, *alive*, goddammit!

He goofed off, started midnight soccer games in the hall. The food was bad and he spoke of hoping a prison riot would break out in the dining hall. "I want to put a plate of braised beef through the picture window," he wrote. One night he turned on the fire hose and let it run until it started to fill up the stairwell. His freshman counselor finally went to see him in his room. He suggested that Eric get his mind on "serious things."

Eric wrote, "Well, I grabbed him and said the pressure of college was just too great and I couldn't take it any more (like when Tyrone Power cracks up in the trenches and Jimmy Stewart slaps him. 'Thanks, I needed that.')."

The counselor went on to tell Eric he'd better find something constructive to do.

"How about throwing shoes through the window?" asked Eric.

"You know you wouldn't do that."

"Watch me," said Eric. He whipped off his loafer and sent it crashing through the pane. The noise was enormous. Faces appeared in the doorway. Glass was all over the place. One piece stuck up out of the wastebasket. Eric indicated it admiringly. "Two points."

The counselor managed to get up and brush a few slivers off his trousers. "Of course we'll have to do something about this," he said grimly, and walked quickly to the doorway. But the sweatshirted spectators were knotted together closely, and the counselor tripped over somebody's sneaker as he made his exit. Somebody else guffawed.

The authorities told Eric they were going to charge him $15 for the window and write a letter home telling us that our son had damaged college property. Eric then went out and bought an 80-cent pane of glass, a 40-cent can of putty, and repaired the window himself. "The resident adviser was impressed with my workmanship," he wrote me with some pride. The college dropped the matter.

I thought, so he smashed something. But then he fixed it. His control wavered but it's holding. The day after getting that letter I flew home.

It was one of those flights—a jammed hatch, a late departure, no air conditioning, engine trouble over New Jersey—so they put us down at Kennedy, which could take us immediately, instead of La Guardia, where our friends or relatives waited with cars. A bus ride. Then my baggage disappeared from the sidewalk one minute after I put it down. I was sure it was stolen. But Sidney found it an hour later in another airline building half a mile away.

With this reentry, I was in a mood to find Eric stretched out on a couch like an invalid poet when I got home. Instead he was practicing hoop shots in the driveway. Even in the half-dark I could see he looked fit, strong, energetic as usual. His eyes were not ringed. Only in the too-full curve of his cheek could you see the puffiness of prednisone beginning to show.

"Mom," he said, "will you drive in with me to Memorial in the morning?"

"Sure, Eric. Of course."

"It's like this: Dr. Burchenal is going to let me have asparaginase every day as an outpatient. It's okay for me to do the driving in if I feel like it. But I have to hang around the hospital all day till four or five so they can watch out for side effects. They don't know all that much about how asparaginase affects people yet. I might get sick or something, so they think you ought to do the driving back from New York."

"All right. I'll be glad to. When do you want to leave?"

"About seven. I have to be there by eight thirty for sure."

"Seven o'clock. It's a date."

"Do you want me to go in with you?" Sidney asked after we went inside together.

"No, I'll be fine." I knew he'd been working on a big job that was due to be turned in in a few days. I was, at that moment, pretty well caught up on my own work. "If I need some relief later in the week, I'll let you know."

CHAPTER 6

MEMORIAL HOSPITAL AT THE TIME Eric and I drove in to keep our rendezvous with asparaginase, was just beginning a mammoth reconstruction project. The old hospital was being torn down, section by section, while a new one was erected on the same site—something like putting on a new suit without removing your overcoat. The groans of falling timbers, the chatter of jackhammers, the roar of rubble crashing down through wooden chutes still fill my ears when I think of Memorial. The sidewalk along York Avenue was protected by a crude tunnel of boards, but it was gritty with bits of mortar and I picked my way along, keeping an eye out for possible flying bricks. Eric, who'd been here many times, was, as usual, ahead of me.

"Come on," he said. "I've got a date at the lab for blood tests. After that you can go to Clinic with me if you want to."

"Sure I want to. I'm coming."

We went up the broad stone steps of the main entrance. Eric left me in the first-floor waiting room. "See you," he said. "This won't take too long."

In about half an hour he was back. He dropped down beside me, picked up a discarded *New York Times* from a nearby seat, read it for about fifteen minutes, then got up. "Let's go," he said.

This was a familiar routine to him, I could see, as he guided me briskly through a labyrinth of old halls with many double doors opening into other halls until at last we came to an ancient room with dark stained woodwork and row upon row of splintery wooden benches jammed with people. It looked like a cross between a condemned school building and an obsolete ferryboat. This was the outpatient clinic, the place where leukemia patients and many other cancer patients had their first contact with the great Memorial. Cancer, the final equalizer, had brought them all to these benches to wait their turn. There were old men and women. Housewives knitting or reading magazines. Students with open notebooks trying to study. A few businessmen reading the morning papers as if they were merely waiting to see a customer. There was one young workman with heavily muscled arms. (Could *he* be sick?) Next to him a chic matron in pearls kept her pose of aloofness, a look that said she was late for an appointment somewhere else. Then there were the mothers, too many mothers, holding sick infants or little children who sat too passively on their laps. These people had come from all over the city, all parts of the country—some from as far away as Greece or South Africa—seeking the best medical care they could find. They were getting it here in this dingy room.

Behind screens at the far end of the room, doctors and nurses worked in crowded bedlam. They examined, diagnosed, treated, and prescribed in tiny curtained booths, bumping each other's elbows as they tried to deal with the flow of patients.

"You gotta watch it when you go in there," Eric said wryly. "We were jammed in so close the other day I nearly got a bone marrow meant for some other guy."

There is today a handsome, modern clinic in full use for outpatients in the new Memorial. But even in the days when it was an overcrowded old ferryboat, you could see right away that the clinic was a vital arm of the big hospital. Here, the results of laboratory tests which measured the patients' blood count (white cells, platelets, hemoglobin, and possible wild cells) were evaluated. In some hospitals it may take hours or even a full day to get such blood work done. In Memorial, where the need is constant, lab experts can often give results to the doctors in half an hour. Periodic bone marrows were also performed routinely in the clinic, for it is in the bone marrow that cell changes are first detected, and immediate diagnosis and treatment offer the best hope of staying ahead of the cancer.

On the basis of lab tests, bone marrows, and general health (weight, temperature, heart, lungs, etc.) decisions had to be made by the doctors for every patient appearing at the clinic. Did his dose of medication seem to be the right strength for him? Too much? Too little? Was he tolerating it without too many serious side effects? Did he now require a change of medication or, perhaps, additional drugs? Most important, was the patient still in good remission or did he show signs of coming out? The first appearance of immature, nonconforming cells was a serious matter to be followed closely. The patient, in this case, might be asked to return in just a few days for a further check, instead of coming back at the usual one- or two-week intervals. When remission was over, usually the patient had to "come in."

This was bad news for all concerned. Memorial's ability to treat hundreds of patients in the outpatient clinic releases many needed beds, saves thousands of dollars, saves the time of overworked doctors, nurses, and hospital workers. Most important, from the patients' point of view, the outpatient clinic is emotionally part of the outside world. Despite the drugs, bone marrows, checkups, and restrictions, cancer patients attending Clinic were usually still holding down jobs, going to school, raising families, and trying to live good lives.

During that first visit I noticed that while a few people, especially the mothers of very young patients, seemed quite frightened, on the whole there was a lot of warmth in the clinic. Many of the regulars greeted each other as friends, gossiping across the benches, telling of vacations and good times, new jobs and new medications all in the same matter-of-fact way. Sometimes there was a moment of shared triumph for a remission achieved. Sometimes voices were subdued as they spoke of a comrade who'd had a serious setback, who'd had to "go in" upstairs. I watched Eric, waving to friends, greeting some by name, and thought, he's one of them now.

Before too long, Eric's name was called and he went up to one of the curtained booths where a nurse and a doctor waited for him. When he reappeared some time later, he was waving a prescription blank. "Asparaginase! Go!" he said.

Eric held the door for me and we began to retrace our steps through double doors and long hallways. He handed me the prescription for a moment.

"Take a look."

"Where on earth will you get *that* filled?" I asked, mystified, as I handed it back.

"At the Memorial Super Rexall Drugstore, where else?"

I had thought of asparaginase as being locked up in a vault like the gold bricks at Fort Knox. "That must be some drugstore."

"It is," said Eric. "But the prescription counter is too close to the snack bar. Some porter on a break from pushing his broom is going to get thirty thousand dollars' worth of asparaginase, and I'm going to get thirty cc's of coffee with cream to go. Well—I'll see you later this afternoon. When I get this filled I have to report back to the doctor's office. Then we go to work. You be somewhere around here? Okay?"

We were once again near the waiting room.

"Okay."

I watched him go off to the pharmacy with his jaunty, quick walk. I went outside to get some lunch, stood blinking in the sunshine for a few moments, then decided to wait for a while. It was getting close to twelve, but I didn't feel hungry.

The main waiting room at Memorial holds little joy. The visitors, sitting alone or clumped together on cracked leather sofas, stare inward or glance blankly out windows as they wait for word from upstairs. Or perhaps they wait to take home a relative, saved or doomed or with the verdict possibly in doubt. Waiting is an illness all its own, and I came down with it myself as the afternoon dragged on. My spine seemed to be entirely the wrong construction for any of the sofas or chairs I tried. My head felt heavy but I couldn't lean it back. Reading was no good; my eyelids threatened to fall down with each new sentence.

Suddenly Eric appeared, walking slowly toward me. I sprang up. "No, no," he said, sinking down in the nearest chair. "Not yet. Have to wait around for observation." I realized from the way he was talking that he was fighting nausea. An extra word might tip him over the brink. He moved at last to an empty couch where he stretched out under an open window. There was a faint breeze coming in from the hot city. A young woman in a lab coat—not a nurse; a technician, I assumed—came out, bent over Eric, said something to him. He shook his head. She left and several minutes later a nurse appeared and took his pulse. She said a few words, he nodded in my direction, then she came over to me. "Watch him, Mrs. Lund," she said. "Let me know if his breathing alters or if anything changes."

This startled me. "Where will you be?"

"Last room at the end of the hall." She walked away.

I wasn't sure what I was watching for, but I knew enough to be frightened. When anyone takes a new drug there can be unpleasant surprises. The doctors who used chemotherapy on their very sick patients walked the tightrope every day between possible death from overdose and slow death from underdose which left the disease unchecked, the patient still vulnerable. In 1969 most of the major drugs used to combat leukemia could also truthfully have been labeled poisons. There were very few drug-induced deaths, considering the potency. But the risk remained. Asparaginase, despite its favorable publicity and "new look," was no exception. I knew how important it was for the doctors to guess what might be the right dose for Eric. By now I also knew that Eric had a tendency to overreact to drugs, so whatever the doctors knew—or thought they knew—about their exciting new drug, it still might not apply to him.

After several hours, a nurse summoned Eric into the doctor's office. They checked him out for allergic or other unfavorable reactions. Apparently he was out of danger. We were free to go. I got our car out of hock from the garage some blocks away and drove it around to Memorial's front door. Eric got himself down to the street and crawled in the back seat, where we had towels and a pillow. Then we moved out into traffic to fight for our lives all over again on the East River Drive and Bruckner Boulevard.

There are a few things in this world I am afraid of. In those days the unfinished Bruckner Boulevard left me numb with terror. The traffic braiding itself in and around the stalled trucks, concrete mixers, and giant pillars moved much too fast for me. Eric bravely lifted his head from time to time to help me. "Watch out for that bastard passing you on the right." Once, after a stop, I managed to fake out a taxi driver who'd been crowding me at every light. "That's the way to go," Eric cheered me in a croaky voice. Out the window he called to the driver, "Don't choose my mom. She'll take you every time."

Eric fought off his nausea until we pulled into home port. Then he was instantly sick and went straight to bed. Around midnight, however, he came downstairs and began foraging in the icebox.

Next morning he was up early, ready to go. We set off again. He did the driving in. Again, at the end of the day, I did the driving home. I was braced for a long daily haul, perhaps many weeks of Memorial, asparaginase, and Bruckner Boulevard. But after a time the doctors decided to hospitalize Eric for a few days, in order to desensitize him to the drug.

A very important thing happened when Eric went into the hospital, something which I did not learn about until much later. He came under the protective umbrella of CRF, or Clinical Research Facility. From then on, his care was totally paid for by the United States Government, which provides what is called an "investigational fund," to hospitals that are using experimental drugs.

Eric was not a specially privileged patient. Everyone on Ewing Eight was a ward of CRF and carried a little plastic credit card, almost exactly like a Bloomingdale's charge-a-plate, in his wallet to prove it. We had earlier paid doctor and hospital costs. We had managed to afford the simpler antileukemic drugs such as mercaptopurine and methotrexate. If we had not been able to, Eric would still have received excellent treatment. No patient in need was turned away. Almost no one, however, could pay for the cost of administering the newer, often more dangerous, drugs. Or the cost of the many studies, intensive nursing care, special diets, and other things which went along with such therapy. The tab might run ten or fifteen thousand dollars a day, week after week, month after month, and that would be prohibitive even for a millionaire. But CRF, from its desire to understand all the manifestations of experimental drug use, willingly paid the check.

Asparaginase was not only a costly drug but a potentially lethal one if not used properly. The process of desensitization, I learned later, was a bit like the course of allergy shots one gets from a doctor to help overcome an unfortunate sensitivity to house dust or ragweed. Only in Eric's case, desensitization, which took only one day, was a continuous process lasting over a period of many hours, whereby drops of asparaginase were added to a bottle of fluid and the mixture was administered intravenously by means of a needle in his arm. The bottle was popularly referred to as an "I.V." The drops were added at intervals of fifteen minutes and the amount was doubled each time: one drop was followed by two drops, two was followed by four, four by eight, and so on.

There was always danger of anaphylactic shock, which can cause instant death from allergic reaction, so a doctor always stayed with the patient to administer the drops. The doctor in attendance for Eric was Dr. Lynn Ratner, Chief Medical Resident at that time. It turned out to be a happy assignment for both doctor and patient.

Dr. Ratner, whose major interest besides medicine was photography, usually found himself responsible for writing, producing, and filming a yearly movie for Memorial's Christmas party. Now, tied to the side of a young patient for most of the day, he invited him to collaborate on a story for the following Christmas. Eric rose to the occasion at once. Between them they hatched a plot revolving around Dr. Ratner's supposed fiendish attempts to infiltrate the hospital with his own private cancer cure—an unlikely mixture called Bubbamycin. Nobody liked Bubbamycin. It tasted awful. Its effects were violent. In the end, Santa Claus saved the day by descending to the floors of Ewing, confiscating Bubbamycin, and giving the patients back their old standard drugs—which were welcomed joyfully—as Christmas presents.

I am told that when Dr. Ratner and crew finally got around to shooting this epic, they first set out for Bloomingdale's very early one Saturday during the pre-Christmas season. Their hope was to find a properly dressed-up Santa on the premises that they could use for a few shots. To their astonishment, they arrived at the very moment that the bus from the employment agency drove up to the front door of the store and disgorged eleven Santa Clauses! The movie, entitled "Remission Impossible," turned out to be one of Dr. Ratner's best.

At the time Eric was first desensitized to asparaginase, I didn't understand the process and I was in no position to watch it. I had gone to a local hospital myself for a minor operation and had been told to take it easy for a few days. While this was going on, I kept asking Sidney how Eric was. The invariable answer was, "Fine." I found this infuriatingly brief. When I asked for more specific medical information, Sidney often got very upset. He hated to guess, he refused to be inaccurate, and he didn't like quizzing doctors. "Fine"

I took to mean that Eric's spirit was good, but somehow I never doubted that it would be. He was not "fine" in my book, though, as long as asparaginase was partly a danger for him, as long as he wasn't in remission, as long as he still had leukemia. I was impatient to take the train to New York and see for myself what was going on. Finally my doctor said I could go.

I was used to the waiting-room scene at Memorial. But I'd never yet been on the upper floors. Now I found I was breathing too fast as I went up the familiar stone steps and walked over to the huge circular information desk. There was a man with a suitcase ahead of me, apparently saying good-bye to one of the reception-ists. There was something a bit strange about her look as she talked to him. I waited. Just then a doctor, walking across the lobby, was hailed by this same man. "See you in a few weeks, Doc!" The doctor waved, but something in his look also made me pause. The man said a final few words to the lady at the desk and turned around to leave. He had no nose. Just a black hole. He walked briskly out to the main door. "So long," he said to the doorman, then went down the steps and out into the world.

"Yes?" The receptionist was looking at me.

"Oh—I want to see Eric Lund."

She flipped through a card file. "Room eight-thirty," she said.

An elevator took me to the eighth floor. There was an imme-diate sense of urgency there, of crises around every corner. A patient whose entire head was swathed in bandages rolled past me on a stretcher pushed by a casual-looking orderly. "Going down! X-ray!" the orderly shouted to the elevator operator.

I looked around, confused, and saw the front office where

nurses worked quietly, busy with charts, not talking. I stuck my head in. A dark-haired nurse with glasses looked up.

"I'd like to see Eric Lund?"

"Room eight-thirty. Halfway down on your left."

I found my way. A sign beside the door of 830 said CAUTION! NO SMOKING! OXYGEN. Inside were two beds. Oxygen tents over both. Mummylike figures lay under the taut white sheets. Both very still. The rasp of breathing filled the room. My God, could it have come to this so quickly? Horrified, I went up to the first tent and peered in. Open mouth. Beak nose. Face of a dying bird. I made myself look more closely. It was the face of an old woman. Those wisps of gray-white hair were definitely not Eric's. I turned to the other bed—another old woman.

"*Who* is it you're looking for?"

I jumped. The dark-haired nurse with glasses was right behind me.

"Eric Lund."

"*Eric* Lund? I thought you said Carrie Young. Just a minute."

We went back to the office. I stood in the doorway, shaken, while the nurse went to a phone at the back and dialed. In a moment she returned. "Eric Lund is in eight-thirty on the eighth floor of Ewing."

"Ewing? Where is that?"

She gestured vaguely. "You have to go all the way down and take the other elevators."

I took an elevator going down. Carrie Young. Eric Lund. My head was full of a strange buzzing. My feet moved very well, though; when the door opened, they carried me out. There was a long hall. I decided it must lead to Ewing. Finally I came to another bank of elevators, got on one just as the door was closing, and immediately went down three more floors. Without thinking, I got out, and before I could pull myself together and ask the operator's help, he'd gone back up. I was somewhere in Memorial's basement. Big pipes running overhead in all directions. Valves. Switch boxes. Doors that said KEEP OUT. I'm tired and I'm getting stupid, I thought. Suddenly I wanted to be home in bed myself, being cared for, far away from this place. But there was another long gray hall and, at the end of it, a porter was mopping a floor. I walked the long hall to ask him, "Where is Ewing? Can I get there from here?"

"You have to go back up, lady. Can't get there from here."

Back at the big information desk on the main floor, I explained my problem and received some good solid directions. Ten minutes later I was on the eighth floor of Ewing Pavilion, a tall red-brick building attached to Memorial Hospital on its western flank, facing First Avenue between 67th and 68th Streets. Room 830 turned out to be a six-bed ward of young and old men, most of whom were lying down and some of whom were obviously very sick. In the middle bed on the left side of the room, Eric, wearing a yellow button-down oxford shirt, slightly flared black-and-white plaid pants, and Adidas running shoes, was sitting up on top of his bed covers. In spite of the I.V. bottle dripping fluid into his right arm, his irritated expression clearly said, "I don't belong here in this place, in this bed; there's been some mistake."

"Hello, Eric," I said. "How are you?"

"Great!" he said. "I'm fine. I'm going to blast out of here as soon as the doctors come."

"Are you sure? Did they say so?"

He shrugged, meaning that wasn't my problem. Meaning he doesn't really know, I thought. I was so relieved to see him still Eric, still defiant and whole, sitting up fully dressed, that suddenly I felt close to tears. There was a chair next to his bed. I sank into it.

"The Burch told me I can have asparaginase at home. That would be better than driving in every day. They're going to start me on it all over again soon. And I want out of here."

"The Burch?"

"Dr. Burchenal. He's in Paris right now. At a conference or something. But before he left he said I could get out. He was going to fix it up so a doctor could give me asparaginase in the hospital at home and—Ah!" Eric interrupted himself. "Here comes Dr. Salem. Hi, Dr. Salem!"

A very small, dark-haired man with dark sad eyes approached the bed. Eric introduced us. In the process I forgot the ground rules and said to the doctor. "Eric wants to go home. Are you planning to let him out?"

"Mom!" There was fire in Eric's eye. "I don't want you asking that. I'll take care of things myself."

"Eric," soothed Dr. Salem. "A mother has a right to her questions, her concerns—"

"Excuse me." I could laugh at this point. "I'm going to bow out. I'll be in the lobby."

I went out to the eighth-floor lobby but it was crowded, so I walked down to the end of the hall where there was a big south window. Four plastic chairs and several wheelchairs were drawn up close to the windowsill. A young man in white pajamas sat in one of the wheelchairs smoking, leaning forward to look down on the traffic pouring up First Avenue. I sat down across from him. Our knees were almost touching. His eyes didn't move. He went on staring at the city.

"Mrs. Lund?"

I turned around. A tall distinguished-looking man was there. Dr. Salem was at his side. "I'm Dr. Clarkson."

I'd heard his name before. Dr. Bayard Clarkson was Chief of the Hematology Service at Memorial.

"We've got a little problem," said Dr. Clarkson. "Eric wants to go home and get his asparaginase every day as an outpatient in the hospital there. I understand Dr. Burchenal more or less promised him he could do this."

"Yes, he was just telling me about it. And he was getting it here as an outpatient, after all, when you first started."

"I know," said Dr. Clarkson. "But that's a little different. We're set up to take care of any emergency here. And if we want to increase the dose we might run into trouble. Asparaginase is a relatively new drug, and we still have lots to learn about using it."

"I understand that."

"What do you think, Phil?" Dr. Clarkson turned to Dr. Salem.

Dr. Salem's large eyes rolled unhappily. "I think this is a mistake," he said. "I prefer to have him here where I watch him." His accent was Middle Eastern. I wondered from what country.

"Will you talk to Eric?" Dr. Clarkson seemed to be addressing me.

"Me? Goodness, no! I'm afraid of him," I said, laughing. "I'm his mother, after all."

The doctors smiled.

"Are you afraid of him?" I challenged Dr. Clarkson.

He laughed too. "Just a little bit, maybe. He can be very persuasive."

"I think he'd listen to you far better than he would to me," I said. "He'd think I was trying to run his show or that I was too worried about him to let him come home. But I'm certainly willing to have him home if *you* are. I know how much it means to him to get outdoors and run and be himself when he feels up to it. But it's your decision. You know the risks. I don't."

"Well—" Dr. Clarkson looked again at Dr. Salem. "I'd still be happier with him in here. But I don't know. Let's go talk to him together, Phil."

They disappeared into Room 830.

Fifteen minutes later they both came out shaking their heads and laughing. "He won. He's going home."

"What about the asparaginase?"

"Well, we're giving him a two-day rest. Then he'll have to come back in on Monday just for a few hours and we'll work something out so he can get the drug administered at the hospital out there."

We said good-bye. They disappeared around a corner. In a few minutes Eric came out and walked over to the elevators. He had his small TV set in one hand, his duffel bag in the other. He threw me a look of fury. We rode down to the main floor in silence. Once we were out in the street, he exploded. "I'm mad as hell at you. You talked to the doctors. They were ready to keep me locked up in there!"

"Look, Eric, I didn't talk to them. They talked to *me*. I didn't say one word except I'd be happy to have you home if they agreed. I told them it was their decision."

He walked swiftly along, several paces ahead of me, swinging the TV and the duffel bag as if they were clubs.

"Okay," he said finally. "But you stay out of it."

We half walked, half ran, all the way to Grand Central. Eric was wrought up and wanted to move. If his hospital stay had slowed him down any, I certainly couldn't see it. Once we were on the train, however, he began to relax. In a voice almost pleading, he said, "Don't you see? I'm not like the others in there. I've got to fight it, and I can do it better outside. Then I can keep in shape. I don't want people messing me up. It's my attitude that counts. They took a guy out of our room yesterday. I heard he died last night. I don't know what his problem was. But I do know he stopped fighting. Now, Richard, on the other side of me, he's going to make it. I like the way he takes it. Strictly day at a time. No sweat. He doesn't let anything get to him. He's got a wife and two little girls back in Cleveland. He's going to get out Sunday and go home to them. He's all right, Richard, a very nice guy."

Eric talked and talked. He talked about what he wanted to do with his life, how he wanted to work with kids some day, how his big dream was to go around the world. But first how he and his friend, Eddie Kline, were going to drive all the way to California and maybe even Mexico in Eddie's van this summer just as soon as he got finished with asparaginase. They'd planned to go in June but Eddie was hanging around now, waiting for Eric, and they were going to go for sure the minute the doctors let him off the hook. Our station came up. We got off, found our car in the parking lot, and when I handed him the keys, Eric said, "Thanks for listening, Mom. I think maybe you understand."

I understand nothing, I thought wearily, except that I love you, I trust you, and I want you to do it your way.

CHAPTER 7

THE NEXT MORNING, Eric went up and got his old job back, part time, at Fox's Funeral Home. That afternoon he mowed their big lawn and started trimming their hedges. When he came home about five, he was flushed with sun, his blue eyes clear and happy.

"I'll do our hedges when I get time," he told me.

Sunday was another good June day. The trees held still. Down at the beach the water held still, too, mirroring the rocks, the buoys, the scallops of boats. Eric went out running through his world. I drove back and forth to town on errands and I saw him several times, running past the summer fields, past little boys fishing from the Sammis Street bridge (where he once fished, too), past the school pond where once again mother ducks sailed ahead of six or seven new ducklings, past the landmarks of his childhood: the cannon, the boatyards, the post office.

When he came in he was glowing. "It felt so good to run again. You know, I love this town. This was a great place to grow up."

A few moments later I saw him go by with his spear gun headed for the beach. I looked at the calendar. Full tide just about now. Maybe a fish would be waiting for Eric down among the dark, crusted rocks.

Eric caught no fish that day. As he came home from the beach, however, five girls dropped by to see him, spilling out of a VW convertible. They went out on our porch to wait for him while he changed clothes. Then I carried his supper out there on a tray.

"Want Cokes? Or Seven-Ups?" I asked the girls.

"Yes, please!" "Oh, yes!" "Thank you!"

I cleaned up the kitchen to their laughter, to summer sounds and the music from somebody's portable. This is better. So much better than a hospital bed. Plain old everyday life may help him as much as the most expensive wonder drug.

On Monday Eric rose early and took the train in to Memorial. Around three in the afternoon he called from New York.

"I'll be on the three thirty," he said. "Meet me? I've got some asparaginase which ought to get in the icebox right away."

Eric jumped off the train an hour and a half later with a brown paper bag which looked like somebody's lunch. "Thirty thousand dollars' worth," he said, tossing it to me. "Stick it in when we get home."

For the next few weeks we had thousands of dollars' worth of asparaginase in our icebox. At first it made me nervous, in spite of the fact that the little vials were sealed and nested safely in their carton like Christmas tree ornaments. The asparaginase we'd seen in Dr. Burchenal's office had been in tablet form. This was a frothy liquid that looked almost exactly like soap-bubble mix. Eric told me it was asparaginase, all right, perhaps a bit more purified than the earlier stuff we'd seen, and now mixed with sugar and water. I finally got used to seeing the asparaginase in there among the hamburger patties, hot dogs, carrots and celery, and bottles of Coke.

And I had to admit that the do-it-yourself-at-home scheme was working. There were fewer side effects now, and Eric felt better every day. From time to time he had to go into the city for fresh supplies of the drug. But most days he was busy outdoors, doing his job at the funeral home, cutting our own grass and hedges, running up at the track, or swimming and spearfishing. Once every day he would drop by the kitchen, wearing cut-offs and T-shirt, casually pick up the day's dose of asparaginase, and take off for the hospital. The young doctor who administered the drug became Eric's friend. I learned that he had once been the resident doctor on Ewing's eighth floor. He still spent a day a week at Memorial in order to keep up with latest proceedings in cancer control and also in order to help his own local patients get the benefit of Memorial's doctors' evaluation of their cases. Memorial had enlisted his help to make it possible for Eric to remain at home.

Dr. Grann was sympathetic and resourceful. Giving asparaginase was not as simple as giving a flu shot. Each little vial had to be added to a larger bottle of I.V. solution. This meant the whole business had to be done in a hospital. But Dr. Grann, knowing our financial squeeze and trying to save us unnecessary costs, took Eric directly to the hospital basement lab. Then, after he'd fixed the needle in place and hung the bottle from one of the overhead pipes, the two of them would sit around talking, laughing, philosophizing a little, while the asparaginase dripped slowly into Eric's arm. "That Dr. Grann's a nice guy," Eric said.

Once I found doctor and patient both in their swim trunks, both very hot with fresh, glowing suntans, standing in front of the icebox gulping down lemonade. "We've got to make a little stop"—he pulled out some asparaginase—"then we're going back out."

Yes, Dr. Grann was a nice guy. The Memorial doctors who dared, weighed, and risked, and who finally let Eric stay on the outside, were understanding, nice guys, too. It would have been easier for all of them to turn him into a patient in pajamas, put him in the hospital where he could only drift from bed to hallway and back again, where they wouldn't have had to worry about him so much, where they wouldn't have been taking chances with their expensive drug. But half the summer would have gone by. They gave Eric wonderful, long summer days in his own world.

Suddenly we learned he was in remission—his third. Just as suddenly the doctors decided Eric must come in again. It was the old irony of leukemia treatment—what makes you better often in some ways makes you worse. Blood tests showed his wild cells in retreat; unfortunately, so were his good cells. The doctors now had no choice but to hospitalize him for his own safety. Eric went right on planning his West Coast trip for midsummer, however. And his doctors went right on helping him as best they could. They gave him transfusions. They watched him carefully for signs of infections. They checked his lab tests every day to see if his counts were coming up. When the news was good, they let him out for half a day or sometimes a whole day on pass. Eric would rush out to the country, grab a sandwich and a glass of milk, then go up to Fox's to cut the grass and trim the hedges. He'd managed to hold onto this part-time job all through June and July by having Mark fill in for him whenever he was stuck in the hospital. Mark hoped to take over the job if Eric finally got to go west.

One evening toward the end of July, Eric pushed open the front door with a shout. (He'd gone to the hospital that morning and I hadn't expected him back for several days.)

"I'm okay to go!" he cried. "Three more days! One more lab check—then we blast off!" He ran upstairs to call Eddie and give him the good news.

"What do you suppose he'll do for money?" I said to Sidney. We were lingering at the dinner table over a last cup of coffee. "Did you give him any?"

Sidney shook his head. "He never mentioned money to me. I thought maybe you'd given him some."

It was never easy to give Eric money. He bought his own clothes. He usually filled the gas tank whenever he used the family car. He paid for his own beers on the few occasions when he went out. But next morning I cornered him over an early breakfast. "Hey, wouldn't you like some money? We'd really like to give you some for this trip."

"Thanks, but I've got enough." Eric pushed back his chair. "We're not planning to do anything splashy. We'll be sleeping in the van, cooking most of our own meals. We figure about a hundred and fifty apiece ought to get us to Mexico and back. Gotta run now. I'm putting in two more days at Fox's. Sunday we pack. Monday we take off." The screen door slammed.

I sat down at the kitchen table. Eric had apparently earned all his vacation money at the funeral home while he was out on passes from Memorial Hospital. He didn't need any of ours. I sat there for a while and I cried.

Eddie's van was an ancient Falcon with nearly 100,000 miles on it. It had a homey, well-used look. Little curtains at the windows. Pots, pans, dishes, cutlery stowed away inside. Eric and Eddie were in high spirits as they packed the van the day before takeoff. Sleeping bags. Duffel bags. Eddie's camera. Canned goods, a few staples. Lots of vitamins. (Eric took them all, from A to E, just in case.)

"That thing will never get off the ground if you don't cut down on the vitamins."

"Wait'll you see what else we've got coming."

They fiddled with racks on top of the van. Half an hour later two surfboards were lashed in place. Then, cap to the climax, they wheeled out Eddie's motorcycle.

"Oh, no! You're kidding!" I said, pretending to be upset. The year Eric was sixteen we'd had a long, hot summer of daily arguments over whether Eric could buy a motorcycle on time. He was determined, even bitter. We held firm. Motorcycles were dangerous. Besides, we thought he ought to learn to drive an automobile well first. And so he had. But, in the summer of 1969, I watched calmly while Eric and Eddie stowed it inside the van and tied it down.

"Give me a ride on that thing when you get back?"

"Too dangerous," Eric said, shooting me a look. "You're not cut out for the motorcycle life, Mom."

"Why not? I once rode an alligator." This was true. At age seven I'd been persuaded to climb aboard a grandfather alligator and ride him for several minutes so my father could record the event for posterity on his brand new Filmo movie camera. Posterity—my sons—had been forever impressed.

"Yeah, that's right. Eddie, how 'bout that? My mom once rode an alligator."

"Really? Automatic transmission?" Eddie had a fast, warm smile, sunny red-gold hair like our own kids. Lisa wanted him for an extra brother.

"You don't believe me."

"Sure I believe you. What make?"

"It was a genuine alligator with four on the floor. Feet, I mean."

• • •

Eric and Eddie took off to see the world the next morning. It was a perfect summer day: gold, blue, still. Their first stop was Memorial Hospital for a few last blood tests and one last checkup by the doctors. A flock of nurses came out to see them off. They stood on the steps of Memorial waving goodbye, smiling, blowing kisses. Then the van took off across 67th Street and headed into the west.

We were able to piece together bits of the trip from a few letters, postcards, snapshots.

Letter from his sister, Meredith, and her husband, Jimmy (postmark, Evanston, Illinois):

> *Eric and Eddie arrived last night. Jim's parents invited us all over for a meal. During dinner Jim's mother remarked that she'd been longing to travel across country ever since she'd read Steinbeck's* Travels with Charley.
>
> *"Well," said Eric, "our trip may be more like* The Grapes of Wrath. *"*

Postcard from Eric (someplace in Kansas):

> *We've been sleeping in fields, cooking out. Or else we buy hot dogs & sauerkraut. (Good stuff, sauerkraut! Cheap & lots of vitamins.) This country is BIG! FLAT!*

Letter from Eric (someplace in Colorado):

> *We're going to try to find a Sears Roebuck in Denver tomorrow night so we can put our noses up against the*

window and watch TV when the astronauts land on the
moon.

Later, they admitted it had been easier to find a tavern and watch the show over a few beers. Never mind how you did it, I thought, it was a miracle watching a miracle. It had taken billions of dollars to put those astronauts on the moon. It had taken millions in medical research to put Eric Lund, very much alive and well, in a Colorado tavern nearly two years after he was stricken with leukemia. Not too many years before, his life would have been over five or six weeks after diagnosis. Science had given him a gift of years. Because of that gift, Eric got to watch the greatest event of his time.

Snapshot from Eric. Taken someplace between Denver and Las Vegas. Eric and Eddie standing in a mountain lake, water up to their waists, smiling in the bright sunshine.

"Who took that?" I asked later.

"Eddie's camera. We set the timer, cocked it, put the camera on a rock, dashed back into the water, and started grinning."

Postcard from Eric and Eddie (postmark, Las Vegas, Nevada):

> *Thought of trying to double our money in a casino*
> *like Frank Sinatra and Sammy Davis, Jr. Thought*
> *better of it. Heading for Los Angeles. . . .*

No word from Los Angeles. No word from anywhere after that.

Eric told us later, "We didn't dig Los Angeles, didn't stop. Just kept heading down the coast toward Balboa. Finally we came to a spot that wasn't so crowded. So we parked the van and scrambled up one of the dunes to look at the Pacific. Some ocean!

"We just stood there a while. Then Eddie said, 'Well, here we are!' And I said, 'Yeah, this is it.'

"Then we surfed the beaches all the way to Mexico wherever the waves looked good."

Eric and Eddie had their greatest adventure on the homeward trip. They decided to head east by first going north to Yosemite. They'd only been there half a day when Eddie's van broke down. It was the first real trouble they'd run into. They walked down the road to a service station, but the attendant just shook his head. "Can't help you out. Not on a Sunday," he said. "Come back Monday when the mechanic's here."

"So then we just said. 'What the hell, let's enjoy,'" Eric told us. "We got out the motorcycle and tore all around those curvy mountain roads. Yosemite is heavy on scenery and big hills. We had a great time. But Monday came and this dude mechanic didn't know what to do with the van. We hung around three days and every day he had a new idea that didn't work.

"We'd about had it with the motorcycle, and we were getting low on food. So we were just sitting there on the road, by the side of this dead van, feeling kinda sunk, when a whole bunch of kids came over the hill. From then on, it was a ball."

The kids were hitching, seeing the country. According to Eric, some were male, some female, but all were dressed alike with beads, backpacks, hair, fringe, patches, and hiking boots. They had guitars, recorders, a few other instruments, and a jug of red wine. More than all this, they had fresh enthusiasm for Eric's and Eddie's problem. One of the group, a lean-faced, bearded youth, even claimed to know something about engines.

"It's your distributor cap," he announced after poking around under the hood for a few minutes. "I seen this before with these old Falcons. You won't get any help 'round here. But there's a real good service station 'bout four miles down the road. We'll give you a hand."

And so the caravan set off, Eddie at the wheel, the rest of them— there were nine of them besides Eric—pushing, heaving, hollering. This was hilly country. They yelled when the van began to move. They yelled louder when they got to the top of each peak. Sometimes going downhill everybody piled in, laughing, swearing, encouraging the old van. Once in a while there was enough momentum to carry them over the next rise. Cries of "Yea! Yea!" But usually they fell back. Then Eddie had to call, "Okay, everybody out! 'Nother hill coming up!"

In this ragged but cheerful manner the group finally reached their destination, a large, businesslike gas station which had a well-equipped garage. The mechanic just happened to have the proper distributor cap.

Eric and Eddie spent the next two days and nights driving all over the West, going several hundred miles out of their way to return members of the expedition to their various hometowns. The detour, made in the spirit of gratitude, turned out to be the best part of the trip. There was continuous live music and song in the back of the van. There was no shortage of tall stories or wine, the original jug having been replaced several times.

•   •   •

Eric and Eddie arrived home on an August afternoon. All brown and gold, with the same light blue eyes. They looked like brothers. They said goodbye like brothers, while making plans for a homecoming blast that evening with a few buddies.

But Mark was the brother who'd held the fort and who'd hung on to the job at Fox's Funeral Home. He came around the corner of the house where he'd just parked the car after work. As he sauntered over, I saw with surprise—why, now he's taller than Eric!

"It's good to see you," he said, looking hard at Eric.

How tough it must be for Mark, I thought. Always worried because he loves him, always second because Eric's problems have to come first, and always waiting, as we all are waiting, to see if Eric will make it. He was a boy who kept his troubles to himself. He had never discussed Eric's illness with us. I knew Eric must have told him by now. Besides, there was no way Mark could escape knowing the seriousness of the problem. There were the trips to Memorial, the transfusions, the news clipping about asparaginase which had been around the house for a while, and the asparaginase itself that had been in our icebox most of the summer.

Now they ran off together to shoot a few baskets in the driveway. It was good to hear Mark's real laugh again, good to watch them bumping each other, wrestling to get hold of the ball.

CHAPTER 8

THAT NIGHT, for the first time in many weeks, I sank into sleep without tossing awhile and then finally reaching for the sleeping pill. He was safely home. Maybe he was also home free. After all, he'd had half a million dollars' worth of asparaginase. I held that thought as I went down and let sleep wash over me.

The ringing blasted me out of a dream about 2:30 A.M.

Groping for the phone, I knocked over my glass of water, dropped the phone, had to pick it up again and start over.

"This is Greenwich Hospital," said the voice at the other end. "We have Eric Lund. . . ."

"You can't have Eric Lund," I finally said. What was going on here anyway? "Memorial has him."

No, Memorial doesn't. He's home in bed. No! No—suddenly I remembered—Eric and Eddie had gone out celebrating somewhere with their friends. I was beginning to come to, and now I was afraid.

"Is this Mrs. Lund?"

"Yes, it is."

"There's been an accident, Mrs. Lund. Who is the plastic surgeon of your choice?"

Hysteria almost climbed out of my throat. This woman must be an idiot. Would I win a color TV, or a vacation for two, all expenses paid, if I answered this question? I pulled myself together and gave her a name. I just happened to know the name of an excellent plastic surgeon in Greenwich, Connecticut. Then suddenly I was totally wide awake.

"Look here," I said into the phone, "Eric Lund has leukemia. You'd better check his blood right away. He may need some transfusions—"

"What is it? What's happened?" Sidney, who usually can sleep through anything, was struggling to wake up. The urgency in my voice had pierced his dreams.

"An automobile accident. Eric's in Greenwich Hospital."

Turning back to the phone, I said to the voice at the other end, "Did you get that about checking his blood?"

"Yes, Mrs. Lund. We'll take care of it. Right now he's being X-rayed for possible skull fracture—"

"We'll get there as soon as we can," I interrupted her. Sidney was out of bed, looking scared, running for the closet. I reached for my slacks, but I couldn't seem to get my leg to go in the right place.

"Mom, you're not going to faint, are you? Mom, you're okay, aren't you?"

"Don't talk, Eric. Keep that thing on your mouth till the doctor gets here. I'm not going to faint."

He lay stretched on the table of Greenwich Hospital's emergency room. His upper lip was split clear through from nose to mouth in two places, a double harelip. His nose—well, it was a nose but not Eric's. His eyes were beginning to blacken and close. A nurse was trying to get the blood out of his hair.

"Where's the doctor?"

The plastic surgeon of my choice, it turned out, was on vacation. But another doctor was coming. In fact, suddenly he was there beside us, a keen-eyed gentleman who swiftly took in the situation and began removing his expensive sports jacket.

"This will take some time," he said.

Sidney and I retreated to the waiting room where the survivors of the outing sat stunned. Eddie hadn't been touched, not a scratch. He shook his head sadly. "Why did it have to be Eric?"

"Anybody else hurt?"

"Jay has a broken nose, maybe. He's in the other emergency room. But he didn't get it like Eric. Carl loosened a coupla teeth. He was driving. But it sure wasn't his fault. Some crazy fool came right at us, forced us off the road. We hit a pole—"

"Then what?" said Sidney.

"Eric was sitting up front on the right. He'd just been turning around to talk to us in back. When we hit the pole, he was whipped around and his face smashed the windshield. Jesus, it was awful. So much blood! But Eric's some guy; he knew what to do. He told us to call an ambulance fast, then he took off his T-shirt, held it against his mouth, and lay down in the grass."

"'S awful," mumbled Carl, his eyes rolling off.

"Carl, are you sure you're all right?" I didn't like the way Carl looked. He nodded, but his eyes seemed glazed.

I went out to the desk where two nurses were going over charts. "Are you sure Carl, that dark-haired boy, is all right? He could be in shock. Maybe it's just that he's afraid he's hurt Eric. He was the driver. It wasn't his fault, but I don't like the way he looks."

One of them put down her pencil and went in to take a look at Carl.

An hour and a half later we were still there in the waiting room. Carl, covered with a blanket, was lying down on a couch. The doctor came out of the emergency room. Sidney and I stood up.

"How's Eric? What about that skull fracture? Did he need blood?"

"He's all right. No fracture. No transfusions. It took quite a few stitches—"

"Oh! How's he going to look?"

"How did he look before?" The doctor delivered that remark with some sharpness. This was a proud man.

"Good. Wonderful!"

"Well, that's the way he's going to look, then." The doctor smiled faintly, with a trace of irritation. "It would have been easier if I could have got him to stop talking. He kept asking me how soon he could work out and get back in shape. What does he play, anyhow?"

"Soccer. For the University of Connecticut."

"Absolutely no running for at least ten days," said the doctor. "His nose isn't broken, by the way. I put a splint on it just to anchor the bandage on his lip. I want those stitches to stay *in*. If he moves around too much or starts to sweat, the whole thing could work loose."

"No running," I said. "Believe me, I'll sit on him personally."

Lisa took one look at Eric the next morning and began to cry.

"He's all right," I said. "I told you he's all right."

"He looks like a penguin," she sobbed. "A penguin who's been in a fight." Then she began to laugh and cry all at once. "It's too bad we can't save him for Halloween. He looks so scary."

The nose bandage did give Eric the look of an angry penguin. His black eyes were now swollen almost shut. His mouth, stiff with tape, stuck out like a beak about two inches in front of the rest of his face. Underneath all the construction, however, he was still very much Eric, and during the week that followed, he did his best to get around the doctor's restrictions. He wore laced weights on his ankles just making a trip from his bedroom to the bathroom. Soon he was wearing them most of the day.

"What do you think you're doing in those things?"

"They're good for my leg muscles. So lay off, will you?" He'd worked out a way of talking by having his lower lip do all the moving. He now sounded like a penguin with a bad cold.

One morning I noticed that he'd been up and down stairs at least eight times. "You're working out!" I accused him.

"Like hell I am!" he croaked. "Twenty times up and down the stadium steps is working out. I haven't even worked up a good sweat."

"No, and you'd better not. That's absolutely against orders."

He mumbled a word fiercely. Suddenly I was full of silent laughter.

His doctors at Memorial did not laugh when they got their first look at Eric the following week. They were angry and worried. Their prize patient, full of all that expensive asparaginase, had gone out and got himself smashed up. They had to admit it was not his fault. They also had to admit that they couldn't find anything else wrong with him. His marrow was still very clean. At that time Eric was not taking any drugs. At that time the doctors were hoping that asparaginase by itself might be a cure.

They agreed to let him head back to school as soon as his surgeon was ready to let him go. Eric's face healed remarkably quickly. The doctor had kept his word; he looked as good as new. It was possible to see only two faint hairline scars on either side of his upper lip.

"My lip feels numb," he said wonderingly, touching it. "Like I've just come from the dentist." (The numbness lasted for several months.) His mouth had always been humorous, sensitive. Now his expression was slightly different.

"You're talking like a British lieutenant, Eric. Stiff upper lip. All that sort of rot."

"I'm talking, that's the main thing," Eric said a bit grimly. He was not amused by this recent brush with Fate, the necessity to take it easy, to slow down the training program he'd set for himself. Besides, by now the new term was under way and he'd missed several days of preseason soccer practice. When the doctor finally released him, he took off within the hour. He left his room scrupulously clean, nothing lying around. He was saying, I'm gone.

Looking back, I wonder if it was the automobile accident that did it? Or was the trouble that waited for Eric just another predictable point in the long journey of this disease? I do remember that Carl's insurance company, which paid Eric's hospital and plastic surgery bills, went out of their way to be generous. The agent even made a date to come and deliver the check in person. It was for $600 over Eric's medical expenses. The agent was extremely anxious that we sign a release stating that Eric was in good shape and free of any aftereffects of the accident.

"What was that all about, do you suppose?" I said to Sidney as the agent went down our front walk.

"Hmmm, I'm not sure," said Sidney, looking at the check.

"I think he was afraid we might sue for a lot of money. After all, the company knew about Eric's leukemia. Some of the hospital bills were for blood work and for checking him out in that department. If he'd come out of remission, we could have claimed it was because of the shock and the injury."

"Well, he didn't come out. He's okay. That's the important thing."

So Eric had gone back to school, supposedly in good shape. And I'd returned shortly after that to Florida on business. I had another project in mind, too. We'd decided to take a small plunge. A long-awaited royalty check from one of my books had come in the mail. I wanted to put it in something solid. Our savings were fast melting away. We had no company pension to look forward to. But for $2,000 down I thought I could probably buy a small, almost new, furnished house. The winter season rental would carry the mortgage. Meanwhile, I could use it for business trips, avoiding hotel expenses, and maybe we would eventually want to live there most of the year. Most important, a house wouldn't go down the drain, as everything else seemed to be going. It was one way we might even come out ahead in the scary battle with inflation. Sidney thought it was a good plan.

I did a few jobs and got a few others. In some ways, work was easier to find in this little Florida town, where I was almost the only writer around, than it was in the ad jungle of Fairfield County. When I wasn't typing, I went house hunting. At last I found a small white house full of sun and promise, and the price was right. It included some good and bad furniture, one palm tree, and three pines. And a fine big yard.

"Where is it?" Sidney asked, when I described it over the phone.

"Well, it's west of town. Within walking distance of a good neighborhood," I said. "It's on a peaceful little street. Nothing pretentious around. But the yards aren't full of old automobile parts or 1927 wringer washing machines, either."

"How much? Say that again?" asked Sidney.

I told him.

"Get it. You can't go wrong on that."

So I visited a lawyer and put down a binder. A day or so later I hung up two new dish towels in the kitchen of the little house and moved in. I had just three days to make it mine before I was due to fly back home again. During those days, I had time to discover the biggest joy of being away—letters from home. There were letters from Eric at college, too. I hadn't been gone long, but long enough for relaxation to set in and some of the defenses between mother and son to melt. With distance between us, he could come closer.

> Like everyone else up here [he wrote], I'm too caught up in daily life to take in everything. . . . I can only catch glimpses and say "My God, this is actually happening!" When I can reach a point of being aware of what's around me, instead of just reacting to it, I'll be happier. . . . The people in this place kind of rush through, like water going through a rapids. Then at the bottom, everyone surfaces and says, "Wow! What happened?" That's the way most people live their lives. One reason I might drop out next year is so I can catch my breath and

see where I want to go. . . . I've had some mail from Ralph Farrell [Ralph was the father of one of Eric's close friends] and he's pretty sure I can get a job as a student observer on a Farrell Line ship. There are trips to Africa, Australia. You learn navigation, engine room procedure, etc. . . .

I've certainly realized how much I enjoy writing to both you and Daddy because you take me seriously and I value your opinions. I wish I could digest the impact of all the crazy things that have happened. The mind is too good at forgetting. . . .

I might come back here, instead of travel, next fall just to play soccer. I'm not closing the door. The things I want to do most are read and draw. . . . The one thing that could shift the whole scene would be if I run into some great chick. Many people up here establish relationships quickly and cling to them very tightly for security. I think in a way that's sad. I dislike the tremendous phoniness on both sides of the sex line in this place. . . . Some of the greatest girls I've ever met were the nurses in Memorial this past summer. Too bad they were all 24 or 25.

In Eric's next letter, he was once again the happy jock and hustling soccer player. The philosopher, for the moment, was taking a rest. He wrote me about playing in "what has to be the most fantastic soccer game" he'd ever been involved with.

Actually it wasn't soccer . . . I don't know what it was. You see, it started raining last Sunday and it was still raining Wednesday. Oh Man, was it raining Wednesday! It was 38° out and the rain was coming down as hard as it could. Daddy drove up to see the game and he can tell you—there was easily 3–6 inches of water on the field. We were playing Yale but they showed up and wanted no part of it. We were all psyched up and went out to "warm up" (our fatal mistake) just before game time. We were all soaked to the bone within 5 minutes and the enthusiasm began to dwindle. . . . Yale stalled around and finally came out. They were still warm and scored two very quick goals. Once the cold hit them, they died. We were already numb. The hands didn't work . . . and the feet said good-bye about the 1st quarter. The wind was cold and all in all it was the sort of a day no mother would even let her children stand by the window, let alone go out. But it was fun . . . painful but fun. Everyone was falling in huge pools and the ball would spin and skip in the water. You couldn't dribble, let alone pass or shoot. I knew I was in trouble when the ball floated by . . . it was like a game played out by the float at our beach at low tide. Coach Morrone, who looked like a cod fisherman from Nova Scotia all bundled up, was enjoying it and, as he told us, "We played because it was a game we'll remember all our lives." He's right. . . . I've never enjoyed a postgame shower so much in my life. Everyone stayed in the showers for about 40 minutes. Afterward, I had dinner with Daddy. I hope Dad didn't get chilled watching. I took my Vitamin C that night and I feel fine today. Practice was canceled today and I expect penicillin rationing will begin tomorrow. Actually everyone was having fun so I don't think anyone will get sick.

I tucked the letters in my purse and reread them several times on the flight home. To my surprise it was not Sidney but Eric who met my plane. His smile and his hug were warm.

"Hey! This is nice! What are you doing home from school?"

"I came down for a few days. Had a checkup last week, and I have to get a few little things taken care of."

I looked at him and saw his eyes had the beginnings of the dark shadows I'd come to associate with drugs. It was hard to keep quiet and not bombard him with questions immediately. My baggage finally came off the carousel. We threaded our way through the parking lots. It took some time to find the turns that led us out of the terminal and get on the parkway for the Whitestone Bridge. Eric was driving steadily but rather slowly, not passing anyone. I noticed he kept touching his left eye.

"It really bugs me," he said at last, "not to be able to see out of this thing."

"What's going on with that eye?" I said as calmly as I could. My heart was jolting me.

"Well, it started hurting a week or so ago. I thought maybe it was because I banged my head again, same place I got it in the accident. It was during a home game. Johnny and I were both moving back after the ball, trying to head it—"

"So? Did you have it looked at?"

"Yeah. They couldn't find anything at first. But it's been gaining on me. I've been losing vision all week. Dr. Grann isn't worried, though. He says it's just a group of cells behind the eyeball, he thinks. This happens sometimes. He said you could call him if you wanted to have it explained to you so you won't worry."

This was the code I'd finally worked out with the doctors. In the name of reassuring the mother, they'd agreed to suggest to Eric that I might call when something new came up. That way Eric felt he was in charge, while I wasn't kept in the dark. Now I knew something was really wrong.

"You okay to drive?"

"Sure, I'm okay. I'm not going to break any speed records, though. I can't see a damn thing out of this left eye. Just blurry light and dark. But it's more annoying than serious."

"How's everything else?"

"Oh, fine, I guess. I feel great. But they're giving me some stuff right now. Just preventive, really. I've got a few cells floating around that weren't there before. They showed up in last week's blood tests. But I'm not losing any sleep over it. They know what to do."

Eric changed the subject swiftly then.

"Tell me about the house. Dad says you found a good one. That's great! You guys have to make plans for the future, you know. Writing is a tough way to make a living."

"I couldn't agree with you more."

"I wish somehow we could all get up the bread for a Christmas vacation in the sun again. Do you think we might? And maybe Meredith and Jimmy could come down, too?"

"Who knows?" I said. "Let's dream big."

"I need to swim and run if I'm gonna stay in shape," said Eric. "It gets really cold up at Storrs. Then you can't run much. Either it's too icy underfoot or it's just too hard on your lungs."

We drove silently through the night for a while, a soft blue night with ropes of lights strung from the bridge towers. "Do you remember what Lisa said about these towers when she was a very little girl?" I asked Eric. "She said they were kings and queens dressed up, wearing their pearls and holding hands."

"I never heard that." He smiled. "But she's right. Lisa's a good girl. She's going to be a great person. . . . The big thing in my life," he said suddenly, "is finding the right chick. That would be so tremendous!"

He talked on about what he wanted to do with his life, the big hopes he had, the sort of girl he'd like to find, the traveling he wanted to do to learn how people lived all over the world. "I'm not going to get stuck in some rat race chasing after dough," he said. "I know what's valuable now. I think I know how to live."

CHAPTER 9

SIDNEY AND I TALKED about Eric's problem that night. "I think I'd better call Dr. Grann first thing in the morning," I said.

"Yes, do," he said. It usually relieved him that I was willing to take on the telephoning. He said once, "I'd always prefer to walk four miles and talk to somebody face to face."

Dr. Grann was in his office, and his nurse put him right on when I called the next day. "Eric tells me he can't see out of his left eye. He says it's just because he has a few cells behind the eye." I stopped and then said, "That's just another way of saying he's got a tumor, isn't it?"

"I'm afraid it is," said Dr. Grann. "There are leukemic tumors, you know."

"What happens now?"

"We have to determine whether the tumor is actually behind the eyeball and still accessible. If it is, there's a good chance we can take care of it."

"And if it's not?"

"Well, if it's in the brain and attacking the central nervous system, that's something else again."

"That sounds pretty serious. Are you worried about Eric?"

Dr. Grann was a quiet man. Whenever possible he underplayed

his statements. But now he said, "Yes, I'm worried about him. It could be very serious. He's going into Memorial tomorrow, and they'll have to get to the bottom of it. By afternoon they ought to know the score. You'll probably hear from them as soon as they have the answer."

The twenty-four-hour day was replaced the following morning with the hundred-year day. I saw seconds, I felt seconds in the pulse of my wrist, but they refused to add up and make an hour. And the hours refused to become a day. Somehow I couldn't move. Trying to get a few things done around the house, I felt as if I were dragging through heavy seaweed under water. Sidney couldn't stay still. Where he normally takes two or three very long walks every day, that day I heard the front door slam every half hour. He ate his lunch standing up, walking around the kitchen. We didn't talk. We couldn't.

In a way I'd faced the fact long ago that Eric was probably going to die. But suddenly I was crying out, "Not now, not yet!" In the back of the mind one always carries the hope of a miracle. There might be a new drug. There might be a complete spontaneous remission. But if Eric had a brain tumor, all would soon be lost. He would never even get a chance to fight.

By the time the hands of the clock finally inched their way to four, I went to the phone and started dialing doctors in Memorial. If Eric had been more confiding, I would have known by this time that the doctor mainly in charge of his case, and the person with whom he was developing a close rapport, was Dr. Monroe Dowling, Chief of Memorial's Hematology Clinic. I had heard Dowling's name as I'd heard many other names. Interns come and go. Residents are apt to spend some months on the floor and then move on. The top doctors confer, make rounds together, substitute for each other often. So my impression, not entirely false, was of a team of experts who, together, did their best for each patient. This team situation exists in many hospitals and is both a blessing and a problem for relatives and patients as they struggle to communicate. But I know now that I would have been supported and informed by Dr. Dowling had I known enough to ask for his help. As it was, in near panic, I called all the big names I'd ever heard of. None of the doctors could be found. None of their secretaries seemed to be at their desks. I got aides or nurses who knew nothing and urged me to call back. Finally at five o'clock I reached Dr. Burchenal's secretary, who told me that most of the doctors had left for the weekend. She herself had had no report on Eric.

I said, "Look, this is absolutely intolerable. I simply cannot live through another hour without knowing if Eric has a brain tumor."

She said, "I'm going to look into it for you. I promise I'll call you back the minute I find out what's happened."

She kept her word. At 5:35 the phone rang. I snatched it up, and she said, "Eric has a tumor behind his left eyeball. He's been admitted and he's already had pinpoint radiation to treat it. They think the treatment will be successful, but he'll have to have some more."

I ran downstairs to Sidney's office where he was standing by a desk littered with work, just staring at it, and told him the news.

The miracle, as usual, was conditional, but it was a miracle all the same. When you think of using something as powerful and potentially lethal as radiation with such precision that you spare the eye and destroy the tumor, you have to admire the technicians who are brave enough and skilled enough to go in there and do it. I know it happens every day, but it hadn't happened to us before.

Thank you, I said silently when Eric came home a few days later, got out his soccer ball, and went off for a back-lot game with the little kids in the neighborhood. Thank you, I said many times in the week that followed, as he reported that he was able to see nearly as well as ever with that left eye. No matter that his hair was falling out all around his head from the ears down, an aftereffect of the radiation. He looked strange but he also looked good because he was moving, running, doing.

But I had hardly finished giving thanks when Eric lost his third remission. This time he could no longer be treated as an outpatient. We had reached the point where drugs of severe toxicity would have to be used, drugs more dangerous than any we'd faced before. He had to come in. And he had to stay in—how long nobody could say.

I was beginning to know my way around. I pushed through the heavy double doors of Ewing's First Avenue entrance and walked thirty feet to one of the big elevators at the right. The elevator was jammed with interns, nurses, hospital workers, worried husbands holding paper-wrapped flowers, bleak-faced ladies holding each other. Somewhere between the third and fourth floors an alarm bell went off. The car stopped immediately and the operator, a black lady in blue uniform, picked up the elevator telephone.

"Sixth floor?" she said. "Yes. Right away."

She replaced the phone and we shot up to the sixth floor.

"Everybody off, please, for patient in bed." It was a brisk command.

We poured into the lobby of Ewing Six. No jostling, no complaints. We were silent, respectful, awed by the sight of the young man who lay crumpled on his side behind the high bars of his hospital bed. He was bleeding through the heavy bandages wrapped around his head. The orderlies swung him quickly, skillfully, through the crowd and into the elevator.

"Stand back, please. . . . Watch it, ma'am. . . . This way—"

In the flash of the moment I saw he was a young man of striking beauty. Proud arched nose. Short, curly black beard. Long black lashes closed on a hollow ivory cheek. They will stay closed, I thought. He will not look out upon the world again.

Another elevator took me to the eighth floor. The office nurse told me that Eric was in a two-bed room at the end of the hall. But when I found the room, another nurse barred my way. She seemed a bit flustered.

"Eric's not here," she said. "We sent him into Chemotherapy to be with the girls."

I must have looked puzzled.

"You can knock on that door." She pointed. "It's all right. He can come out and sit in the lobby as long as you're here."

I knocked. The door swung open, and I saw Eric sitting on top of a desk talking to several girls. They were nurses or technicians or perhaps both, I guessed. It was the first time I'd seen Eric in white hospital pajamas. He seemed smaller, more vulnerable. His neck looked delicate.

"Mom!" He was glad to see me. He jumped down, and we went out to the lobby and found two chairs by the elevators.

"What's going on?"

"Well—" Eric seemed hesitant, almost apologetic. "I guess the guy in my room was dead for quite a while and I didn't know it. I thought he was taking a nap. So I was being kinda quiet so as not to disturb him. Not playing my radio. But then I looked over at him and—well, I called the nurse. She took a look and a lot of stuff began to happen fast. They sent me into Chemotherapy. But I hear they couldn't bring him around. I guess he's gone."

Eric spoke very quietly, looking down. "Sorta shakes you a little," he said. "I mean, that I was there all that time and I didn't know." Then he shook his head. "But he was a pretty old guy. They say he had a lot of heart trouble on top of his leukemia. That makes a difference."

Two pretty nurses walked down the hall and came up to us. They stood by Eric's chair on either side of him. "Is this your mom, Eric?"

"This is my mom. Mom, this is . . . "

There was talk: friendly, light, easy. There was laughter. And there was a stretcher coming down the hall on its silent rubber tires, heading right this way toward the elevators where the nurses stood protectively beside our chairs. A blank-faced orderly was pushing the stretcher. But there was no figure under the white sheet. The sheet stretched flat as a board across the stretcher, hanging way down on either side. I didn't know then that the body was hidden on a shelf underneath. I only saw the empty stretcher silently disappearing into the elevator. I hadn't yet learned that the dead vanish tactfully at Memorial. There are too many of them for anyone to bear.

One of the head nurses came up to us. Vigorous, cheerful. "You can take your mother back to your room now if you like, Eric."

We looked at each other.

"Okay?" he asked.

"Sure." Maybe it'll help if I go in with him and stay awhile, I thought. "Dad's coming by to see you on his way home from New Jersey this evening," I said.

"Good," he said.

There were two empty, spotless beds in the room. Freshly made, the sheets pulled taut. Eric's stuff was piled in one corner. Only an hour ago there had been a second living, breathing human being in this room, someone with possessions—probably a small shaving kit, a suitcase, shoes, maybe a few books—and a lifetime of experience stored up in his head. Now there was not the slightest sign that this other person had ever existed, had really occupied this space.

"You want to move to the bed by the window, Eric?" A young nurse's aide had come in behind us.

"Uh—no, thanks," said Eric. "I think I'll stay where I've been."

I sat with Eric for quite a while. I sat on the foot of the bed by the window, swinging my feet as we talked. Maybe I should have kept that bed absolutely clean and untouched for the next patient. But I figured it was more important to have it become an ordinary piece of furniture again, something your mother could sit on casually while she chatted about nothing important, instead of the bed where a man Eric hardly knew had died before his eyes.

The next time I came to visit Eric he was sitting up in the bed by the window, drawing with a felt marker on a large pad.

"Hi!"

"Hi, Mom."

I smiled at him. He smiled back with a slight shrug.

"I figured why not? The light's much better. And they've got some kid coming in this afternoon."

"Do you mind if I see what you're drawing?"

He showed me. The sketch was titled "Dr. Vin Cristine."

Vincristine, I knew, was the name of one of the superbomb drugs the high command liked to drop on leukemia cells. Eric had turned it into a proper name and drawn one of his typical caricatures—a bald old man who looked like a hardened lifer in a penitentiary.

"I brought you a poster for over your bed. I saw it in a window on Lexington."

"Let's see."

It was a Joan Miró. Vermilion, black, white, a dash of yellow.

"I like it! I've got some tape in the drawer. . . ."

We put it up together. He's feeling pretty good, I thought. Maybe things are working out. I asked no questions. He knew no answers. After all, he was now out on the edge where no one had any real answers. They were trying. He was trying. What more could we do?

A brown-haired boy appeared in the doorway. He was wearing a windbreaker, carrying a suitcase. He looked like some of the soccer players from school who often came home with Eric. How well he moved! How vital and healthy he seemed! There were shy introductions. The boy, whose name was Terry, went off to look for his father, who'd been parking the car and wouldn't know where to find him.

Shortly after he left, a harassed-looking intern showed up.

"Did Terry come in yet?" he wanted to know.

"Sure. That's his suitcase," said Eric.

"How did he seem? Was he carrying his own suitcase? Did he come in a wheelchair?"

"He's fine. Good as you or me," said Eric. "Of course he carried his own suitcase."

The intern grinned and went out fast. The interns at Memorial never walked or sauntered; they wheeled, dashed, spun, and ran.

Shortly afterward Terry's father showed up. He was walking slowly, just out of the hospital himself, he explained. He'd missed connections with Terry but somehow found his way to the room. He was quiet, kindly, unflustered.

In the days that followed I learned that Terry had leukemic cells in the brain. The doctors were considering putting a small valve into the top of his skull with a screw-on cap, like a radiator cap, which could be removed to administer methotrexate drip directly into the brain. I knew that methotrexate was one of the most effective antileukemic drugs. What I did not know was that the brain presents a problem that's different from the rest of the body for patients with advanced leukemia. There is a barrier in the fluid of the spinal column which protects the brain from many infections. This same barrier also prevents ordinary methods of treatment from being effective against leukemic cells in the brain. The drugs are simply filtered out before they can reach their target.

Terry did not, as it turned out, get his "radiator cap" while he was Eric's roommate. Something else was tried. Something else, for the moment, seemed to be working. The next time I went in to visit Eric, a few days later, Terry's bed was empty. He was home on pass.

It was the first time I'd been in alone to Ewing Eight on a weekend. Sidney and I had fallen into a sort of pattern of sharing the responsibility for weekday visits. It was easier to alternate for reasons of time and energy and expense. Often I went in the early afternoons so I could get back home in time to cook dinner. Many times Sidney stopped by to see Eric in the early evenings on his way home from business trips to New Jersey. The previous Sunday, Eric's first Sunday in the hospital, we'd driven in together to see him and then had supper in a nearby restaurant.

Today Sidney was staying home to finish a rush job, and suddenly I found the atmosphere on the floor strangely hollow. There were quite a few patients out on pass. While their pictures and small personal things remained on the bed tables, the beds themselves looked flat as ironing boards as you walked by the wards. Some of the doctors and regular staff were always away on weekends too, I learned. The chemotherapy offices were locked. The meeting room was dark. There were a few visitors coming and going, of course, but the halls had lost their normal bustle.

I found Eric sitting up in bed drawing on his big pad. I went over and sat on the windowsill to be nearer the world. A plume from the power plant smokestack floated lazily across a gray-blue sky. The city in the light of late afternoon was a smudgy watercolor. Lovely! Lovely pollution. When I moved here when I was thirteen, we'd never even heard the word "pollution."

"Could you move, Mom? You're cutting off my light a little."

"I'm sorry, Eric." I moved to a chair.

"That's okay. I hate to turn on all the lights before I have to. It makes the evening seem so long."

He drew silently. I leaned my head against the wall. Then I heard it. Not exactly a groan. It was a monotonous, steady protest. A woman's voice gasping as if in a bad dream.

"No! . . . No! . . . No!"

I tried not to hear it. The hoarse gasp came at regular intervals. There was no blotting it out. After a few minutes I moved to a chair on the other side of the room. It was still there.

"No! . . . No!"

121

I looked at Eric. His face was quiet. He was trying to concentrate on his drawing.

Perhaps the door was open in the next room? Letting the sound out? Maybe I could do something.

"I'm going to go get a drink of water."

"Okay."

I went down the hall to the fountain, came back, took a look at the door. Closed. NO VISITORS sign. NO SMOKING! OXYGEN! sign. Well, then, there was nothing to be done. I sat down again in the chair by the wall.

"No! . . . No!"

Eric looked up, caught my eye.

"Does that bother you?" I asked him.

"It'll bother me more if she stops," he said. "At least she's still fighting. Hang in there, lady!" he said to the wall, and went back to his drawing.

CHAPTER 10

THREE DAYS LATER Eric was moved to 830, the six-bed ward where he'd first been admitted for desensitization for asparaginase. Only now, in the chance game of musical beds, he'd landed in the last bed far left. Fortunately it also had a window. During my first visits there I was glad to see that the ward was partly empty. Two beds were unoccupied. Two more always seemed to have their striped curtains pulled shut all the way around. This made it easier for me not to see what was happening to the others, to go on with a partial denial that Eric at this moment belonged in this place. Yet I was finally made aware of a presence in the sixth bed right by the door. One day I couldn't resist looking right at him. A wizened, impish-looking man in his sixties looked back at me.

"I'm Eric's mother," I said. "The boy by the window."

"Sure," he said. "I know."

I stared at the card on the foot of the bed. "W. Murphy," it said.

"W. Murphy. That's me." He gave me a crooked smile. "Still here. They haven't been able to do me in yet."

I smiled back. "I'll bet they never do," I said.

This was my introduction to life in the wards, the real life on Ewing Eight.

• • •

Although there was a social room with pool table, fish tank, and a few stiff couches at the end of the hall on Ewing Eight, it always had a faintly dismal, abandoned look. The real social center for both patients and visitors was the cluster of chairs, upholstered in institutional green or brown plastic, which formed a loose circle right opposite the three elevators. There were several standing ashtrays, usually overflowing with cigarette butts. There were Formica-topped tables with slightly out-of-date magazines. A big TV set on casters stood against one wall. A pay telephone hung in an open niche on the opposite wall. The TV, while usually turned on, often ran skipping and flipping from one commercial to another, through hours of daytime dramas, cops and robbers, or evening talk shows, without anyone paying too much attention. It was the pay phone and the elevators which held the deep interest of the inmates.

The phone, a battered, capricious, overworked instrument which preferred dimes to nickels, was the only phone on the entire floor available to the patients. Every evening they began to swarm around the open niche, hoping for a chance to call home. At the same time, relatives were sitting at their phones out in New Jersey, the Bronx, Connecticut, or wherever, trying to call in and getting a continuous busy signal. There was no other way to reach a loved one confined to Ewing Eight. The phone number of the nurses' station was never given out. The main Memorial switchboard, like that of most hospitals, had no information about patients beyond the fact that one was, or was not, on the critical list. So for the latest news you just went on dialing, hoping for a break in the evening's business. Eventually, you got someone, usually another patient. Doctors, of course, never answered the pay phone, and nurses seldom. But the walking wounded took some pride in tending the phone themselves, taking and giving back messages. Sometimes the messages, given in broken or heavily accented English, were brief and upsetting. "No. He no can come to phone now. He very sick." Pause. "Yes, I tell him wife call, give love." End of conversation.

While keeping one ear on the telephone, patients sitting in the Ewing Eight lobby watched the elevator traffic come and go. At any moment the door might open, bringing you a visitor or perhaps a doctor who might grant a weekend pass. Even if you expected nothing, hoped for nothing, you sat by the elevators because it was as close to life as you could get. Bright short skirts. Shiny boots. Hiphuggers. Long swinging coats. Fur hats. The styles of the time were a dazzling relief from white uniforms, saggy pajamas, and the faded seersucker bathrobes of the hospital compound.

One day I sat by the elevators with Eric as he waited for a doctor. He had not been out of Ewing for ten days. He wanted a pass to go home. For half an hour he'd been watching elevator doors open and close without reward; now he was looking at the floor to conceal his disappointment. Just then a girl with scarlet miniskirt and long mane of blond-white hair swung out of an elevator and disappeared down the hall. He failed to notice her.

"Eric! Come on, now! You're losing your grip."

The speaker was the wizened man I'd seen in the bed, near right, by the door. Murphy, that was his name.

Eric smiled faintly.

"You missed something pretty hot, let me tell you!" jabbed Murphy.

"How would you know?" said Eric, finally picking up a cudgel. "You're way over the hill."

"Me?" Murphy's voice rose in wrath. "Just because there's snow on the roof doesn't mean the fire's out."

The joke was old, but coming from this shrunken fellow whose sparse gray hair was a worn-out scrub brush, whose ankles were made of galvanized pipe, it struck me as high courage. I looked at him with interest.

At that moment the pay phone on the wall rang loudly. Then rang again. No one seemed about to answer it. So Murphy rose, clutching his flimsy bathrobe around his shanks, and plucked the instrument from its hook.

"Murphy's Mortuary," he said into the phone. "Murphy speaking."

Eric looked extremely pleased. "Old Murphy's all right," he said.

It was from W. Murphy that Eric—and I, too—learned some of the ropes about being a long-term insider on Ewing's eighth floor. Murphy's real-life job, I discovered, was working in a sewage treatment plant somewhere on Long Island. This figured. Saints and philosophers understand dirty jobs. While other people argue about whose turn it is, they get on with the garbage and carry it out.

Murphy deplored his own close ties with the human race, but he was unable to dissolve them. "This is a terrible floor to make friends," he confided once, shaking his head. "Make 'em, you lose 'em. But what you gonna do? I get involved. I get involved, that's all there is to it."

Murphy did not have simple leukemia, he explained to me. He had something a bit fancier which had necessitated the removal of several important organs, and from the look of him at the time we met, he had very little blood left in his veins. Just battery acid and a few drops of mother's milk. The essential Murphy, the spirit of the man, however, seemed to have survived every assault. He belonged in an Irish pub. He needed the banter of a bunch of cronies, the comfort of raw whiskey and tall stories. Instead, he found himself improbably in hospital pajamas on the eighth floor of Ewing Pavilion. He made the most of it. Gathering the more active patients around him, he organized a loose floating group known as Murphy's Mob. The professed goal of the Mob was, at all times, to prevent hospital procedure from rolling along smoothly. Nurses were to be paid off to prevent temperature-taking at 5 A.M. Interns were to be slipped a few bucks to prevent bone marrows. Doctors were to be bribed regularly to provide weekend passes.

In fact, Murphy's Mob only talked insurrection. They could have put their clothes on and simply walked out the door, as some patients did. But they were survivors at heart. They took their medicine. They did not take it meekly lying down, however. They gave Fate a poke in the eye first.

Eric did not get his pass that day, or for many days thereafter. He ran low-grade fevers so he had to be watched for infection. His counts were dropping because of the shots of vincristine and a new drug, daunomycin. And yet remission eluded him. So of course he did the natural thing. He joined W. Murphy and other irreverent members of the Mob in efforts to raise patient morale by pretending to screw up the organization.

There was no generation gap on the eighth floor. All the other gaps of race, color, religion, or country also tended to disappear in the face of the great common enemy—cancer. A few patients on the floor couldn't speak a word of English, so sometimes language barriers presented a problem. Yet compassion and courtesy often overcame even this. As for class distinction or economic superiority, they bought you nothing on Ewing Eight. Everyone was poor in the one thing that mattered most—health. But everyone was rich, too, for when costs ran high, care was free. And so, as in a shipwreck or other large-scale disaster, when life came down to basics, the things that counted were bravery, humor, and the will to live.

There were complainers and groaners, of course. And they were not always the sickest patients. I remember sitting in my usual spot in the lobby with Eric one afternoon when a terrible sound, almost a roar, came from a nearby ward. I was shaken; it must have shown. But Eric just shook his head and smiled.

"That's Mr. Gross. He's really not all that sick, not right now anyway. He can walk. He can eat. But he hates being left alone a minute. He figures he'll get more attention if he roars."

"Does he get more?"

"No. The nurses are on to him, and they've got plenty of patients who are sicker."

I remember many things from those long afternoons. Mostly I remember not groans or moans but many kinds of courage. There was Mrs. Golden, who sometimes wore an ice bag, full of what must have been melted ice water, on her rusty dyed locks. It was green rubber and matched the green of her jungle print housecoat. "How are you, dear?" she always called to me (I was "dear" as soon as we met), and she'd wave her free arm, short, fat, jiggly, in happy greeting while she pushed her rolling I.V. hat rack with the other, which had a needle in it attached by tube to the bottle above.

"Some lady! Some fighter!" said Eric. "She's been in and out of here for twelve years, but you never see her down."

Then there was Abby, slim, pale, with a long waterfall of dark hair down to her waist. Married just a year to a man I privately called Mustache. (I'd never seen such a big one.) Mustache's great mournful eyes followed Abby every minute, as if by looking at her long enough or hard enough he might somehow make her well or at least protect her. She was very frail but always insisted, "No, I'm fine. Really! Let's try it one more time." Then she'd cling to the hall railing with one hand, Mustache with the other, while they made another painful journey up and down the long hall. Abby wanted to go home. She knew they'd never let her out unless she got stronger.

Eileen was, in Eric's words, "something else." A black girl from upstate New York with such style and vitality, such a quick wide smile, that I couldn't help saying to Eric, "There must be some mistake. She doesn't belong in here!"

"Who does?" said Eric wryly. "Would you believe Eileen has four things wrong with her right now, all at once? But she's had this thing licked before and she'll do it again. We spend a lot of time together. She's a real friend."

Ricardo was another who wore his illness lightly, swinging around the halls as if he were playing truant from school and on his way to the pool hall.

"What's he doing on the phone all the time?" I asked Eric. "He's got it tied up fifty percent of the time."

"Playing the horses. Placing bets."

So Ricardo was trying to make his fortune from a phone booth on Ewing Eight. In the meantime he did his best to alter the atmosphere around his corner of the ward, playing his radio, poring over the racing form, flipping through old magazines for pinups. At one time the entire wall around his bed was plastered with *Playboy* centerfolds. An improvement, I thought, over the grim gray paint. But then two nurses, who happened to be Marine sergeant types, made him take them down. Ricardo was sad. Murphy was outraged to see them go.

"I'll get those biddies when I come back!" he fumed. Rigged out in a green suit and green and purple tie, W. Murphy was the proud possessor of a weekend pass.

"The old lady has gone out to buy a roast beef as big as a trunk," he announced. "I'm gonna eat it all myself."

"Eat some for me," said Eric, looking a bit wan. Food wasn't big on his list that week. He'd been fighting nausea.

"Run the Mob till Monday, Eric," said Murphy. "See if you can organize a strike."

"Okay. What are we striking for?"

"Who knows?" said Murphy cheerfully. "We'll think of something." He disappeared into an elevator.

I caught a bad cold soon after that. It hung on. Sidney managed to get in to see Eric every other day. "He's all right," he told me in answer to my questions. "Sometimes he wants me to go off while he's eating. He's fighting nausea and trying to eat at the same time."

Then we learned that at long last Eric was getting out on pass. He wasn't in remission. But he was being given a rest from drugs.

Sidney went to meet his train. I heard them come in as I was getting dressed after a bath. When I came downstairs, Eric was sitting in the living room. He didn't move. We said hello. He's changed, I thought. His eyes have a look that wasn't there before.

"I'm just starting dinner. Do you want something to hold you? It'll take about forty-five minutes."

"No, thanks."

I went into the kitchen, turned on the oven, put in the chicken, washed some lettuce. When I went back in the living room, Eric still hadn't moved. I sat down.

He looked at me. "Abby died last night," he said.

"Oh, no!"

"We sat up till four o'clock with her. Eileen and I. Murphy sat up some of the time, too. We wanted to help her. And we wanted to help her husband."

I was stunned. Abby. And poor Mustache. You know this can happen yet you don't believe it when it does.

"Her husband was so great," Eric said gently. "He brought *us* coffee! How do you like that? We wanted to do something for him—and he was thinking of us. He told us, 'Now you mustn't give up, you mustn't let this get you down. You've got to go on with the fight. Don't think you can't make it just because this happened to Abby.'"

"I'm so sorry."

"Richard died, too."

"Richard!"

"You remember he was in the bed next to me last summer? He went home to Cleveland."

"I remember. You told me he had two little girls."

"Yeah. He came back in ten days ago. He got hepatitis. He went very fast."

This was too much all at once.

"That's awful. I remember you thought he was making it."

"Yes. I thought so." Eric spoke quietly, looking at the floor.

"Well—" I did something very stupid then. I was trying to

recover, fumbling for something to say when I should have said nothing. I said, "I'm sure Mrs. Golden is still walking around with that wonderful ice pack."

Eric's eyes flashed. "Mrs. Golden is dead."

Now I saw how angry he was at death, how angry at all that courage counting for nothing, and how angry at me for being an outsider who dared to speak of things I didn't understand.

I sat humble before his anger. I made a vow then never to speak of such things again, to let him tell me—if he would. I don't know how long we sat there. I was frozen by shock and by my own blunder. He was lost in his own sadness.

Suddenly he got up and started walking around the worn living room carpet in a small circle, as if around a hole.

"Mom, that's the *deep shit.* The deep shit," he repeated, looking down in horror, shaking his head. "And some of the people are down there. No way out. No way back. You say to yourself, 'Not for *me*. No, sir!' But still—you've got to look at what's down there. And you've got to face it." His upper lip was trembling. He touched it to make it stop.

He said no more. I put my hand lightly on his shoulder, and then I went back to the kitchen. My arms felt weak as I opened the oven door and pulled out the rack to check on my dinner. He was afraid. It was the first time I'd seen it. And he was afraid of being afraid. I remembered my struggle by the window that long-ago day when he went off in the falling snow. Once again I wanted to hold him, comfort him, save him. But save him I could not. All any of us could do was help him live or die with dignity. Because that was what he really asked of us. He was still trying to be a man even though he might be dying. It took all my strength to do nothing, to turn my back and walk away.

• • •

The next afternoon Lisa came out to the kitchen where I was peeling some oranges for supper and sat, drooping, on a stool. Her lower lip was out, her eyes dangerously close to brimming over. I waited.

"Mom," she said at last in the little-girl whine she hadn't used for years, "Eric's awful to me."

"Mmmm hmm," I said. "What's he done?"

There followed a usual brother-sister tale of fighting for possession of the bathroom, the TV, and general ground and air rights throughout the house. "But that's not all," she complained. "He never says anything nice to me any more, he just growls."

I sat down on the other stool. "Lisa," I said. "Do you know what's wrong with Eric?"

Her eyes got big and round. "Anemia?" she said in a small voice.

"He has leukemia." I was pretty sure she had escaped the full understanding of her brother's illness up to that time. But it was time to fill her in. She was twelve.

"Is that—will that kill him?" She looked frightened.

"We certainly hope not. But they don't have a cure for it right now, although they're working hard on different things that might help. It's pretty scary for Eric. He's just seen some of his friends die. It takes a lot of energy for him to go on fighting. Now we can all help him by being patient. Just go round him when he's growly. Remember he's got a lot on his mind. And remember he loves you, because he does."

She nodded and immediately went downstairs and began to play her piano. She played the loudest piece she knew.

• • •

Eric's furlough was up in five days. He went back to the firing line, but not before he'd spoken once again about a Florida Christmas in our little house.

"I need the sun and the beach. I want us to be all together. I want to see Meredith and Jimmy."

"Do you think you can get out for a week at Christmas on pass?" Of course he couldn't possibly know yet—this was late November—but I had to raise this question.

"Sure I can. They're going to hit me hard when I go back in. I can take it now. I'm ready. It was good to be home. But I've got work to do. I've got to get in remission."

He was looking better. The vacation from drugs let him eat. The good food, the change of scene, the fooling around with a soccer ball with his brother had helped a lot. But now and then his eyes still looked back at the unspeakable.

And so Sidney and I began to plan for the Christmas he wanted. What was money? What were problems? We'd make it somehow. I'd go down and get the place ready. We could use it, then maybe rent it when the tourist season came along. But I wasn't taking off until I saw how he fared with this new course of drugs. At the end of the week I headed in for Ewing Eight.

Eric was taping surfing posters to the gray tile walls of the lobby when I came out of the elevator. Murphy, back in his old plaid bathrobe, hooked up once again to an I.V., was kibitzing. "Up a little, Eric. Over to the left. That's it."

"I'm running this museum," said Eric.

He taped up the last one, which said "Come to Hawaii!"; then he came over and threw himself down beside me on the plastic sofa.

"That looks better," I said. "All you need now is a Swiss Alp and an African elephant." I glanced around the walls. There wasn't much more room. Between the elevators was a large hospital sign about platelets. I'd heard the word but was vague about what they were. They must be important. That sign was on the main floor, too, right between the elevators. I got up and wandered over to read it. It said in red capitals, two and a half inches high, PLATELETS MUST BE REPLACED EVERY 24 HOURS. ONLY *YOU* CAN GIVE PLATELETS—THE GIFT OF LIFE. I went back and sat down.

Murphy got up and headed back toward the ward. "Gonna get my beauty sleep," he said. "If I don't get a nap I start showin' my age."

Eric was restless. Soon he jumped up and began bouncing a little red rubber ball, playing handball against the tiles. Once or twice he faked a pass to a nurse going by. Then he sent the ball winging sharply just under the nurses' front office window. One nurse smiled and waved. Another shook her head. He laughed. He must be feeling pretty good anyway. Or was it nervousness? Or bravado? I noticed he had a large red paper rose pinned on the front of his white hospital pajamas. Ah! He missed a shot and went dashing off to retrieve the ball from under an empty stretcher.

"Eric!" A young doctor came round the corner at just that moment. He motioned Eric over to sit down. "I don't want you jumping around so much. I've just had the lab report on your counts. I think I'd better order you some platelets."

"Okay," said Eric, sitting down. "They're low, huh?"

"Well, they're on the edge of the danger zone. If you cracked your head—" The doctor didn't go on. He smiled and patted him on the shoulder as he headed for the stairs. "Take it easy now."

"What would happen if you cracked your head?" I asked.

"I could end up like Joey. He fell out of bed when his platelets were down. Without platelets, you can bleed anywhere. Joey got a brain hemorrhage. You've seen him go by strapped in his wheelchair. He was a nice guy. I used to see him last year in Clinic on Mondays. He was a football player, big fellow. Now he weighs about ninety pounds. He can't even push his own chair."

My throat felt dry. I remembered Joey. I remembered his mother, too, a stoic-faced little woman in a gray sweater pushing Joey, like a ruined baby, in his wheelchair. I looked at Eric. He was a little pale, perhaps. But his arms were round and strong, and his legs were much too long for the pajama bottoms. He was following orders, he was sitting still. But his foot tapped restlessly.

The elevator door opened. A short, sturdy nurse stepped out and headed straight for us. "I'm from the Donor Room," she said. "And we're going to need sixteen donors for Eric tomorrow."

"Sixteen! Tomorrow? But I thought he needed platelets right away."

"He does. And he'll get them this afternoon. But we have to replace what we give him. And also he might need more this week."

"But why *sixteen?*" It sounded frightening. So many! Where would we get sixteen people to donate blood by tomorrow?

"It takes sixteen people to provide platelets for a hundred-and-sixty-pound man. Can you give blood yourself?"

"No," I said sadly. "My doctor told me recently I shouldn't."

"What about your husband?"

"He tried twice a few years ago. But the last time it didn't work out. They told him not to try again. I don't know why."

A little nurse who'd been standing near us waiting for an elevator suddenly ran over and touched Eric's arm. "I'll run down and give for you, Eric. During my break." She looked like a pretty high school freshman with her short brown curls and pink cardigan tossed over the uniform, her arms full of notebooks and papers. But the papers were charts and drug records of cancer patients.

"Cathy," Eric said. "I can't let you do that."

"Why not?" She laughed. "I do it all the time. I'd like to do it for you, Eric." She took his hand. "I mean it."

"Thank you, Cathy," Eric said quietly. She ran off into the elevator, waved good-bye. Eric looked upset. "That gets me. The people here are so great. How am I ever going to pay them back?"

"You'll find a way." The sturdy nurse smiled. To me she said, "I'll hear from you then?"

"We'll find some donors somehow," I said.

The elevator was slow in coming. I felt depressed, defeated by the task ahead, when I finally boarded it. Going down I could see people drooping in their bathrobes, sunk in wheelchairs around the lobby TVs on every floor. Second floor, Pediatrics. We stopped. A slim black youth got on with his father. He must have been about fourteen. The friendly black elevator lady smiled at the boy. He lifted his hand—it was the only smile he had. His entire face was gone from the nose down. Mouth, teeth, jaw— gone. There was a tube dangling from his nose. His warmth, grace, and shy politeness still came through. My heart froze.

In the lobby I hesitated, wondering whether to take a taxi. It was a bitter day. Then I saw the young boy peer out of the lobby window and wave to someone excitedly. In a battered station wagon parked at the curb, a little black boy, about five or six, was bouncing up and down in the back seat, waving back. The father, who was carrying a suitcase and a gift-wrapped package, started to open the heavy hospital doors. The boy with half a face stopped him. He pointed at the gift package and wound an imaginary scarf around his throat. The father put down the suitcase, opened the package, and unfurled a new muffler. Together they put it around his throat. The muffler was beautiful. Rich paisley silk. It didn't help. Above the scarf I could still see the eaten-away face of the boy. Yet his gentle eyes glowed as he bent once more to wave to his brother.

They were going now. The father held the car door open. Even twenty feet away I could see the little boy backing away as the older one got in. He huddled in the farthest corner of the back seat, looking. And he stayed there a long minute. Then suddenly he threw himself in his big brother's lap. Their heads were close together, their arms hugging each other as the car pulled away from the curb.

CHAPTER 11

FRIENDS COME TO YOUR RESCUE. I'd thought we were alone and suddenly people we knew were coming from everywhere to give blood, to help in any way they could. Friends told friends, and before the week was out we had several times the sixteen donors Eric needed.

"You ought to go down to the Donor Room," said an old friend of mine who'd called to tell me she'd just given platelets for Eric. "Even if you can't give blood yourself, you ought to go. It's a fantastic place."

"Fantastic? What do you mean? Impressive? Giant laboratory of the future?"

"Heavens, no! It's a hole in the wall. I don't know how those girls who run it manage. But they're terrific. It's the spirit of the place that's so great. It's more like a circus act than a hospital lab. But don't think they don't know what they're doing. Those are crack nurses in there."

I was intrigued. I meant to go. But Eric was out of immediate danger, and it was time for me to head south to put the little house in shape, to put Christmas together. Meredith and Jimmy planned to fly down from Chicago. Lisa and Mark would take a plane as soon as the school Christmas vacation began. Sidney would pick up

Eric from the hospital and drive straight through. This way he could bring a lot of the baggage, the surfboards, the wet suit Eric would need for winter swimming, other stuff.

Sidney appeared at the front door in Florida four days before Christmas. Alone. He had all the baggage and equipment. He didn't have Eric.

"But when is he getting out on pass? Have they told him? How's he going to get here?"

"Well, he's not sure. But he didn't seem too worried. He told me to go on ahead. He figures he'll get on a plane somehow."

I went to the phone that night and started dialing. Somehow I managed to blast my way through all the dozens of other people dialing and redialing that miserable Ewing Eight pay telephone without getting a busy signal; I could hear the phone ringing right away. Then the miracle happened. Eric answered.

"Mom! I've been sitting right here. I knew you'd call."

"Eric! I'm so glad I got you. What's the scoop?"

"They don't want to let me out. I guess they're afraid something will go wrong."

"Oh, no! Jesus! I'm going to fly back then—"

"Mom, it's okay. I'll be all *right*." In fact, he sounded like a very disappointed small boy. But he was not whining, not a bit. "You've got to stay there and make Christmas for everybody else," he said.

"Eric, can you talk to the doctors again? How do you feel, anyway? Are you okay?"

"I feel pretty good. Little sick from so much prednisone and other stuff. But no big deal. I'm all right."

"Do you want to come?"

"Sure do. I'm still trying. But—I dunno. Doesn't look like I'm going to make it."

"Call us tomorrow noon? Collect. Promise?" Tomorrow was Christmas Eve.

"Okay. I promise. Give my love to everybody. Say hello." He sounded very far away.

"I will. Love to you, too."

I hung up, crying, cursing. Then I pushed open the sliding door and walked out on the spongy, unreal Florida grass into the soft unreal night, so blue, so bright from the huge, foolish moon. What were we doing in this place? Eric needed his family at Christmas, and now he might have to spend it alone in the hospital. What could we do *now?* Should I try to fly back? Let Sidney make Christmas for the others and eventually drive the car home? I probably couldn't get on a plane. Oh, what a mess!

Nobody got much sleep that night.

The next day Eric telephoned at noon to say he had a Christmas pass for the whole week. He was going out to the airport and somehow (he didn't know just how but count on it; it was going to happen, he said) he was going to be on that plane when it touched down in West Palm Beach at 9:30 P.M. Christmas Eve.

We were late getting to the airport. We missed the exit to get off the turnpike at West Palm Beach and went fourteen miles out of the way. Sid went to park the car while I ran up the wide marble steps, ran all across the huge airport lobby as fast as I could. I ran right past Eric.

"Mom! Hey!"

I turned.

"Didn't know me, did you?"

His face was lost in the swelling of prednisone once again. But he was Eric. He was here. And he was very happy. He drove us the seventy miles home. I was worried that he might be tired.

Besides, he didn't know the roads. But I kept my mouth shut. Sid calmly assumed Eric would want to drive, and he was right. It was the best thing he could have done. Driving helped Eric relax. Sidney coached him gently on the turns as they came up. At last we pulled into the driveway.

Lisa had decorated the Christmas tree while we were gone, hanging all the old ornaments that Sidney had brought down in the back of the car. There was the little goldfish, the two tiny wine bottles from my mother's Christmas tree, the broken angel with silk wings, the blue and red drum, the silver horn, the real glass icicle that we'd hung on all our Christmas trees year after year. We were all together, and it was going to be Christmas after all. The phonograph went through the old carols, and when it came to "Silent Night," Eric began to cry. He cried hard, and when he'd managed to stop he said, "It's because we're all here and I'm so happy. I'm just crying because I'm happy."

Eric got into his fourth remission early in January. He also ran into trouble. It is unusual to have remissions after three or four. Each remission becomes harder to achieve, harder and harder to hold. Eric's doctors had had a three-month struggle getting him into this one; they didn't want him to lose it. There were some new words in leukemia treatment at that time, and I began to hear them frequently. Protocol. Maintenance. Consolidation. Soon enough I learned what they all meant.

Protocol was the fancy, rather military term for a whole procedure of drug treatment agreed upon by Memorial's top doctors. There are some hospitals which share protocols with each other, but it is a limited exchange because of the difficulty of following patients closely in different hospitals. Occasionally Memorial patients might have different programs of drugs designed and tailored for their needs. In general, however, protocol was standard and was followed with most patients. Protocol might mean you would not use Drug B before using Drug A. Or it might mean that, after studying the case histories of hundreds of patients, both inpatients and outpatients, you had discovered that Drugs C, D, and E should be used in combination to give you the best results. The patient's response to the drugs, his general condition and blood tests, would determine whether, according to protocol, you would stick with the program he was on or whether a change was indicated. I learned that one reason Eric's doctors had been reluctant to let him fly down for Christmas was that at that time there was only one doctor in all of Florida—over a hundred miles away on the other side of the state—who had trained at Memorial and was familiar with their protocol. Fortunately, Eric's condition had seemed to stabilize at the last moment to the point where the doctors dared to let him go for a week.

Maintenance was, as the word implies, a course of drug therapy given after the patient was in good remission to help him maintain that remission. I grew to like the word "maintenance." The maintenance drugs were, on the whole, gentler, the side effects less. You could take the pills at home, at school, or wherever you might be, and go on with your life.

It was the word "consolidation" that soon struck terror to my heart. Consolidation was a necessary evil; I understood that well enough. But in my mind it was a euphemism for nearly killing the patient. The doctors were bravely trying for total kill of leukemic cells, of course. It was still very painful, though, to watch your patient, who had finally achieved remission, being submitted to the powerful battering of poisonous drugs week after week, sometimes month after month. Eric's consolidation, following his remission, lasted from mid-January 1970 until the first of April. The drugs used were some of the most ferocious and most effective in the whole antileukemic arsenal: cytosine arabinoside and thioguanine. Popularly known to those who've endured them as CA and TG. By the end of February, after six weeks of nearly continuous vomiting, after low blood counts which had made it necessary several times to resort to transfusions of both whole blood and platelets, Eric seemed to have become a different person.

There were occasional short rest periods of a day or two or three when the drugs were stopped to let the patient recover from their effects. But Eric no longer used his rest time, or his passes, to come home. Instead, when he felt well enough, he went out and plunged into the life of the city. Sometimes, he told us, he walked the streets alone, looking in shop windows along Lexington, listening to the music blaring out of the record shops, studying the faces of people on the streets. Sometimes he took a nurse or a hospital technician to one of the bars along First Avenue. Drinking, he discovered, did not combine well with drugs. Even a single beer sometimes could make him very sick. But it was good to sit in the dark, talking, sticking a few quarters in the jukebox, forgetting for a while that he'd ever been in a hospital. He always managed to slip off the hospital ID bracelet. He didn't want to feel like a patient, he didn't want strangers asking him questions. The best times were when he felt well enough to run. Then he felt he was holding his own, could get his strength back, get in shape; it would just take time.

But well or sick, Eric did not often tell us his plans these days, and he did not seem to want visitors from home. When he was very ill, wrestling with the nausea, he definitely wanted to be alone. He said, "If I concentrate, sometimes I can beat it." He willed very hard not to vomit. He knew that with every episode he lost weight, lost strength, and so with his will he fought it off as long as possible. Sometimes he succeeded.

Sidney was perhaps a more welcome visitor than I during those months. He had occasional business in New York or New Jersey, and when he stopped off at the hospital on the way home, he managed to make it look like a casual five-minute errand. His cool dignity and his Scandinavian calm were a help. Besides, he was nobody's mother.

I tried to find out how things were going on the eighth floor. Sidney doesn't remember names too well, but with my guessing here and his supplying parts of the puzzle there, we pieced the news together.

"That gray fellow, the dried-up Irishman, is back on the floor."

"Mr. Murphy!"

"Yes. He looks just the same as ever."

"Then there's that tall black girl Eric's always liked—"

"Eileen?" Oh, no, I thought, that's too bad. She must be having some trouble again.

"And Eric spends some time with the boy who was in the double room a long time ago. They went out on a pass once to try to throw a ball around in Central Park."

"Oh, you must mean Terry. The boy who was going to have a valve put in his head. Has he got it yet?"

"No, I don't think so."

• • •

One day in mid-February, hearing from a young friend of Eric's that he'd been in to see him and found him feeling better, I thought, "Now maybe he'll be ready to see me." I got on a train the next day, went into the city, and walked the long blocks up to Ewing Pavilion. I'd also heard he was still in the same old six-bed ward, in the bed on the far right. I rode up to the eighth floor, found the ward, and looked for the bed. The curtains were pulled shut around it. I waited ten, fifteen minutes, then peered hesitantly around the flap. The bed was empty. Freshly made, pulled taut. There were posters, pictures, drawings on every inch of the wall above the bed, however. I recognized the style. This was Eric's place.

Feeling let down, a bit forlorn, and somewhat foolish, I went out and sat in the lobby. Was I being an overpossessive mother? I didn't think so, but then mothers never did think so. On the other hand, I'd stayed away almost three weeks, following Eric's wishes, and now I felt out of touch, almost neglectful of him. What was going on, anyway? I had to see him, even if it took all afternoon before he showed up.

Twenty minutes later he appeared out of an elevator, and the moment he saw me I could tell he was angry.

"What are you doing here? I didn't ask you to come."

"I know. Maybe it was a mistake coming in. But I wanted to see you."

"Look, dammit, I don't want to have to feel guilty because my mother shows up to visit me and I'm somewhere else. Can't you think of me as living my own life in the city? You wouldn't come in and sit on my doorstep if I had my own pad. Well, that's what I've got. It just happens to be a pad on Sixty-seventh Street and First Avenue."

"Okay. I'm sorry. I get the message."

We stood together silently for a minute. He looked miserable. "I'm sorry for taking your head off," he said at last. "But don't you see how it is? People have been dying in here all week. The guy next to me went out last night. When they let me up, I want off this floor fast. I want to move!"

"I do understand," I said, suddenly seeing it more clearly. "I'm really sorry if I bugged you. Now I'm going to go shopping. Call us up collect any evening when you feel like it."

"Sure," he said. "Have a good time shopping." He lifted his hand in good-bye, turned, and went back to the ward, his pad on First Avenue and 67th Street.

One evening Sid came home and said Eric had asked if I'd like to come in and say hello. Any day would be okay.

"How is he?" I asked right away.

"Fine, I guess," said Sidney. "But he hasn't been out of there at all this week so far."

"Was he in bed?"

"Yes. He said he felt a little tired."

"I'll go in tomorrow."

Mr. Murphy was wearing his ancient plaid bathrobe, sitting in his same old place next to the pay telephone, when I came off the elevator at Ewing Eight.

"Well, hello," I said. "I'm sorry to see they canceled your shore leave."

"They couldn't run the ship without me was why," said Murphy, looking pleased with himself. "I've had a hard time gettin' things back to normal, let me tell you. The patients fergit about

147

their rights when I'm gone." Then he said, "You lookin' for Eric, he's takin' a shower."

I nodded and sat down beside him. At that moment a door opened down the hall and Eric emerged in a hospital bathrobe with a huge white towel wound Arab fashion around his head. He came toward us.

"Hey, Eric!" called Murphy. "Where's your camel?"

Eric smiled. "Ralph?" he said, looking over his shoulder. "Why, he's right behind me. Can't you see him?"

And so I was witness to the birth of Ralph the Camel. This melancholy dromedary later went on to star in a series of underground comic books that were widely distributed throughout the hospital. Written and illustrated by Eric, the series was known as "The Adventures of Ewing 8."

But in the beginning Ralph was not on paper. He simply spoke and acted for Eric whenever Eric couldn't speak and act for himself. If Eric was confined to bed, Ralph went out on pass to the bars along First Avenue or went running along the trails of Central Park. Ralph was a very good runner in spite of suffering from humpomeia, a disease which baffled Memorial's best experts. While Ralph had a friendly, open personality which endeared him to many, he was suspicious of doctors. He also had a low threshold of pain which later, in the cartoon comic, allowed him to groan "Ooooooh!" whenever he was on the receiving end of a needle—a reaction Eric did not permit himself.

All this I did not know when I saw Eric leading Ralph, his new invisible camel, back to the ward. But I said, playing along, "Nice-looking camel you've got there. Does he bite?"

"Not usually," said Eric. "Not unless he's very annoyed."

"How long have you been an Arab?"

"Since I heard all my counts were down. I'm not crazy about catching a cold after a shower. My hair's wet."

What he was saying, I knew, was that he didn't want pneumonia. Leukemia patients were often easy marks for lung infections, and Eric had already had pneumonia three times as a little boy. This could make him more susceptible now. He walks the line well between fear and false bravado, I thought. He's not taking chances. But he's not trembling in his boots, either.

Eric got into bed and pulled the covers up to his chest. He looked pale and I realized he was cold, even though I felt too warm in the rather overheated ward. Suddenly he looked at me and said, "Have you thought any about going back to Florida?"

"Yes. But no. I should go, I guess. I've got some work to do. But I'm not going right now, not while you're in here."

"Mom." He looked annoyed, but he carefully kept his tone gentle. "I partly asked you to come in because I get this feeling you're not living your life on account of me. You've got to do what you have to do, what you want to do. You can't be waiting around all the time, waiting to see—"

He struggled and went on.

"What I'm trying to say is go ahead and be you. All the way. Go to Florida if you want to. It's not all that far away if something happens."

"I'll think about it," I said. "You're a good guy, Eric."

The CA and TG made Eric very sick that week. He came home to rest for a few days. It'd been a long time. "New York's too much for me right now," he said by way of explanation. "The air makes me cough. I don't like breathing that stuff."

I'd bought a plane ticket south for the following Sunday. That week we had steak, we had turkey, we had blueberry pie, we had everything Eric loved best. Slowly his appetite picked up; he began to eat. How can I go anywhere? I thought. I tried to talk to him about it.

"I have to go back into the hospital Sunday night anyway," Eric said. "But first I want to drive you to the airport."

I started to demur. He looked at me hard. "Thank you," I said.

I felt shaky that Sunday. I felt wrong, confused. But Eric seemed calm, even content, as we drove toward Kennedy. He still looked frail, though. We got the bags checked and picked up my boarding pass. There was still a little time.

"Let's go in the bar," he said.

I was pleased as we sat down. We'd never done this before. It seemed like an important ceremony to have a drink with my son.

"I think I'm okay for a beer," he said. "It's been long enough since the drugs. What'll you have?"

"Bourbon and water."

He ordered for us. We touched glasses and sat together quietly for a few moments. Then he leaned forward earnestly and said, "Try to understand something. If I have to die, I want to die alone. I want to be with my friends on the eighth floor. Can you understand that?"

"I'm trying to." I swallowed.

"What I mean is, I can do a better job alone. It's better if I'm not looking at you and worrying about what it's doing to you. I want to think of you as okay. I want you to be you, remember?"

"But Eric—"

He knew what I wanted to protest. "I'm not giving up." He smiled. "Not yet. Not by a long shot."

He looked away out the big window of the bar, where a plane was lumbering by.

"I know what's coming these next few weeks," he said. "The big bombs. But I'm ready now. So you just go do your work. Stay there as long as you have to."

I couldn't speak. I didn't know what to say.

"Listen," said Eric suddenly. "I'll come down to see you. Man, that's a great idea! Will I be able to use the beach by April! And the ocean!" He stood up. "We'd better go now."

He walked me to the roped-off area where passengers were showing their tickets before boarding. "Think about it," he said. "April. I'll make it. So be ready for me."

I kissed him good-bye then. It hurt to walk away. I didn't look back.

CHAPTER 12

THE AIRPORT IN MELBOURNE, FLORIDA, is the right size for an airport, big enough to be reassuring, small enough to be rural and neighborly. The crowd gathers every afternoon to wait for the four o'clock plane from New York much as crowds might have gathered long ago to meet the stagecoach in Laramie or the arrival of a steamer in Boston. They are family people, for the most part, in sandals, sneakers, sleeveless dresses, or jeans. I was among them one April afternoon, waiting for Eric, when someone cried, "Here she comes!" The little children climbing the chain link fence complained that they couldn't see.

Now I've spotted it, a bumblebee in the pale western sky. Slowly it floats in, gradually becoming a plane, settling gently down at last, circling around and then suddenly turning into a 727.

As the hatch broke open and stairs shot out, I held my breath painfully. I'd talked to my family nearly every evening during the past weeks—but not to Eric. I'd tried to reach him, but he never could come to the phone when I was trying. I'd nearly flown home two or three times. I knew that Eric had been surrounded by death, close to death himself. I'd seen what the drugs can do. Would I even recognize him?

Then in the stream of people slowly filing down the steps and over to the gate where we waited, I saw a tall figure. Very thin. Although the April day was warm, the figure had on a navy wool cap pulled down very close over the ears and a heavy, dark wool jacket. Was it Eric? Had he lost all his hair? Was he freezing because he had so little blood? The figure came closer; the face was white, gaunt, with terrible hooded eyes. He passed right by me and I felt nearly faint. It was not Eric! It was somebody else who resembled him closely and who also must have been very ill.

Then at last I saw him, the last one out of the plane. He was wearing his old plain jeans, a pale blue button-down shirt with rolled-up sleeves, and sneakers; he was swinging the same old duffel bag. As he came up to me I saw that his eyes were black-rimmed but they were Eric's eyes. He was very thin but he had not lost his style. His hair was all there, too, gold and a bit shaggy in the afternoon sunlight. Holding him, I thought, this is joy.

In the parking lot, handing him the car keys as usual, I said, "Let's go down A-One-A. It takes a little longer but it runs along the ocean."

With a few turns we were clear of the town traffic and heading south. The houses thinned out at last, and we were on the long white road that unrolls along the shore. Nothing but pure blue-green water. A few ruffles of foam. Gulls wheeling, gliding.

Eric glanced at the beach. "It's too beautiful. I can't take it in. I don't really believe it yet."

We drove peacefully for about ten minutes. Suddenly he said, "That's some place, that hospital!" His tone was light. "We had quite a ball. Before that stuff really hit me, and knocked me out, we managed some good shows."

One night, he told me, he and Terry decided to "escape."

They made their plans and waited for the right moment. Then they jumped into two laundry carts and hid under the piles of dirty linen.

"We went all the way down nine floors to the street." He laughed. "They trundled us right out to the sidewalk and were about to load us in the truck when we had a few second thoughts. We might have waked up in Consolidated Laundry's plant out in Westchester or someplace. So we gave ourselves up at the last minute. What the hell—we'd proved we could do it."

There was no escape, I thought. The disease was your jail, not the hospital. I said nothing.

"We pulled plenty of other stuff, too, when we felt up to it. Remind me to tell you about the I.V. caper sometime."

I learned later that this stunt occurred one Monday morning when Memorial's top ten doctors came into the ward on grand rounds. They stopped by Eric's bed and were surprised to see him huddled miserably under the covers. Even at his sickest, Eric usually tried to banter with them, get his laugh some way. Now he lay with eyes closed.

"Eric? What's wrong?" asked one concerned doctor. "How do you feel?"

"Scaly," came the mumbled reply.

Only then was the doctor's eye caught by the live goldfish swimming around in Eric's I.V. bottle overhead. The plastic tube ran down under the covers; of course it wasn't hooked up to Eric's arm but it looked very convincing. The doctors broke up. The ward cheered. It was a glorious moment on Ewing Eight.

As we rode back to our little house, I didn't press for details about anything. I'd learned my lesson, or tried to. Let him tell me what he wants to. His eyes were so black-rimmed, he must be exhausted, I thought. But it was a keyed-up exhaustion. I waited. Soon he began to talk some more.

"You should have seen that place the last few days. The whole of Memorial was in an uproar. They were up for accrediting, that's why. The state's examiners were coming. What a scene! Nurses were running around with their pastry caps on. Some of those dolls hadn't had a cap on all year. Everybody was trying to be busy, busy. The supervisor had a list of about a hundred and eighty things that had to be done immediately. Overhaul the boiler. Put some toilet paper in the patients' johns, for Chrissake. And do you know what the last thing on the list was? Put a hospital bracelet on Eric Lund and see that he keeps it on. They clamped one on me at suppertime. Then they came around with a flashlight and snapped another one on me in the middle of the night. I wound up with three bracelets after breakfast!"

He's rattling, I thought. I've never seen him quite like this.

"They made me take my stuff off the windowsill—"

I remembered Eric's collection. Besides, the usual books and magazines, he had his Adidas running shoes. His favorite soccer ball. Dumbbells. They were good for fixing up your arms after too many needles, Eric told me once. He thought that the hospital ought to have a real gym. "It would encourage people to work out as soon as they could. They'd get going again." Eric used to run up and down several flights of stairs every day when he could. I doubted if he'd been doing that lately.

"—then they made me take down my posters. All of them!" Eric was saying. "That made me sore. Then this lady head nurse came along and wanted me to take off my Marjorie Webster shirt—"

I remembered that shirt. A scarlet T-shirt with long flappy

tails which said in white letters across its chest, "Good night, Marjorie Webster, good night!"

"—so I said to her, 'You make me get back in hospital pajamas again and I'll get in bed and start pressing the buzzer every five minutes for a bedpan. What do you think I am? A *patient?*'

"You see, I was on my way out then," he went on, "and I knew I was going to make it. So why the hell shouldn't I get out of those crappy pajamas and wear my own shirt? Anyway, I fixed them good." Eric's face for a moment had the small smile he used to wear when he'd pulled off some particularly wicked business with his brother Mark's help; he and Mark would always begin to giggle the minute they saw me because, as they said, I would never, never know.

"How?" I asked in spite of myself. "How did you fix them?"

"Well, they came in and gave everybody thermometers to stick in their mouths so we'd look good when the examiners walked through. You know, see what fancy care we're taking of our patients. So I just turned my thermometer around so the bulb was sticking out." He began to laugh.

"Did they spot it?"

"No. But the head floor nurse did. She was dying. Frowning. Shaking her head at me."

He's probably making half this up, I thought, but good for him.

We drove along in silence for a while. Then we began the long beautiful climb to the bridge over the Sebastian Inlet. It soars over the black rocks of the jetty, and when you come off at the other end you're flying. It's a downhill glide all the way into town.

"You know," Eric said at last, and his voice was different, quietly serious, "it's not all bad. You might think I've been unlucky or something, having to spend over three months in the hospital. I don't see it that way. I've been fortunate to know so many great people. In a way, I feel I've been really privileged. If I hadn't been sick, I'd never have known them. And they're the best. . . .

"They got me through," he said, wondering. "There were times—some times, well—" Then he began to tell me about the new dead.

"Henry's gone. You didn't know him. He was the first. Then the kid across from me by the other window, the one who was so scared he shook all the time. Manny. Remember him?"

I hadn't known his name. I remembered his fright. I remembered his mother was always there rubbing his back.

"Terry died a week ago."

There is nothing I can say.

"I was mad when Terry died. He was a great guy. You know what he did? He was in another room, really sick, and he heard I wasn't in great shape, so he sent his girl in to cheer *me* up for a while. How 'bout that?

"And Mr. Murphy died," he said.

The sheer numbers of the dead finally dull your capacity to respond. Yet I am astonished now. I can't imagine Ewing Eight without Mr. Murphy.

"That must have been hard to believe."

"It was, sort of." Eric smiled sadly. "He was just wire and bones all along. You never saw him getting any worse because he was already there. But one day he died just like that. It surprised everybody. Old Murphy was all right."

We were on the outskirts of town now. Eric needed help with a few turns. I was glad of the distraction. "Next right. Then left at the canal—"

He recognized our street and swung the car into the driveway beside a small white house with a yellow door. Our house. He turned off the ignition and sat still a moment. "Eileen died last night," he said.

His last friend is gone. All the patients he was close to are gone. Of that gallant group, he alone survived the long winter on Ewing Eight. He is alive and a thousand miles away. He is here, and he can still see the sun.

Eric went out each day trying to find his way back to the world. He ran the beaches. He plunged again and again into the surf. He lay flat on the hot sand. But when I looked in his eyes, I saw him looking at death. *This* was unreal, this postcard world of palm trees and pretty people sauntering along the ocean's edge, picking up shells, exclaiming at the sandpipers or the gulls or the temperature of the water. What had he to do with this? His dead were still too alive to be put aside. I let him alone. I tried hard to stay out of his way because I saw his need. But he couldn't mourn while he stayed in my house. Three days later he moved out and took the small upstairs room, the cheapest room in the old Drift-wood Inn. I knew that room well. Once, long ago, I'd lived in it for a while. I was happy to think of him there with the rough old boards letting in chinks of light right through the walls in the morning. The washbasin mirror would be too low for him; it had been too low even for me. The front door lock, heavy bronze and green with age, was a holy terror to open. Well, wrestling with locks, wrestling with himself, was something Eric had to do alone. I felt sure he'd find his way eventually. In the meantime I yearned to give him things—homemade brownies, maybe some new clothes, a transistor radio, a good dinner. But what could I give him compared to what he'd lost? Even when I gave him money, which after all was necessity, I just passed it to him quietly with no comment. Sometimes I gave him my car for half a day so he could take off. He was gravely sweet, appreciative, but his eyes still held their look. He couldn't be close yet.

So I watched from a distance when I was sure he couldn't see me. How beautiful it was to see him running again! Or to see his brown legs strolling down one of the side streets off Ocean Boulevard. Then one night I caught a glimpse of him through a doorway hunched over on a rattan stool in the Bahia Bar. It had to be Eric. I knew that faded blue denim shirt, the cut of those white jeans. Something in the way he was sitting there made him look so vulnerable, so terribly lonely, that I almost went in and spoke to him. Instead, feeling distressed, I went home.

The next afternoon Eric appeared on my doorstep about four thirty. "Do you feel like giving me dinner?"

"Sure do." I'd been keeping a steak, hoping he'd show up. I had frozen rolls, string beans, a little head of Bibb lettuce. Even fresh strawberries.

We watched the news at five, and he accepted a beer while I began to get things ready. There wasn't much to do. As I turned off the TV, suddenly he said, "Is there something funny about me?"

This stopped me. I must have looked astonished.

"I mean," he said, "do I look okay to you?"

I nodded, still not getting the drift.

"Well"—he laughed a little nervously—"I've had some experiences that make you wonder. I've been going into the Bahia at night. You know, just to nurse a beer and see a little of the outside world before hitting the sack. Two nights ago this older guy comes up to me and starts talking. He was a nice-enough-looking guy, little too dressy maybe, gray hair. Anyway, it turns out he was trying to pick me up. It sorta shook me. I mean, do I look like I'm inviting that?"

"No, of course not," I said. Yet I could see why the attempt had been made. The things he'd endured set him apart, gave him a look you do not often see in the young.

"That's not all," said Eric. Again he laughed, but he began to look a little more relaxed. "I thought maybe I wouldn't go back in there. But what the hell, it can't happen twice. Besides, the bartender at the Bahia is used to me and doesn't challenge me. I'm not twenty-one after all, and down here it's a different scene from New York. Well . . . "

Eric told me the story over dinner. This is what happened:

It began about 10 P.M. Eric wasn't sleepy enough to turn in. He thought about dropping into the Bahia. There was a TV over the bar he could watch for a while. At first he was afraid the gray-haired man might be there, but then again it didn't seem likely. In his shyness and surprise, Eric had rebuffed him pretty coldly. So he pulled on his blue shirt, his white jeans, and decided to go. For just one beer. There was a crowd of kids, late teens, early twenties, sitting around a table feeding the jukebox when he went in. Nobody was at the bar except for an older couple down at the other end. Eric sat down, ordered his beer. Two of the kids got up to dance on the little dusty square between tables. The rest were laughing, arguing about the next record to play.

About halfway through his beer, Eric noticed a nice-looking young guy get up and leave the group to come over and sit down on a barstool next to him. "He was a Yalie type—or what I used to think of as Yalie, anyhow," said Eric, describing him. "Good clothes. Striped button-down shirt. The works. Good features. He looked a little square but pleasant."

The guy said to Eric, "You're not from around here, are you?"

Eric smiled and said, "No. New York."

"Down here on a vacation?"

Surprisingly, Eric heard himself saying, "No. I'm down here on an assignment." (He explained this to me a bit shamefacedly, saying, "My current lie is that I'm a writer. I keep writing in my head all the time about everything I've seen, wanting to get it down.")

The guy introduced himself. His name was Pat. His grandmother had a place over near the yacht club, he said. He'd come down for Easter vacation. What, he wanted to know, was Eric's assignment? Eric, after a week of being totally alone, suddenly found himself wanting to talk.

"I've been interviewing this young guy in Memorial Hospital," he said. "He's got cancer. Leukemia, in fact. I've been talking to him off and on for weeks. Now I'm supposed to write a story about him. I've come down here to think about it."

Pat gave him a strange, hard look, Eric said. Then he smiled and ordered another beer. "Can I buy you another?" he asked.

Eric saw he'd reached the bottom of his own glass. "Well, thanks," he said. ("I hesitated a second," Eric told me. "Then I decided I must be getting paranoid if I start seeing trouble every time a friendly guy offers me a beer.")

Pat went on pressing for more details about the story. The more Eric talked, the less he found he wanted to. It was one thing to imagine himself writing about scenes and happenings in the hospital; it was another to share this imaginary writing with someone before the material had jelled. Finally he finished his beer, thanked Pat, and said good night. He walked down the boardwalk for several blocks, trying to shake off a feeling of annoyance with himself. At last he turned and went back toward the inn.

The Driftwood Inn is full of shapes and shadows by night. Soft orange lights glow in the old lanterns along the passageways. Eric crossed the tile courtyard and started up the rickety wooden stairs to his balcony bedroom. Suddenly he heard thudding footsteps behind him. He glanced around but saw only the shadows. Then he heard a voice.

"Hey, Eric, wait up!" Pat came running out from behind the sea grape that grew in the center of the driveway. "Can I talk to you a minute?"

"Sure," said Eric. "Come on in. Now I can buy *you* a beer." He was somehow glad to be able to return the favor, as if it would cancel his deception and the abrupt way he'd said good-bye. The bronze lock turned; they stepped into the small room. Eric had borrowed my Styrofoam picnic chest for a temporary icebox. He kept it filled with chips from the hotel ice machine so he could always have cold fruit juice and a few snacks in his room. Now he went to the corner of the room, bent over the chest, and pulled out a can of beer. As he turned back, he saw that Pat had opened his belt and was unzipping his pants.

("Oh, man!" Eric said to me, as he told the story. "Was I mad at myself for being so dumb two nights in a row! But I was also pretty scared. I thought, what if he has a knife? I really didn't know how to handle it.")

"You've got me wrong," Eric said to Pat. "I'm sorry, but it's just not my thing. I've got nothing against it for somebody else. I don't mean to put you down. But it's not for me."

Pat took the beer out of Eric's hand and sat down, half undressed, on the bed. "You know, Eric," he said, "You're just being defensive. You're afraid to get close to people. Why can't you relax and open up a little?"

Eric's fear passed and he felt anger. "I'm not afraid to be close, dammit," he said. "I'll be as close as you like in conversation. But that's it. So what do you want me to be open about? We can talk all night. I'm not going anywhere."

"You're a phony, Eric," Pat said, changing his tactics. "You're nothing *but* talk. You're not even a writer. And I'll tell you something else. You don't know any kid with leukemia. You've never even seen the inside of a cancer hospital."

Eric pulled out his wallet and took out his CRF card, his magic credit card which had entitled him to live free in the world of Ewing Eight. It was made out in the name of Eric Lund. "I'm the guy with leukemia," he said. "This is my card. I may not be a writer, but I've just spent nearly four months in Memorial Hospital."

Pat stared at the card.

"Now get out of here," said Eric.

To his dismay, Pat suddenly broke into sobs. In a moment, when he was able, he stood up, buckled his pants, and opened the door to the balcony.

"I guess I don't understand your problem," Eric said, feeling that he'd really messed things up and that he was somehow responsible. "But I'm sorry."

Pat suddenly turned on the balcony. "No, you don't understand," he said, tears still in his eyes. "But let me ask you something. Do you have a brother, Eric?"

"Yes," said Eric, surprised. "I have a brother."

"How old?"

"Mark is seventeen."

"Then listen to me," said Pat, beginning to cry again. "Take care of him, Eric. That's all I can say—"

Is he drunk? wondered Eric. We didn't have all that much.

"Take care of him now while you can, before it's too late," Pat went on. "You see, my brother died of leukemia four years ago. I was the younger one. I got left behind." He turned and stumbled down the stairs before Eric could say another word.

I knew that Eric had worried about Mark—about all of us, in fact—being affected by his illness. Up until that time, for instance, he'd absolutely refused to let Mark visit him in the hospital. "I don't want him in this place," he'd said. Now I waited to see if Pat's story, with its implied suggestion, had upset him.

"Poor guy," Eric said at last. "Pat's got a problem, but why tangle it up with his brother's death? It doesn't follow. At least not necessarily."

"Maybe the brother was the family favorite or something. Maybe Pat feels guilty because *he* should have been the one."

"Well, we don't have that problem," said Eric decisively. "Mark's probably the best kid in the family. What a head! He's really smart and he's the best looking. So no contest. Remember, I told you a long time ago I was glad Mark hadn't been the one to get sick?"

I nodded, relieved that Eric hadn't been thrown off course. I was amused, too, because whenever Eric talked about his brother or either of his two sisters, the one under discussion was always "the greatest, the smartest, the best looking." He meant it at the time, too. I looked for jealousy; I expected it to turn up in the normal process of raising kids, like chicken pox or skinned knees. But I never found it in Eric.

A bit of good fortune came Eric's way the following day. We were invited to dinner by friends of mine, a talented man and his wife, both in their early thirties. They hit it off with Eric immediately. Ted was a burly, sensitive man with a thousand interests, an artist, designer, writer, and theatrical director, as well as a skilled photographer. He was also a man who was challenged by sports and the unknown. Ted wanted a companion for a skin-diving and deep-sea fishing expedition in the Florida Keys. He had the tanks, enough equipment, and he also knew the area. "Beautiful fish!" he said. "I promise you you've never seen anything like this."

Eric was ready to set out immediately. There was a catch, however. He'd been on maintenance drugs ever since he'd come to Florida. Now the time had arrived when he must pay a visit to the Memorial-trained doctor across the state in Sarasota, Dr. Phyllis Stevenson. She would then decide, according to protocol and on the basis of blood tests done in her office, whether Eric's remission was holding well, whether he needed more of the same drugs or possibly different ones. Several days later Eric set off on the long drive to see her. He had a packet of papers giving her all the information she would need about his recent treatment in the hospital.

While Eric was gone, Ted dropped in. "You know, it's a helluva long drive to the Keys. If the doctor gives Eric some new drugs and he has a bad reaction, I wonder if it'll be okay for him to be so far away?"

"Um—I don't know. I see what you mean."

"I'm game to go. I've been looking forward to it. But I'd sure hate to have something happen to him. I mean, when you're skin diving, especially at some real depth, there's pressure and stuff. What do you think?"

"Well, I don't think he'd take chances. He's pretty interested in surviving. Up to now he's always done whatever he felt he could do."

We puzzled over this for a while, and when Ted finally left, he said, "I've got an idea. I'll give you a call later."

That afternoon the phone rang. "Listen to this," Ted said when I picked up the receiver. "A friend of mine is a pilot, has his own plane. I've been up with him several times. He's agreed to fly down to the Keys to get Eric if he gets in any trouble, and then we can rush him right back to Sarasota. All I have to do is give my friend a call if we need him."

"That's quite something," I said, amazed at the trouble people were willing to go to to help Eric. Again, I tried to think what the hazards might be. Nosebleeds? He wouldn't be allowed out of a hospital if his platelets were way down. Nausea? He was an old hand at dealing with that. Other things? I couldn't guess what they might be.

"I think it's great, Ted," I said finally. "Go ahead and go. I bet you won't have any trouble. And please thank your friend for me. But listen, do we have to tell Eric about the plane? In advance, I mean? I think it might upset him."

"Why should we tell him?" said Ted. "If we don't run into trouble, he never has to know. But I'll feel more comfortable knowing I've got an ace in the hole. If something should happen, that plane can get Eric out of there and into a hospital."

Ted, Eric, Ted's ten-year-old son, and another friend took off in a VW camper the following day for the Keys. They were loaded to the roof with tanks, spear guns, flippers, rods, tackle, the works. Dr.

Stevenson had given Eric a shot and some new pills. He wasn't feeling very good when they left, but he was determined to go. Ted told me later that Eric was pretty sick the first day. He lay in the shade watching the others strap on their tanks, dive into the clear, sunlit water, and then return, telling of the many-colored fish, the beautiful plants that opened and closed. That night the party cooked some of the bigger fish, as well as a five-pound Florida lobster that Ted had caught. Eric couldn't eat. The next day he felt better and was able to try a little diving. By the time he returned to the Driftwood three days later, he'd explored the underwater world for himself; he'd been out on the ocean in bumpy weather, too, fishing from the boat for big stuff. He and Ted had become close friends. They spent some time together nearly every day from then on. It was with Ted that Eric was finally able to let go and share the burden of his grief for his dead friends.

It didn't happen right away. Eric often dropped in at Ted's house for dinner. They'd talk way into the night or perhaps drive around the countryside, eventually stopping in at some little roadside spot for a midnight hamburger or a beer. When the time came for Eric to fly back north on a dawn flight from Melbourne, Ted stayed up with him all the night before and drove him to the airport himself. Then Ted stopped in to see me on his way home. The mission was accomplished.

"You look exhausted. But a little triumphant, too," I said.

"I'm exhausted, all right." Ted leaned back on the sofa. "But I think Eric's going to be okay. He's some guy! He finally got it all out. He started talking about his friends on the eighth floor, and pretty soon he began to cry. He cried and cried. He said he just couldn't accept it that they had to die.

"In a way I wish I'd never met Eric," Ted went on, "because

now I'm involved, too. It's going to hurt like hell if something happens to him. I'll be the one who can't accept it. You know, I've never let anything like this get close to me before. Illness was something that happened out there to other people. In my family we're used to living forever. My parents are still alive, and both sets of my grandparents are still alive, too. I've never had to face up to losing anybody, and now all of a sudden I care."

"It's not all that bad—caring," I said. "When you run the risks of loving, you get a lot back."

CHAPTER 13

SOON AFTER ERIC LEFT, I rented the house and flew home myself. The summer of 1970 should have been peaceful. Eric was in good remission. We should have been able to relax, to enjoy, to be a family. Instead, whenever we got together, especially at dinner, we all started sawing away against each other like an out-of-tune high school band.

At first I couldn't see what was wrong. Eric had a fine job lined up for six weeks, starting the first week in July, working as one of the head counselors in a summer camp nearby for inner-city children of our town. It was the sort of thing he loved. It would also give him the $1,000 he wanted to help with college and personal expenses. Mark had just been accepted at Yale. This was the first year we would have two in college. Nobody needed a crystal ball to predict that we were going to have a serious shortage of money around the house. I was frightened but hoping we'd skate through somehow. Sidney, as was his custom, was bland on top, tense underneath. Still, no one was shouting blame. We all knew that Eric's illness, even with CRF assistance, free drugs, and hospitalization, had been a financial blow to the family. If Sidney and I hadn't been free-lancers it might have been easier. It was hard to hunt for new work or follow through with old projects when we were limp with worry as we'd been most of the year. And even if we only made two or three trips to the city a week when Eric was hospitalized, it knocked the slats out of our budget.

Yet money wasn't the crux of the trouble that summer. I began to understand what might be wrong one afternoon when Eric came out to the kitchen looking for a stamp. I dug around in a household drawer, found a little book with a few left in it, then glanced at the letter he'd laid on the table while he tore out the stamp. He caught my glance and instantly resented it. Now I was a prying mother.

"If you want to know," he said, "I'm writing to ask for that job from Ralph Farrell. On a ship to Africa."

I remembered his talking about it long ago. But now? I was astonished. I almost asked, "What for?" Eric had felt lucky and happy to land the counselor job. The director was understanding. Every Monday when Eric had to report to the Memorial clinic, and every Monday afternoon when he was apt to be ill from drugs, the director just assigned another counselor to his spot. In return, Eric went in earlier to set things up and stayed later to put things away on the other four days a week. It had seemed like a good deal.

But suddenly I saw that being tied to Memorial's maintenance program was keeping Eric on a very short leash. No wonder in recent days my simple question, "Will you be home for dinner?" had produced a barely civil answer, "Where else would I be?" Here we were again. The mother-son syndrome. Only now there was a difference. He had earned his freedom but couldn't use it. At twenty he was a man. He knew more of life and death than many men do at fifty. He also knew that time was precious and might be short. There was so much he'd never seen. Longing to be thousands of miles away, longing for adventures, he found himself still staring at the tired walls of home.

"I think you ought to go to Africa," I said, knowing sadly it would probably be impossible.

Eric shrugged. "I'll have three weeks after camp closes and before soccer practice starts up at Storrs. I could work my way to Africa and back on a round trip. Anyway," he growled, "whatever happens, I'm damned if I'm going to spend those three weeks hanging around here."

Amen, I thought. I was having some struggles of my own getting out of various cages of my own making. I could sympathize with Eric, but I didn't enjoy the flak I was catching. I thought, "Go! Take off! The sooner the better."

My problem was not just the housewife's daily hang-up of how to divide two pounds of hamburger by x number of people every night. Like most women, I can make a meat loaf in my sleep or spot a leftover in the back of the icebox, multiply it by two green peppers and a can of soup, and get a passing grade in kitchen arithmetic. I even like cooking. What I like best is cooking and writing together. I write on the backs of grocery lists, brown paper bags, cash register tapes from the A&P. Sometimes I've ended up with twenty-eight scraps of paper stapled together (which can give you an original draft eight feet long and two inches wide). But the point was, I ended up with *something*. Not that summer. I even bought new pads. New yellow pencils. (Always a sign of desperation.) There was no action. I was a writer in irons.

The things that had been happening to Eric the past few years had also been happening to me. He'd had to grow up fast; he was changed forever by what he'd lived through. I'd been growing and changing, too—but with a difference. By the nature of the situation, I was always an outsider. There'd been rare conversations, a few letters when Eric let me in. There was all I could see for myself whenever I went to the hospital. Yet I felt as if I'd sat out the whole drama in the waiting room.

I wanted to be more involved. The huge struggle of life and death had struck me hard. I couldn't simply put it aside. So when I ended up complaining, as writers are apt to do, that I was blocked, done for, my writer friends just said, "You're overtired from strain." Sure. Of course. But lying feet up in a hammock or dozing on a beach turned out to be the last things I wanted to do.

All I really wanted to do was work. God, I longed to sit down, pull an idea over my head like a tent, and stay safely inside it for a month. No way. The things I'd been working on before summer began turned limp and pale the minute I tried to go at them.

It was in this fractured frame of mind that I went in to New York to have lunch with my oldest friend, Carla, one day. Carla lived at the lower end of the village, but she picked a restaurant in the East Sixties for our lunch.

"What are you doing up here?" I asked her when we met. "Aren't you off your beat?"

"I've just been over giving platelets at Memorial."

"Not again! This is too much. You don't have *another* friend in Memorial who needs blood?" Carla had given several times for Eric the winter before.

"No, dummy. They need donors every day. I told you it was a great place. I like going there. I can't explain it. You give blood—but somehow it fills you up."

We talked about many things: her kids, mine, her work, mine—or rather my not-work. We caught up, sympathized, reminisced, and left each other comforted. She went off to keep another appointment. I went off to Bloomingdale's, where my malaise quickly returned in the world of merchandise and three-way mirrors. Everything cost a fortune. Nothing seemed to fit. Suddenly I thought I knew what I wanted to do. I pushed my way out of the store and headed across 59th Street.

About quarter to two, I arrived in front of the plain brick building that fills the block from 67th Street to 68th on First Avenue. Ewing Pavilion. Strange to be coming here on my own with Eric home working in Connecticut. All at once I felt like an imposter. If only I could give blood! The heavy glass doors were wedged open to let the crowd of summer visitors flow freely in and out of the hospital. I drifted in with them. Without knowing exactly what I had in mind, I crossed the lobby and found myself standing for the first time in front of the door which said in large black capitals, DONOR ROOM. Underneath, a card tacked to the door gave the schedule of days and hours for donors, including Sundays and holidays. Running the Donor Room was apparently a seven-day-a-week all-year job. The need for blood did not disappear just because it was Christmas or the fourth of July. I saw I had arrived close to the end of a day session. Well. Feeling somewhat timid, I grasped the doorknob and went in.

There was a nurse sitting at a desk at the other end of the small waiting room. She had dark, short curls, lively eyes. When she saw me she raised her arm and cried, "Aha! Another donor! Just what we need! You can help us wind up our day."

"I'm sorry. I'm afraid I'm not a donor. I'm not allowed to give blood. But I am the mother of one of your beneficiaries—Eric Lund. I guess I've just come to thank you and see what goes on here, see if there's anything I can do."

"Oh, Eric. Of course! Well, hello!"

During the next few minutes I discovered that Eric and Ralph the Camel were already well known to the Donor Room nurses.

They had all read Eric's "Adventures of Ewing 8." The nurse at the desk was Jeanne Miller, head of the Donor Room. In a moment she introduced her second-in-command, a vivacious English girl named Margaret Hooper. Margaret, it turned out, was from Liverpool, home of many a great soccer team.

"Eric's not upstairs now, is he?" Margaret asked anxiously.

"No. I'm here on my own."

"Oh, that's good. I know his team is counting on him to come back this fall. We can't have anything happening to a soccer player like Eric."

A young girl of about nineteen had followed me in. She'd come, she explained, hoping to give blood for her boyfriend. While Margaret took down her history and extracted a blood sample, I looked around the waiting room. Posters for Snoopy, Peanuts, Lucy. John Donne's "No man is an island" had been translated into donor language—"Every man is a peninsula." Sign: HUMAN BEINGS HERE—HANDLE WITH CARE. Quotes from Thoreau, J.F.K. and others. A bulletin featured postcards from regular donors now vacationing in the Caribbean or Scandinavia. One led off with, "Dear Gang at Vampire Center. . . ." There were thank-you cards, too, from the relatives of patients. Reading these last cards I realized suddenly that most of the patients were now dead.

Margaret was discovering that the girl could not meet the requirement of 12.5 hemoglobin necessary for female donors who wish to give blood. (The number 12.5 refers to grams of hemoglobin in 100 milliliters of whole blood. I learned later that there is a natural difference in the normal hemoglobin count of males and females. The requirement for male donors is 13.5.)

"Look, love," Margaret said to the girl. "You can't give blood until we get you up to twelve point five. Eat well, now. Lots of red meat. Take a glass of wine with your dinner. Then come back and see us in two weeks. Right?"

"Right," said the girl, looking crestfallen. She went out.

"Some of the girls have a hard time making it. They tend to be anemic. Then the poor things are so disappointed." Margaret walked over and gave the lock on the door a turn. "That's all for today."

I got up quickly. "I should be going. I don't want to keep you. I know it's the end of your session."

"Oh, we've got two inside we're still finishing up. I just locked the door so we won't get any new customers. But we'll be here for another half hour. Wouldn't you like to look around?"

"Sure." I followed her through a doorway.

The Donor Room was actually four tiny rooms opening awkwardly into one another so that you were sure to bump rears with somebody as you went from one place to another. There was less chrome and foam than you'd see in a college infirmary, yet the place had a ragged charm.

Another nurse was helping a lady in her fifties get unhooked from an I.V. apparatus. "See you next week," the lady said, smiling at Margaret.

"Oh, thanks for coming, love. Have a cookie on your way out? More coffee?"

"No, thanks, I'm trying to diet."

Margaret turned her attention to an extremely worried-looking bald little man. Clear liquid dripped slowly from a bottle into the tube in his vein.

"I think we must be about ready." She disappeared around another corner, then returned carrying a dark red plastic sack. It looked like a pound of frozen chicken livers.

"These are packed red cells, you see," she said to me, holding them up. "The donor gets them back after we've used our centrifuge to spin off the platelets from a pint of whole blood. And because he gets them back he's ready to give platelets again in two or three days. If he gave whole blood he'd have to wait eight weeks."

Margaret went up to the worried little man and shut off the I.V. solution bottle. "Mr. Katz," she said, "I'd like you to meet Eric Lund's mother. Eric's one of our patients who's out getting ready for the soccer season right now."

"Yes? Yes?" said Mr. Katz. I could see he didn't believe a word of this.

Mr. Katz, I learned, was giving platelets for the second time that week. His wife was a new leukemia patient upstairs on Ewing Eight. Plainly he was in terror.

"Eric was with us three months last winter, right?" said Margaret. I began to see the method in her chatter.

"Almost four," I said.

"But now he's out and doing beautifully. What's the university he plays for?"

"Connecticut."

"All right now. There you go." Margaret had completed the switch from I.V. fluid to Mr. Katz's own red cells without removing the needle or tube. It was a quick operation the way she did it, using snips and clamps. She inspected the flow, then disappeared into the next room.

Mr. Katz eyed the needle nervously. Finally he turned his attention to me. "You mean he really plays soccer? On the field? Your son?"

"Absolutely. He's very good. He was only a sophomore last

year but he traveled with the varsity all season and played in every game. When he isn't playing, I mean when it's off season, sometimes he runs ten miles a day just to stay in shape."

"Ah! Ah! Wonderful!" Mr. Katz relaxed enough to smile slightly. I saw him thinking this over, expanding his frightened view of a world, recently shrunken with serious illness, to include the possibility of some normal life again. His wife might come home again, might actually be able to move around. They still might do things together.

"They say it is all right for your son to play? The doctors?"

"They think it's great. They want him to do everything he feels he can do."

We talked a few more minutes. As I got up to go, suddenly he took my hand. "I'm glad to have talked with you. You must have a wonderful boy. Good luck to you. Good luck to you both!" His eyes were now alive with emotion, hope.

"Good luck to you, too," I said. The warmth I felt for him, for all struggling people, filled me. I was connected again. In this mood, I was as grateful to Mr. Katz as he was to me. I yearned to say something extravagant. What I did say was, "I know you'll have some wonderful days when your wife gets out."

I knew nothing of the sort. And perhaps she would never get out. But there was a conspiracy of hope I subscribed to in that moment and from then on.

I went out to say good-bye to Jeanne and Margaret. They were finishing up the day's work, totaling the donations for whole blood and platelets.

"Forty-eight donors. Not bad for a day as hot as this."

"I suppose you must have trouble in summer, getting enough people in here," I hazarded. "Everybody goes away—"

"Some trouble, sure. But it's not too bad. Our donors are real dolls. They're so faithful."

"Would you believe that one of our donors, a man on vacation, called in from Long Island today to see if we needed him?" Margaret cut in. "He'd heard about the shortage of blood over the radio. He wanted to be sure we were okay."

"Was there a shortage? I didn't get the word. But then I'm not much of a radio listener."

They told me about it. During the preceding hot summer days, all the great hospitals of New York had been growing desperately short of blood. Early that very morning the radio had begun broadcasting an urgent appeal for donors. Throughout the day the appeal had been repeated many times. The situation had been nearly critical.

"But haven't you felt the shortage?" I asked them.

"Well," said Jeanne, "we had forty-eight donors today. That's really good for this time of year. Maybe some of them were walk-ins off the street who heard the broadcast. But a lot of them were our regulars that we can depend on. When other places get in trouble, we still do pretty well. But that doesn't mean we don't appreciate it or that we take it for granted. We need all the help we can get. So we go after it! We lasso anybody who comes in because we want him to come back."

I can understand why Carla keeps coming here, I thought.

"I'd like to come back and meet your centrifuge. Some day when you've got more time," I said. "I want to see the monster that makes all this possible."

"Do come back! Come some evening and you'll really see us in action." Margaret had a bit of a tease in her voice.

"You make it sound like a smashing party."

They both laughed. "Sometimes that's how it is."

I said good-bye again and set off to catch the 4:05 for home. Twenty-six blocks downtown and three over to Grand Central. It went fast, for I was lit with energy, tied in to the world again. I hadn't known what I wanted to do for a long time. Now I had a mission. I wanted to learn all about the new techniques of giving blood and separating it into components. It seemed to me important and exciting that a platelet donor could give two or three times a week. How many people knew this? I was in a hurry to do my homework and find out all I could. I was pretty sure I could interest some magazine in a story about the Donor Room and what went on there. Perhaps in writing about Memorial I could wake up a few more people to the great need for blood. Then hospitals everywhere might have fewer days like the one they'd just lived through, when a shortage had nearly become a crisis, when urgent appeals had had to be broadcast. It was a good hope. I held on to it all the way home.

That night I was so preoccupied with my new plans while I was getting dinner that when Eric came in looking for something cold to drink I made a very stupid mistake.

"Hey, guess what?" I said. "I went in to Memorial's Donor Room today. It's a wonderful place, and I want to learn all about platelets and write something—"

"Listen!" Eric interrupted me with a tone like a smack across the face. "I don't want to hear about it. If you want to do anything at Memorial or write anything, that's strictly your affair. It has nothing to do with me. Don't involve me. Don't talk to me about it." He walked by me angrily, and the thud of his front-door slam closed that subject forever.

He was right. He was an outpatient now. The last thing he

needed to be reminded of was what went on inside the hospital. My needs were real but his came first. It seemed to me I was always blundering. I sat on the kitchen stool, staring at the chicken I'd thawed for supper. It looked naked, unpromising, as if nothing could be done with it.

Sidney came in. His raised eyebrows told me he'd heard the slam. It was not the first door slam of the summer. Sidney suspected me, unfairly I often thought, of not being always tactful with our sons. Now I was wretchedly aware that this time he was right.

"It's not easy to be Eric's mother this summer," I said. "Sometimes I think I can't say anything to him without making him mad."

Sidney said nothing, got out ice cubes, made a drink, left.

"You might comfort me! Or offer me a drink!" I shouted after him.

This was a circle not so much vicious as sad, that was repeated many times that summer. For Sidney to comfort me would have meant admitting the underlying trouble, admitting that Eric was still in very real danger; this he could not bear. For Sidney, each remission was a pardon that could be full and complete, certainly would be sometime soon. He trusted Eric to win. He believed in the triumph of Eric's spirit, the invincibility of his perfect athlete's body. And of course, being an engineer and a scientist at heart, he also had great hope of progress in research and new drugs coming to our aid. I did, too. But I saw things differently. I saw that each remission was harder to achieve than the last. I saw the end implicit in the word itself.

There was another thing that gave us trouble. Illness wasn't very real to Sidney; he had little personal experience of it. He'd been sick only once in nearly twenty-five years of marriage, the time he'd had pneumonia. It was then I had understood at last the real meaning of that old saying, "Ten thousand Swedes marched out of the weeds to battle one sick Norwegian." It takes at least a battalion to cope with a Norwegian who's under the weather. Sidney went out and swam half a mile while waiting for the report on his chest X-rays. He finally got well in spite of having outwitted everybody's efforts to care for him.

The myth or reality of male power and female weakness dominated our household that summer. Eric had many reasons for identifying with his father. His own recent brush with death, his witnessing of the deaths of so many friends, had left him vulnerable; to compensate he now put on the armor of the cold warrior. Nothing could touch Sidney, therefore nothing could touch Eric. No matter how much I suppressed my concern and tenderness, Eric still suspected me of harboring some. He was not abusive, not overtly cruel, he simply behaved most of the time as if I did not matter and did not really exist. I tried to laugh it off, to see how it was for him. Sometimes it was hard.

"You know," I said one day to a friend who was an analyst, "Eric behaves as if the word 'mother' was a dirty word."

"It is, for him," said my analyst friend calmly. "You are the threat. Men have often seen woman as the death figure."

"But why? We give life."

"Well, that's just it. That *is* why. We all come from the unknown, from darkness, from the mother. And we go back into darkness when we die. Don't you remember how the Egyptians painted a mother figure inside the sarcophagus?"

No, I didn't remember.

"It's not *your* fault, see?" said my friend, laughing a bit, with his wry, gentle detachment. "Man has always been scared of the dark mysterious womb. So now you get the blame."

"It's not fair, is it?" I said, smiling.

"No, it's not," he agreed. "But maybe it helps if you understand it."

Part of me understood. Part of me cheered as Eric went his way, defying me, defying death, running, swimming, working out after his long day of work at the camp. He was never still. He was doing everything he could to toughen himself. For we both knew—and here was where our similarity of outlook and temperament, if not of sex, led us to see things the same way—that a fight was coming. Much as Eric yearned to be totally Sidney's child, he had probably always been more like me in many ways. We had had great pleasure from our easy closeness when he was a baby and a little boy. Now, as I lost this closeness, as mothers always must, as I feared to lose him forever, my loneliness went deep. The only cure I knew was work.

CHAPTER 14

IT WAS QUARTER TO SIX on a Tuesday evening when, once again, I found myself opening the door to the Donor Room. The roar, the clatter, the laughing hit me at once. The place sounded like a successful cocktail party in full swing. There were six impatient, eager people in the outer room waiting to be processed. The nurse at the desk was pricking a finger. I peeked in the next room to see how things were going inside. Bedlam. Arms, legs, everywhere I looked. Every couch was occupied, every chair filled. I.V. bottles were flowing, rotators humming, *arrum, arrum, arrum,* as the sacks beside the beds slowly grew dark, filling with blood. A nurse, dashing by with two sacks of blood held high, bumped into a blue-coated volunteer who was trying to make it through the doorway with a tray of paper cups. They both backed off, laughing, and the volunteer finally pushed in and began to circulate.

"Yours was the ginger ale, wasn't it? And yours?"

"Same, thanks."

I spotted Margaret on a stepladder adjusting the tube attached to somebody's arm. She had a disheveled charm and looked rather like a happy plumber fixing a leak, quite a contrast to the glamorous snaps of her on the bulletin board taken at the last

183

Christmas party. She spotted me. "Hullo, love! We're a bit wild tonight, aren't we?"

"Maybe I ought to come back some other time?"

"Don't run away now. You wanted to see us in action. This is it."

I didn't run away. I stayed till they closed their doors. I returned again and again that summer, and I finally learned something about platelets and the way blood can be divided into components.

ONLY *YOU* CAN GIVE PLATELETS, THE GIFT OF LIFE. When I'd first read that urgent sign next to the Memorial elevators, I'd had no idea what platelets were. About all I knew about blood was that if you had a low hemoglobin they said you were anemic. And if you were low in white cells, you'd have a hard time fighting infections.

But when the doctor told Eric not to "jump around so much" and when Eric explained to me that since he was low in platelets he could bleed anywhere, I got the message fast. Platelets were very important. The Donor Room literature described them as "tiny, colorless, disk-shaped particles in the circulating blood which are essential to blood clotting." There were said to be about seven billion in every ounce of blood. But I still didn't understand the difference between giving whole blood and giving platelets. How was it possible for donors to give platelets twice a week while donors of whole blood had to wait eight weeks before giving blood again? The answers to these questions and many others, I discovered, lay in the big centrifuge in the pantry of Memorial's Donor Room and also in the new science of plasmapheresis. The centrifuge looked rather like a cross between a kettledrum and a washing machine. By its whirling action, which was again rather like the spin-dry cycle of a washer, it would separate the plasma and platelets from the whole blood. Plasmapheresis was simply the name for the whole process, which included not only the separation of the blood into components but also the return of the red cells to the donor.

A postwar baby, plasmapheresis was born of the plastics industry that boomed in the late forties and early fifties. During World War II there had been a huge demand for plasma to help the wounded survive. Soon people began to wonder if there wasn't some way to reinfuse donors with their own red cells after the plasma had been extracted. Such an idea held great advantages for both the donor and the patient. If the donor did not lose his red cells, his health would not be at all affected by giving. He would be able to donate platelets as often as twice a week.*

But when the techniques of plasmapheresis were finally developed, a donor room, such as Memorial's, still had many practical problems. It was thought that platelets had to be used within six to eight hours. Not only did scientists believe platelets would lose their viability after that time, it was also feared that bacterial growth would soon begin. Further research showed, however, that under proper conditions platelets could be stored for as long as forty-eight hours without losing their usefulness or purity. Improvements in plastics designing also reduced risks to both donor and recipient.

*Today, in the 1970s, Memorial's Donor Room has a new machine called a Latham cell separator, or "milker," which can withdraw as many as eight units of platelets, or the equivalent of what you would get from eight pints of whole blood, at one time from a suitable donor in order to help a patient in a serious crisis.

Nurses and technicians in today's modern donor room use closed sterile systems whereby donor blood is collected in plastic bags, and the plasma and platelets are then separated from the red cells by the centrifuge. Further separation occurs when the plasma and platelets are expressed via a connecting tube into a separate plastic bag. The tube is sealed at both ends with clips and then cut between the two clips. At this point the red cells are immediately returned to the donor through the needle which has remained in his arm while the centrifuge was doing its job. (The needle has been kept open all this time—about fifteen or twenty minutes—by a continuous I.V. drip.)

As soon as the donor gets all his red cells back, his part in the drama is over. But before the precious platelets are given to a patient, the sack of platelets and plasma is centrifuged once again. When a bead begins to form in the bottom of the sack— much as a drop of nearly cooked icing will harden as it falls from the spoon—the centrifuge is turned off. An extractor presses the platelets, along with about 30 cc's of plasma, through another tube into a third sack. (Without this small amount of plasma, the platelets would simply stick to the walls of the sack.) And it is the third sack, representing one unit of platelets, which is given to the patient.

The sack of pure plasma that remains is put to use too. It's quick-frozen and stored. Then when there is a need—for example, if the New York Blood Center runs short of plasma—it is sent to the rescue. It's thawed, and during that process the cryo-precipitates are formed that are used to treat hemophilia. The astonishing thing about the whole process is that a blood donor at Memorial who is helping a leukemia patient there can also at the same time be helping a hemophilia patient somewhere else.

Neither this awesome fact nor much else about the technology of plasmapheresis was known to me that Tuesday evening at Memorial. I watched everything that was going on around me without really understanding it. The handsome black girl with a huge Afro and a miniskirt who was tending the centrifuge and dealing with dozens of sacks performed all the operations with the offhand deftness of a French chef throwing together a dinner party for eight. This illusion was helped along by an aide who stood right beside her, spreading cheese on crackers and arranging small plates of hors d'oeuvres on the counter right next to the extractors. But for all the party atmosphere, I knew I was watching a miracle—whole blood was being separated into plasma, platelets, and packed red cells right before my eyes, and in perfect sterility, too.

Something else I learned that night: Generally anyone can give platelets for anyone else; you don't have to be the same blood type as you do in giving whole blood. But repeated platelet transfusions of dissimilar types may eventually, for reasons not yet completely understood, lead the patient to produce antibodies and start rejecting. When treatment is just beginning, however, all platelets are more or less compatible.

Margaret told me a story that dramatized this point. One evening in the Donor Room a Yeshiva student came in to give platelets. He found himself in a reclining chair next to a young Arab nationalist who was also giving platelets. "What an uproar!" said Margaret. "They got into an argument right on the spot. But you know what I did? I said, 'Look, you two, I'm going to make sure both your sacks of platelets are given to the same little boy upstairs. Your cells will get together and get along—even if you can't.'"

I found that similar stories were in good supply each time I visited the Donor Room. And while the monster centrifuge, the extractors, and all the plastic apparatus were interesting enough, it was people who really made the place exciting. The connectedness of all human existence came home to me every time I went there. You'd expect to find parents giving for sick children, people giving for their relatives. But here, too, were busy doctors and nurses giving on top of the giving they did all day long. I'll never forget the expert Operating Room nurse who was waiting to get her red cells back, lying back in a donor chair with the clear I.V. fluid dripping into her arm, when a hurry call came in for her from the O.R. upstairs. They had a serious emergency, needed her right away. She yanked out the I.V. needle herself, held her arm aloft with a piece of cotton pressed against the vein, and called as she was running out, "Save my red cells! I'll be back and get them later!"

Doctors and nurses, of course, couldn't help but understand the need. What surprised me was the number of ordinary people who returned week after week to give their blood so that strangers might live. Eric was already in their debt. When he'd needed platelets—sixteen units from sixteen donors—the winter before, he'd received them immediately and without question. No one had known who he was (except Cathy, the little floor nurse who'd offered to run down and give for Eric). Yet something had brought those unknown donors to that place at that time so that platelets would be ready, so that a nineteen-year-old boy would be able to run out in the world and live his life again.

I discovered that some of the regular donors didn't want to know too much about any of the patients upstairs. Others took the risk of getting involved and sometimes then had to face the

losses that were inevitable. A young truck driver told me somewhat sadly that for months he had given blood for Joey, the football player I'd seen strapped in the wheelchair.

"I like football," he said, "and it meant something to me to try
to help Joey. I felt real low when he died. Like he'd let me down
or something. But I see now he just came to the end of the line."
Then he told me cheerfully, "Well, I guess now I've just gotta
pick out somebody else to help."

Some of the regulars surprised me. I remember arriving on the
scene one evening as a very elegant executive was apologizing to
Jeanne for having worn cuff links.

"After coming here for five years, you'd think I'd remember it's
Thursday when I get dressed. I'm sorry to slow you down," he
said, fumbling with the French cuffs of his handsome gold-
striped shirt, trying to get the links out.

"No problem," she said. "But what beautiful cuff links! What
are they? Cerulean?"

"Lapis lazuli."

So he's a five-year man, I thought. I wouldn't have guessed it.
He looked too important, somehow too busy, to be faithful. But
I was beginning to learn I shouldn't generalize. Soon we got into
conversation, and he began telling me why he came.

"You know, parents bring their children here from all over the
country. Then suddenly, when the child needs transfusions,
they're asked to run out and find donors to replace what's used.
Not just one or two donors, but dozens! It's awful for people
from out of town. If they were back home they could call up all
their relatives or the PTA or the Woman's Club. Here they feel so
terribly alone. Last week I heard of this couple from North Carolina whose little girl was in trouble. So I went up and found

them and told them I'd give all the platelets I could for her and that I'd organize some other people, too. They couldn't get over it. Someone in big, cold New York wanting to help a perfect stranger from North Carolina! But it gives me a terrific kick to do that. Their need is so great."

"If you look at the needle marks on the arms of some of our regulars, you'd think they're hooked on hard drugs," Jeanne said one day.

They're hooked on giving life, I thought. But sometimes a faithful donor had to take several months' vacation from giving blood to let his arms heal. Then when he came back, Jeanne and Margaret liked to pretend to punish him for his neglect.

"Lie down!" I heard Jeanne say to a handsome black-haired young man one evening. "It's the electric drill for you! Where have you been hiding yourself anyway?" She knew perfectly well where he'd been and why. I saw her carefully inspecting his arm to see if it was ready to stand new needles. Another time I heard her greet a long-absent donor with, "*You're* going to get it right in the aorta!"

In spite of the banter, anyone who watched could soon see the high peak of professionalism in the Donor Room. These girls were experts. But it was the banter, the informality, the warm spirit of the place that brought donors back to Memorial. After all, there were many other medical centers where blood was needed. Many of them would have been more convenient places for lots of the donors to give. Yet they continued to stop by on their way back to Queens, New Jersey, the Bronx, or Westchester because they felt at home in the crowded little rooms of the Donor Room on the ground floor of Ewing Pavilion.

And so did I. As long as I was there, on the scene, watching people, gathering information, I felt peaceful and competent. I had an editor who was interested. I knew what I wanted to write. But when I got home it wasn't easy to work.

Our house was full of furies those last weeks of August. Camp was over, but Eric could not go to Africa or anywhere else. His doctors would not let him. They were changing his medication, and they didn't want him running around the countryside. He was still in remission, but the new protocol clearly said this was no time to get careless. Like a ring of brilliant criminals, the leukemic cells are likely to be operating again just when you think you've got them on the run. If you can't kill them all, at least you can try to outwit them. Eric had his orders: Report to the outpatient clinic every Monday.

One night somebody said something to somebody else at the dinner table. I can't remember what. Like Desdemona's handkerchief, the thing itself was unimportant, and like a handkerchief I've lost it along the way. But suddenly we were plunged into blood-and-thunder drama. No one hurled dishes, just accusations. No one fought fair. All the blows struck home. There was no right, no wrong, no rhyme, no reasonableness. Pain. Rage. When it was over, when doors had been slammed and various members of the family had escaped in their various ways, Eric and I were left alone at the table. He was eating silently, much too quickly, hoping to escape, too. There was something in his grim, cold withdrawal that moved me, unwisely, to defend myself.

"You expect the impossible," I said. "You want us to be a perfect family. But we're not just Mommy and Daddy and paper-doll children in a coloring book. We're real people with real problems. And you don't help when you take sides. Why should you always be judging *me?*"

He got up without a word, grabbed his dishes, and went by, giving me a look like a blowtorch.

It was too much. Overwhelmed with fatigue and despair, I said, "I wish I were dead."

Eric stopped, whirled around. "Fuck you, Mom," he said.

I suppose he expected me to faint. I said, "Eric, there's something you want to say to me. So say it."

"It's this. If you don't want to be alive, that's *your* problem. I *do* want to be alive. And I've got too many problems of my own, trying to survive, to be involved with yours or to worry about yours. You handle yours. I'll handle mine. Right now I'm checking out."

He went upstairs.

I was shocked that he'd taken me so literally. Suddenly I was in a panic that Eric was going to do something self-destructive. I rushed upstairs. He was throwing clothes in his duffel bag, packing angrily, foolishly, the way people do in bad movies.

"Where are you going?"

"It's none of your business. But I'm going. That's all." Within twenty minutes he was gone. I was left alone with the dishes and the unhappy necessity of telling Sidney that Eric had walked out.

He was gone six days. By Friday I was humbled enough to call Memorial's Social Service worker and tell her Eric had disappeared. I knew he was due in at the clinic that Monday. Would she call me if he didn't show? Would she also call me if he did?

"I have to know if he's all right," I said. There was a disturbing lump just south of my tonsils. In another minute I was going to be sobbing into the telephone.

"I'm sure he's all right, Mrs. Lund." The girl soothed me. "I know Eric. He wouldn't do anything really crazy. He'll be here Monday, I'm sure of it. But I'll call you either way."

"Thank you."

• • •

Sunday evening long after midnight I was still up and prowling around the house. I'd tried to go to sleep three different times. But up is better than down when it's like that. I'd just opened the icebox door to see if there was any cold juice when I heard a sound, the gentle crunch of somebody trying to close our humidity-swollen front door without being heard. I waited, not moving. If he doesn't know I'm here, he'll come out. He'll be hungry.

The kitchen door squeaked. I went on looking in the icebox, finally pulled out a bottle of apple juice.

"Would you like some?" I said, getting down a glass for myself.

"No, thanks." Eric gave me a shy look. He seemed a little embarrassed and very young at that moment.

"There are some fresh jelly doughnuts. In the cake box."

"I'll buy that." He smiled just a little bit.

I took my juice out on the porch and sat down in the dark. The August night was buzzing and grinding away. When I was four, my parents took me to the zoo and asked me what animal I wanted to see. I replied, "A cricket," thinking it surely must be the biggest, most interesting animal in the whole place. When Eric was four or five I'd told him about that. He loved that story. His mother had once been a funny, dumb little girl who didn't even know what a *cricket* looked like! Well, sometimes it seemed to me that I hadn't progressed very far, that I was still that dumb little girl. Only now life was really full of huge monsters, terrors in the dark, terrors in the day. I wished that somehow I could explain to Eric how it was to be me, to ask him to be patient. I made so many mistakes. Yet he was the one who had just looked shy, embarrassed. Why?

"Fuck you, Mom." That was it. That must have shocked him more than it did me. My own mother would never have forgiven me that. But words don't shake me. I'd never heard any of my children use that word before, even though we hadn't over-reacted to swearing around our house. Sidney never swears. If he's really pushed or upset, he says, "Oh, my!" When my control goes, though, which doesn't happen too often, I use every word I can think of. So the kids had heard them all. But somehow they picked up restraint. Or perhaps it was just a matter of style. When you use the strong words too often, they lose their luster. Well, Eric had chosen his moment. He'd captured my full attention; he'd made his point. I sat in the dark, smiling to myself, thinking about all this. All at once I felt more relaxed than I had in months. He was brave. He was a fighter. We were going to have a good fall after all.

CHAPTER 15

September, October, November 1970. It was three years since the diagnosis of his leukemia, and Eric was playing the best soccer of his life. Because of his height and hustle, he had been moved from forward position to fullback. There was less opportunity to score, but there was plenty of action and often the chance for assists.

The Connecticut Huskies opened the season with a few choice wins, but they also had several agonizing close losses. By November 10, however, a newspaper sports lead article cheerfully asserted that "in a matter of weeks, the University of Connecticut has distinguished itself with perhaps the most talked-about soccer team in New England." The article, accompanied by action photos of Eric and Mark Kurimai, his oldest, closest friend and teammate from Brien McMahon High School soccer days as well as college, made no mention of Eric's disease (newsmen were not aware of his problem). It was simply headlined, "Defensive Backs Play Major Role in Husky Wins."

They weren't winning them all, but the Connecticut Huskies were winning more games than they had in the past four years and feeling pretty good about it. On November 12, they scored a 3–1 victory over Boston University and Eric's picture made the papers again. He was shown midair, several feet off the ground, delivering a header. Mark Kurimai and Eric were mentioned for helping to thwart the Boston offense for most of the game.

When the season finally closed with the annual soccer team dinner, held in the Faculty Alumni Center, it was announced by Coach Joseph Morrone that Eric Lund, a junior fullback, had been chosen by his teammates to be captain of the University of Connecticut soccer team for 1971.

Discussing the choice later, Coach Morrone said, "Eric was overwhelmingly elected captain by his teammates because he was the best man for the job. There are certain things you look for in a captain, and unquestionably Eric had those things. He was a natural leader. He always had great rapport with his teammates from the first year on. He could talk to anyone. He could be very down to earth. He cared about the team and he knew what to say. Now you don't pick the best player necessarily. It doesn't usually work out that way. But the captain has to play very well and Eric had that ability.

"The first year when he was elected co-captain of the freshman team, no one knew he was sick. He came to me and told me he had leukemia but he didn't want anyone to know. The second year he played, hardly anyone knew, maybe a few close friends. By the third year more were probably aware of his trouble because he had to drop out of school the winter of 1970, following the soccer season of his sophomore year. But it didn't make any difference. That's not the way we operate. We were all interested in winning, Eric as much as anyone. No one gave him any quarter this past season. No one had to, and Eric wouldn't have allowed it."

This view was borne out by the fact that Eric was also presented at the banquet with the Most Improved Player Award. As Mark

Kurimai put it, "The problem for the rest of us was to keep up. When we were working out, most of us would run two or three days, ten or fifteen miles a day, and then knock off. Eric ran every day, fifteen and sometimes twenty miles. He never let down."

Following that 1970 season, when the National Soccer Coaches Association for the New England area held their midwinter meeting, Eric was named to the All-New England All Stars. Like the newsmen, none of the coaches, with the exception of Joe Morrone, knew of Eric's condition. He was one of three players chosen in the area. The other two who were honored were well known to Eric. Phil Kydes, a former teammate of Eric's at Brien McMahon, was the possessor of a full soccer scholarship to Harvard. Chip Young of Brown University, formerly of Westport's Staples High School, was a fullback who had literally banged heads many times with Eric when they fought against each other for the Fairfield County championship. The head bangings did not occur during the ordinary course of the game, since both played fullback, but during the penalty corner kicks where Eric was assigned to try to score and Chip was assigned to prevent him.

There are thousands of news write-ups, and thousands of awards, medallions, and gold statues given away every year for every sport under the sun. Eric was not the greatest soccer player of his time. But he was good, a natural fighter who loved the game, and he worked harder than most. He had his reasons, of course. He was running to win, and he was running for his life.

Few people knew that the reason he missed practice nearly every Monday was that he had to check into Memorial's outpatient clinic. Fewer still knew that when he played in a Tuesday or Wednesday game, he was usually taking drugs orally, and might even be recovering from a bout of nausea induced by a powerful injection. While Eric never discussed this problem with people at college when he could possibly avoid it, he had no objections to talking about it frankly with interested doctors and nurses. As he told some of them in an open forum once, "It's not always easy to do business with Memorial and do business with my soccer coach at the same time, but we work it out."

There were times when Eric would show up at Clinic and his doctors would want to start a new drug course immediately. But Eric would say, "I have a game tomorrow, so could we hold off a little bit? Because it's not easy to go out and play eighty-eight minutes of soccer after you've been hit with daunomycin." The medical experts were flexible whenever they could be. They respected his spirit. They got great enjoyment from having a former boarder on Ewing Eight out running around on the playing field. They backed him up emotionally and gave him all the help they could. But Eric, his doctors, and his coach all had to accept the fact that once he really started to come out of remission or was on the borderline, there was a limit to flexibility. Then Eric took his shots and did the best he could. His best was not bad. What saved him, what made him able to contribute to the team even under duress, was hustle and drive. He'd always had it.

I remember when I first picked him up—such a skinny little baby, all bones and beating heart!—I couldn't believe the fierce energy in this tiny creature. My first baby, a perfectly healthy girl, had felt limp as a wet washrag, like most new babies. But Eric was trying to climb over my shoulder, active as a little squirrel looking for nuts. At the age of two weeks, he nearly crawled off the examining table in our pediatrician's office. The doctor, who'd turned her back for a moment, grabbed him by the ankle as he went by, face down, over the edge.

"Look at him go!" she said, astonished.

"Look at him go!" we said to ourselves now.

For us the high point of the year came early in the season on November 4 when Connecticut's soccer team went down to New Haven to play against Yale. Sidney's cup was full and running over that afternoon. Both his sons were playing on adjacent fields at the same time. Mark, a Yale freshman fullback, stayed in his game sixty-six minutes, helping his team beat the Connecticut frosh, 1–0. Eric, playing the same position for Connecticut's varsity, stayed in for the whole eighty-eight minutes while his team scored a similar victory over Yale's varsity, 1–0.

The event was recorded in our local newspaper the following evening. "Lund, Kurimai Aid UConn Win. Eric Lund and Mark Kurimai were instrumental Wednesday in UConn's 1–0 win over Yale in New Haven. . . . Lund and Kurimai, both fullbacks, were outstanding in the second half as they prevented Yale from hitting the UConn nets despite enormous pressure as the game neared the finish." The account took note of Mark's appearance on the freshman team and went on to speculate that "it's conceivable that [the Lunds] will be playing against one another next year since Eric is a junior at UConn and Mark is a strong prospect for the Yale varsity."

Reading that made my heart jump a little. I didn't dare look ahead but I couldn't help thinking, wouldn't *that* be a game to see! I had missed the double header in New Haven, being home in bed with a cold. But Sidney needed no encouragement to go into vivid detail in telling me about it. According to his not-at-all impartial version of the varsity contest, "It was a really tough game, close and scary all the way. Yale was all over the UConn goal at one point. UConn, of course, was desperate to protect their one-point lead.

Yale must have made about a dozen good kicks that almost scored, but the Connecticut guys just couldn't seem to get the ball out of there. All of a sudden Eric came charging down the left side of the field all the way from the back. He swooped into the tangle of players, disappeared for a moment, the ball shot out high in the air, and Eric followed it, still on a dead run. He'd gotten off a terrific kick with his left foot and carried the ball out of danger just like that. It was great! One of the best moments I ever lived through."

After both games were over, Mark had jumped in Sidney's car and they'd trailed the Connecticut bus all the way through New Haven traffic and out to the highway, where the team finally stopped at a roadside diner. Mark and Sidney stood in line with the rest, got their hot dogs and soda, then climbed back in the big bus to eat with Eric and his teammates. There are not many times when life holds still and behaves like it's supposed to for a minute. Not many days when you win 'em all. This was one.

That Christmas Mark gave Eric a "Big Apple" hat. It was sort of an oversized golf cap and it sat on Eric's head like a huge, lightly browned pancake. He wore it most of the time from then on, indoors as well as out.

On the last day of Christmas vacation (we'd stayed home this year; the Florida house was rented), I went outdoors to watch the two brothers loading the car to go back to college. Mark was wearing a motorman's cap on the back of his curls, a jacket of undetermined color that looked as if he might have worn it the past ten years hunting for gold in the Yukon, and a six-foot-long scarf that trailed its blue and white stripes along the ground. Somebody might have guessed from the stripes that he went to Yale, but I doubt it. Eric was attired in his usual pancake, a gigantic fuzzy gold sweater knit by a long-ago girl friend, and mattress-ticking, slightly flared pants. Whatever happened to real *clothes?* I wondered, amused and slightly dazed by my sons. They were laughing, pushing each other now and then, pretending to argue about the arrangement of baggage. It'd been fun to have them around, even if they did go through the icebox like vacuum cleaners. All at once, in the midst of happiness, I felt a stab of fear.

There had been a big blizzard New Year's Day. Snow was still high on the ground. Sancho was running around giving joyful leaps in the air—like black exclamation marks on white paper— as he tried to help his "brothers" pack. Lisa was there, too, bundled up, mittened, scarved, enjoying the show, her red-gold hair streaming free against blue sky. Sidney, in red plaid lumberjack shirt and huge black rubber boots, was jumping up on picnic tables or stone walls, or kneeling in the snow with a camera, trying to catch the children in action. Clouds raced by above them in the wild blue air. A snowman stood nearby in the front yard, still wearing the bright muffler and carrot nose bestowed on him three days ago. The playroom windows had snow at their corners like a Christmas card. The wreath on our front door was still shouting its red and green holiday cheer.

And I stood there sick with fear. It was a Kodak ad. I saw the headline: "Moments like these don't last. Capture them now— while you still can!" *Click . . . click.* With every click of the camera, I saw my family changing, dissolving with time. I saw Eric disappearing forever into the frozen pose. He would be captured, yes—in the picture frame, in the pages of the photograph album. It was not enough. I wanted him out of focus, imperfect but alive, blurred in action, angry, happy, shouting, jumping, running free.

The moment passed. A week later I was studying the pictures developed from that roll of film.

"Hey, these are great! You did a beautiful job! And it's so hard to get the right exposure in snow and sunshine. But they're all perfect."

Sidney looked pleased.

"Let me see." Lisa was at my elbow.

It was hard for me to let them go, even for a minute, and pass them around. As soon as Lisa and Sidney had looked at each one, I took them right back and studied them all over again. What had I seen that day? Where was the doom? I couldn't see it now.

"Do you think Eric looks all right?"

"He looks neat in that hat," said Lisa.

"I mean *all right*." I looked at Sidney.

"He looks good to me," Sidney said.

Lisa took the pictures back. "It's the hat, Mommy. He looks small under it, kind of delicate. But it's just because the hat is so big."

We smiled together. She usually knew what I meant, what I wanted to know.

Three weeks later Eric learned that his hard-won fourth remission was at an end. It was January 25, 1971. The fight was on.

On Tuesday morning, January 26, Eric ran downstairs so dressed up that I had to turn off my vacuum cleaner, turn around, and take another look. He'd always said, "If you have to go, go in style"—but this was splendor!

"Eric—you're checking into Ewing? Like that?"

"Not today. Friday. I've got a coupla things to do first." He said no more.

Years later I found the printed announcement.

DEPARTMENT OF NURSING

ANNOUNCING

REGIONAL MEDICAL PROGRAM—

ONCOLOGIC* NURSING

SEMINAR ON "THE PROFESSIONAL NURSE

AND CHEMOTHERAPY"

The seminar was to be held from 1 to 4 P.M. on two different dates, January 26 and January 28, 1971. The panel of experts who would be onstage in the large Memorial auditorium would consist of two of Memorial's chief doctors from the Medical Oncology Service, the head nurse in charge of Adult Chemotherapy, the supervisor of Chemotherapy Research, a resident doctor from the Neuropsychiatric Service, a social worker, and two patients, one of whom was Eric Lund. Besides that announcement, I now have transcripts from the tapes that were made at the time. The program, planned for the benefit of nurses from all over the neighboring eastern areas, was well attended. Perhaps 600 nurses were there. As Barbara Livingston, then Supervisor of Chemotherapy Research, told me later, "It was a real privilege for these people to hear the story straight from the patient's mouth."

The patient who was called upon to speak first was an attractive housewife in her mid-twenties. She had been flown to Memorial about five years before, suffering from a rare form of cancer called choriocarcinoma. The cancer, originating in the

---

*Oncology is the study of tumors. Hematology is the study of blood disorders. As the chemotherapy drugs, originally used to fight tumors, also began to be used as weapons against leukemia, the term oncology broadened to include study of cancers of the blood as well.

placenta of her miscarried four-month baby, was far advanced; it had spread to the lungs. X-rays were shown of the "multiple pulmonary metastases" present at that time. She was described as a "very, very sick young woman." But although she sat quietly on the platform during the seminar, she might have been waving a flag of triumph. As she and her doctors testified, chemotherapy had saved her life. Her present X-rays were normal. She was completely cured.

The other patient on stage, a young man about twenty-one years of age, was wearing the blue blazer with silver buttons, yellow striped shirt, and new necktie that had amazed his mother earlier that morning. He also wore, according to reliable reports, an expression which flickered somewhere between reverence and mischievousness. No one seeing this young man for the first time could have guessed that he was halfway into his fourth year of acute lymphocytic leukemia. Chemotherapy had bought him time, wonderful time in a world he greatly enjoyed. Now chemotherapy was going to have to try again. Friday he would come in for another long stretch on Ewing Eight.

The doctors on the panel knew that Eric had learned only the day before that he was out of remission. They were surprised and impressed, Mrs. Livingston told me, that he could keep his cool in a public seminar while absorbing such a blow. They put serious questions to both patients. At one point Dr. Irving Krakoff, one of Memorial's chief oncologists, asked Eric, "Should a patient be told all the facts about his illness? Should he be helped to face hard reality, and would he usually be strong enough to take it?"

Eric answered, "In my case everything was emphasized toward success from the beginning. And everything that's happened since then, in this place in particular, has been emphasized toward success. Even though you may be dealing with a disease where there's only, say, a ten-percent chance that someone will reach a point where he's considered cured, at least you try to stay ahead of the game. Now that's what I'm doing right now—trying to stay ahead. I could look to the future and say I'm running out of drugs. I'm becoming resistant to certain chemicals. My therapy has gone completely to hell. Maybe I should forget all about the future. But there are doctors working across the street at Sloan-Kettering Institute. Doctors are working around the world who are, at the same time I'm running out of things, perfecting new things. So it's a questionable thing, as far as a doctor or a nurse dealing with somebody's denial of the disease. You might say the patient doesn't accept the fact that he's going to die. Well, in a lot of cases it's questionable about whether somebody's going to die or not. And if you start disputing the fact with patients, you're kind of cutting into their confidence. I know, as a patient, I'm terribly responsive to people around me, especially to my family, especially to people on the eighth floor. If they have doubts about me, I have to rise one step up on the scale and say, well, I have to be strong enough for myself and for them, too, in keeping up my own confidence."

At another point Eric was asked how he was told that he had leukemia and what impact the illness had had on his life.

He replied, "Everything that happened before this was in a fog. I've been forced to think about so much. I just had everything knocked out completely from beneath me. Like—when I first got sick, it was about a week before I was to go away to college, so psychologically I had all the doubts. I was worried about going away to college, but I was also ready for a big change. In other words, I was looking at the fact that I was going to leave the environment I was in and something new and drastic was going to happen to me. So something new and drastic *did* happen to me. I became a patient in a hospital. I wasn't told right off I had leukemia. I was told I was anemic. This was instrumental in forming some of the philosophies I've developed. In other words, at that stage of my life, as a seventeen-year-old, worried about all the things I was worried about, as sick as I was when I was first diagnosed, if somebody had walked in and said, 'You have leukemia, you know,' I probably would have just hung it up right then and there and said, 'Okay, I don't want to play.'"

Eric went on.

"People have asked me, 'Weren't you wary of what was going on?' Well, everything was strange—I had no frame of reference for looking at things analytically. The day-to-day life I was in was just completely new. . . . People ask, 'When is the right time to tell a patient?' In my particular case, it wouldn't have been wise earlier. But you really can't draw general rules about this. There are not really simple answers. And, nurses, you should realize that. It makes it much more difficult on you because each patient presents unique problems that demand a flexible philosophy and outlook on your part. It requires that you be exceptional people."

Eric had never admitted to me that he thought we did the right thing in telling him at first he had anemia. In fact, at the time of our biggest fight, when he disappeared for six days, one of the brickbats he hurled angrily my way was that I'd "interfered in the beginning, kept things from him."

"But weren't you glad in the long run?" I'd protested. "Didn't it work out for the best?"

"I'm not so sure," he said, glaring. "I can handle my problems. I don't want you messing around with them."

One thing came through strong and clear on those tapes. Eric was an appreciator. At one point a member of the audience observed that "most doctors are just as scared of cancer as the patients are and tend to duck the emotional problems." She went on to recall that Eric had said that the nurses can be "the first bulwark" for cancer patients. "Can you tell us what the nurses have done for you, Eric?"

"The nurses are super people," Eric replied. "They're great! What makes Mrs. Livingston and Miss Somerville so great, for instance, is that they always operate one step above what could be expected of an ordinary person. Now I've been a patient here for three and a half years, and during this time I've reached a point where I am not only dealing with these people in a patient-nurse relationship, I am very good friends with them. This is a sticky situation because there are boundaries here which have to be dealt with. There are things which become difficult. . . . In other words, if I were to go up on the floor in the next few weeks and suddenly get into trouble, it would be hard on me, of course, but it would also be hard on these people because they are my friends. They would be concerned. The ordinary person would never establish these relationships to begin with. But the reason these nurses are the great people they are is that they operate above that. They are looking at everything, weighing everything, reacting to everything just at a higher level."

The question was raised as to how the nurses themselves coped emotionally with continuous dealing with cancer patients.

Both Mrs. Livingston and Miss Somerville admitted it was sometimes a very "draining experience." Mrs. Livingston went on to say, "We support each other, and I think we're constantly invigorated by the support our patients give to us. We discuss their illness and their treatment with them, in most cases, on a very honest, open level. And I think we all benefit from this. On the other hand, I'm not ashamed to tell you that sometimes we cry."

As Eric summed it up, "Ewing Eight is both a heaven and a hell. The hell is obvious. The heaven is created by the people who work up there."

CHAPTER 16

FOUR DAYS AFTER he checked into Ewing Eight, Eric was placed in Memorial's new sterile air chamber known as the laminar air-flow room. This room, similar in concept to the Life Island, or sterile bubble, used earlier at Memorial and other large medical centers such as Roswell Park in Buffalo, had been in operation only two months. Both the Life Island and the laminar air-flow room had been developed for the protection of patients whose ability to combat infections had been critically lowered by some factor or other. Leukemia patients, undergoing intensive chemotherapy, of course were logical candidates. But the Life Island, in which a hospital bed was enclosed in a plastic canopy, had been found too restricting to patient activity and too expensive and too complicated to operate. A special nursing team had to be on hand twenty-four hours a day to care for a patient in the Life Island. Injections, blood pressure readings, or whatever had to be carried out through a set of arm-length gloves built into the unit. Memorial's hopes were now centered on the new laminar air-flow unit.

Eric's doctors, faced with the grave problem of getting their patient back into a fifth remission, and planning a long assault with powerful drugs, decided he must have this extra protection. They expected Eric's white counts to start dropping severely once the assault took hold. They didn't want to lose him to pneumonia or some passing bacteria when this happened.

The laminar air-flow room was windowless, very small, in some ways rather like a third-class ship's cabin. It was just possible to fit the usual hospital equipment—bed, nightstand, bed table, and one chair—into the tiny quarters. There was also a washbasin and a portable commode. The patient in this isolation chamber was surrounded by purified air which moved in continuous streams across the width and height of the clean area. In reality, the process was self-cleaning. The concept of laminar air-flow had first originated in the aerospace and electronics industries, where extreme cleanliness was most important. It had also been used before in hospital operating rooms. Memorial's first patient unit, like a separate room with three sides, had been installed in an already existing patient room. The germ-free air was propelled by fans, in a horizontal nonturbulent pattern, through a bank of microfilters along one wall. The speed of the air-flow, 100 feet per minute or about one mile per hour, prevented airborne organisms from moving up against the flow of air toward the patient. Anyone or anything remaining downstream could not infect him. Visitors could stand in the open doorway of the original room, within a small square marked off by yellow tape, and as long as they stayed there downstream of the patient, supposedly their germs would not reach him. Anyone venturing inside the room beyond the yellow tape, however, had to observe the rules for sterile dress.

While the laminar air-flow room was supposed to do its part in saving Eric, Eric was also supposed to help save himself. His survival might even depend on how well he followed instructions and how well he could adapt. The nurses tried to prepare him for this part of the job.

"Don't let anyone come in here, Eric, without sterile clothing—mask, gown, hat, rubber gloves, boots, the works. There's no point in keeping you in a sterile chamber and having some new orderly from the kitchen, who hasn't got the word, push in here with a tray. The rules apply to *everybody.* They apply to doctors who might be from another department and aren't familiar with the procedure. Don't just be polite. We want you to be tough about this."

Since the fewer people who entered his room the better, the nurses also taught Eric how to do his own housework. He was supposed to make his own bed, clean his own washbasin with a special germicidal agent, and replace the gas-sterilized plastic bags which lined his commode. And to reduce the risk of infection still further, Eric was started on antibiotic gut-suppression protocol; the specific oral antibiotics used were supposed to help suppress bacteria in the gastrointestinal tract. All these careful preparations were made in the hope that the patient in the unit would remain in pretty good condition. The laminar air-flow room was not designed for emergencies or intensive care.

Memorial's first patient in the laminar air-flow room had, in some ways, proved to be an ideal test case. She was a young woman with acute leukemia who never became critically ill while she was in the unit. Her greatest problem had seemed to be how she could go on looking pretty while still observing the rules. During a previous course of chemotherapy she had lost all her hair and was very anxious to continue wearing her wig. After much discussion, she was allowed to wash it thoroughly and carry it with her into the room. Another problem was makeup. At first she was told no go; cosmetics were usually not sterile. But the patient's husband happened to work for a leading cosmetic firm. Rallying to the challenge, the firm prepared lipstick and eye makeup for her under sterile conditions.

The result was, as Mrs. Livingston put it, "one very happy and attractive patient."

Now it was Eric's turn to say good-bye to the everyday informal life on the eighth floor and enter the lonely cell. Sidney was on the scene February 3, the day three nurses marched Eric to the shower room to get him ready. The patient could not be boiled, but an effort was made to get him as clean as possible before entering the sterile quarters. Eric, wearing an old bathrobe and scuffed moccasins, walked the length of Ewing Eight's corridor, smiling, joking, and waving to the populace. He might have been a toreador headed for the bullring, accepting the cheers of the crowd.

The shower itself was accompanied by a great deal of laughing, shouting, and stage directions.

"Don't forget to wash behind your ears, Eric. . . . Don't forget your feet! . . . Wash your hair three times, now—"

"Who's taking this shower, anyway? How can I wash everything all at once? I've got my own system."

After a time the tone changed.

"Eric? How are you coming? . . . Eric? Are you almost done, love?"

"Naw, I'm never coming out. I like it in here."

He emerged at last. They had disposed of the bathrobe, the old moccasins. He slipped his feet into new paper slippers, wrapped his head in a sterile towel. The nurses advanced on him giggling, pretending to be greatly worried about preserving his modesty, holding high two sterile sheets. They wrapped him up tightly from neck to ankles and tried to trot him quickly into his new quarters.

"Hey! I can't walk in this outfit. I'm about to tip over."

"Never mind. We'll catch you."

"Hey, Eric, where's Ralph?" called a friend, seeing Eric's towel turban as he crossed the hallway.

"He ran away. He heard they were going to sterilize him."

"How long you s'pose you gotta boil a camel?"

"I dunno. But Ralph didn't want to hang around to find out." Eric finally entered the laminar air-flow chamber, where new sterile clothing awaited him. The nurses shut the door. He closed the curtains on the little window in the door himself. Five minutes later he opened them and sat back ready to receive doctors, nurses, technicians, and other distinguished visitors—provided they were suitably masked and dressed according to regulations. He was sitting up in bed wearing freshly boiled white pajamas—and a large beige pancake hat. Someone, knowing how Eric loved Mark's Christmas-present hat, had put it through the autoclave. Now it, too, was sterile. Eric wore it all that week.

At first it was a lark. There was the challenge of doing it well, not letting it get you. Memorial's psychiatrists were interested in patient reactions, of course. Some of the first patients had been unhappy with the feeling of "being in solitary," the fact that there was no window to the outdoor world. Another, on the contrary, had expressed resentment and anger when she was finally let out into the dangerous, germy world. Why don't they go on protecting me? was her feeling. Then there was the problem of noise. The roar of the air blowers, which never stopped, was considerable, enough so that patients subjected to it for any length of time were given regular hearing tests. Eric cleared all these first hurdles with no difficulty. For one thing, he had the excitement of visitors who waved through the window or sometimes got suited up in sterile clothes to come all the way in. We tried on the outfits, laughing, complaining. At first, for all of us, it was something to play light and easy. I drew a large cartoon of Sancho, our little black dog, in sterile dress wearing a mask, cap, and four white boots on his feet, entitled, "Sancho comes to visit Eric." We tacked it up on the door under the name card that Eric had brought from his place at the panel table at the seminar—"Mr. Eric Lund."

"Who's this guy in here, anyway?" I heard one visitor say to another one afternoon as they strolled past Eric's door on the long hall of Ewing Eight.

"I dunno. Some celebrity, maybe?"

Nobody else on Ewing Eight had his name on the door. And certainly nobody else had a sterile telephone. It was the only private phone on the floor—with a private number, too. It had been given to him so he could call the nurses' station for help, and also just to help him get through the day.

Friends soon learned the number and began calling in from all over. Eric never answered the same way twice.

"This is the Pentagon. . . ."

"Lund's Bar and Grill."

"Sanitation Department."

"Lum Foo Poo Chinese Restaurant, Lum speaking. . . ."

"Demolition Squad, Captain Lund here. . . ."

I paid Eric several visits that first week. Then I had to stay home to fight off a sinus infection and cough. Sidney went in once or twice, but Eric and I still ran up quite a phone bill talking to each other. The phone acted on Eric like a powerful stimulant. He was enjoying the drama. His spirits were high. He talked on and on.

Then one day when I dialed Eric, there were five or six rings and no answer. He *had* to be there. I held on. With the next ring, the phone was picked up. After some delay, I heard Eric's voice gasping, "Can't talk now . . . nosebleed . . . I'm packed." That was all. The phone clicked.

"Oh, Eric—good luck!" I cried into the phone as it went dead. The nosebleeds of leukemia were dreaded by everyone. Occasionally they might be mild and stop of their own accord. More typically they became an athletic event involving a team of three or four nurses and doctors. The first effort was to keep the patient from drowning in his own blood. The second move was to get in there fast with a nose pack. To do this, the doctor went in through the mouth and up behind the soft palate, wedging the pack in place so it couldn't move. With the hemorrhage confined to the front of the nose, the patient had a better chance of surviving it. As it slowed, the front of the nose was also packed. I had no way of knowing how severe Eric's nosebleed was, but it didn't sound trivial.

The next day we drove in early to see him. He was very pale, in a good deal of pain from the pack in his nose; he could not talk.

The doctor visited him while we were there. Later, he took us aside in the hall. "We did a bone marrow today. The marrow was very bad, to be truthful. There hasn't been any response to the drugs, although both white cells and platelets are way down. Of course we've been using CA and TG, which he's had before. We think we'll have to get him ready for asparaginase tomorrow, desensitize him."

The following day Eric, despite the protection of the sterile room, had developed an infection and was running a fever of 102 degrees. He'd received transfusions of both whole blood and platelets. A doctor was with him administering the asparaginase drip, a process that was going to take hours. There were needles in both arms, packs still in the front and back of the nose. Above the grotesque, swollen nose, Eric's eyes were steady with the will to endure.

Mark went with us to Memorial the next day. It was the first time. He put on the paper cap, mask, gloves—we had trouble getting the sterile gown around him and tied, he was so big!—then he went into the room. Sidney and I watched through the little window in the door. Eric looked up and saw Mark's eyes over the mask, Mark's shaggy red-gold curls under the paper cap, and he smiled. Then I saw that he was actually feeling better. His fever had come down a bit in response to some broad-spectrum antibiotics. The nose pack had been removed and replaced with a rubber tube which had a small bulb in it. Inflating the bulb at the outer end very gently kept pressure on the site of the hemorrhage, yet it was much more comfortable than the pack.

The day after that, Eric was feeling well enough to talk a bit. Sidney and I began to feel hopeful. We relaxed and, having relaxed, our defenses went down. We both caught flu that night.

Friday and Saturday we stayed in bed, coughing, taking every remedy we'd ever heard of for aches and fever. In between coughs, I kept trying to reach someone at Memorial who could tell us how Eric was doing. But the following Monday, February 15, was going to be a national holiday (Washington's and Lincoln's birthdays were celebrated together that year), and all the doctors whose names we knew well had gone off for three days' vacation. I'd been given the name of an intern who was supposed to be on call. Later I learned that the schedule had been revised at the last minute, which explained why he never answered his telephone page. I tried twenty-seven times by actual count. No one was to blame, but the communications breakdown between home and hospital was painful during those two days. Mark had gone back to school. We felt cut off, somewhat frightened, but we kept telling ourselves he must be all right or someone would call *us*.

That Saturday afternoon, in an effort to help, our close friend, newspaperman Frank Fay, Jr., went in to the hospital. He found Eric in serious condition, hemorrhaging once again, in semi-coma with wild delirium. He was running the fevers of 105 or 106 which, if prolonged, could lead to brain damage. And although he'd been receiving massive platelet transfusions every day, Eric's count was down to zero. His body had begun to manufacture antibodies and was now rejecting platelets as fast as they entered his bloodstream. (Such a reaction, I learned later, usually occurs only after many transfusions. It is also less likely to happen if family members can be found to give compatible platelets. But even if the doctor has no compatible donors at hand, he often continues giving platelets to the patient as fast as he can, rather the way workers might go on throwing sandbags on a dike that's likely to break anyway. If you can get enough platelets into the bloodstream, you may neutralize the antibodies—knock them out, so to speak. Then when you give still more, some of the good platelets may get through and help the patient. But of all these things we were ignorant as we lay at home trying to get over our flu.)

Frank stayed with Eric far into that Saturday night, trying to calm him down in his delirium, trying to keep him from climbing out of bed. Eric was so wild that he finally had to be sedated, although this was risky in his semi-comatose condition. When Frank finally drove home it was after 3 A.M. He decided not to wake us with such disturbing news at that hour.

The next morning we were startled into terror by a phone call that came before seven.

"Mrs. Lund, this is Dr. Maresh. I've just been in to see Eric, and I think you and your husband had better get in here as fast as you can."

"Is he—?"

"His condition is very serious. I've put him on the critical list. This means you can get a pass and come right up when you arrive."

Throughway traffic. Cars, trucks, bridges, tolls. At last the exit. No place to park. Never any place to park. "All right, put it in the garage. I'll get out and go on up."

"This elevator, please." But the doors closed. Wait for the next elevator. Pushed to the back . . . five . . . six . . . seven . . . I have to get out.

"*Eighth* floor, please." I went running down the hall to the laminar air-flow room, to the moment I'd been fearing for three and a half years. The door was shut, no one in sight. But the curtains were open. I looked through the window.

"Ah . . . ah!" I heard my own gasp. Something fluttered, trembled, and nearly gave way in the center of my body. But I held tightly to the doorknob. Now I have seen him, and now I am sure that this February 14—Valentine's Day!—will be the day of Eric's death. Already he wore its mask. The deep black-purple eyes, the nose black with blood, the open black lips. And this, then, was where the Greeks first got the mask, I saw in a flash— not from the paint pots backstage but from the real and tragic deaths of their heroes on the battlefields. Thermopylae. Marathon. And now, Memorial.

The bed was high and slightly raised. Already Eric seemed to be upon his bier. His red-gold curls against the pillow were lifeless, as if carved in stone. His gray fingers hung down and did not move.

"Who are you?" A nurse, who looked quite frightened, was beside me.

"His mother."

"Oh! I'll get the doctor." She flew away.

Soon she came running back. "He's not there. They're having him paged." She began to put arms into one of the sterile paper gowns that were lying in piles on the stand outside the door.

"Gloves are in the drawer." She showed me. "Put everything on, then you can come in." I already knew the procedure, but I was clumsy; nothing would tie. At last I made it. The nurse was bending over Eric, trying to adjust the flow of an I.V. bottle. Her hands were shaking. I stayed quiet for fear I was making her nervous. The door opened and a young doctor came in, hair dark under the cap, eyes a warm blue.

"Dr. Maresh," he said.

"Hello, doctor."

He went to the other side of the bed, took firm hold of Eric's shoulder. "Eric?" His voice was commanding as he bent to the ear. "Can you hear me? This is Dr. Maresh, Eric. Come on now. Your mother is here, Eric."

"Oh, no! Please!" I cried. "Don't wake him for *me!*" He doesn't know he's dying, I thought. I don't want him to wake and be afraid. Oh, let him die quickly now. Let it be over!

"We've got to bring him back," said the doctor. "We want to get a response. He's been going further into coma for three days now."

"But you don't expect him to live through *this* day, do you? Not looking like that!"

"I don't know," said the young doctor seriously. "But I haven't given up. Sometimes they come back when you wouldn't believe they could. Eric's still very strong. He must have been in fantastic shape when he came in."

"He was. He planned it that way."

Sidney took one look at Eric and went to the telephone. Mark said he'd get the first train down from New Haven. Meredith and Jim said they'd fly in from Chicago as soon as they could. They arrived that afternoon and came right to the laminar air-flow room door still wearing their winter coats, still carrying suitcases. Then Jim, who could not believe what he was seeing, fainted. He went down fast, without a sound. Watching him go, I thought, "That's the first honest reaction of the day." What were the rest of us doing on our feet? This was unendurable.

Not an inch of Eric's body was untouched. Bruises, four and five inches across, covered his chest, arms, and legs. The red and purple dots of petechiae, which are the badges of platelet failure, were everywhere. His tongue, swollen, protruding, was covered with sores. His gums dripped blood.

That afternoon, Eric began to move, trying to struggle out of unconsciousness, and we saw his control go. An intern, probing for a new vein, had gotten the needle through his layer of reserve. Eric, who had borne a thousand needles without a sound, suddenly began to scream.

"Shit! Oh, no—SHIT!"

He pulled away violently, turning in bed. The needle flew free. Firmly the intern grabbed his arm, anchored it, and inserted the needle again.

"Mother-fucker!" screamed Eric.

You could hear his yells down the hall. The intern taped his arm once again to a board, pulled up the side rails on his bed.

"Watch him," he said to the nurse and went out.

Eric began to sob. Just as suddenly he stopped. "Not crying," he said, shaking his head. "That's not the way back. Not crying. No!" He shuddered.

He lay still for a while, then all at once began to sing the victory songs of soccer battles. A drunk with a bloody mouth urging his old teammates on. The words were garbled, but every so often we could catch the refrain "Fight! Fight! Fight!" and this he took as a signal to begin climbing out of bed. Seeing his brother with one leg over the rail, Mark hurriedly put on sterile clothes, went in, and held him down.

"Listen, Eric," he shouted. "We're going to get you out. But you've got to stay here a while. Do you understand?"

Eric went on rolling around the bed, lurching, singing.

Mark hung in there. Eric finally tired and fell back into coma. "He's strong," Mark said, coming out. "You ought to feel his arms. It's hard to hold him down." He tore off the mask, gloves, gown and threw them in the trash with the indifferent gesture I'd seen young interns use.

"Gonna go play some pool," Mark said. There was a pool table in the day room at the end of the hall.

Meredith and Jim got dressed and took over the next time Eric tried to get up.

"Eric—lie down."

"We're going to get you out."

"But not right now, Eric. . . . Eric, can you hear us?"

It began to dawn on me that the battle was far from over, and

221

for the rest of that day and evening we took turns fighting it. How strange we looked to each other, seen through the little window, only our eyes showing above our masks. Sidney looked like a surgeon. I looked, he told me, like a seventeen-year-old playing a nurse in a high school play. But we were not nurses, doctors, miracle workers, or magicians. And Eric, still spiking a fever of 106, still using up sack after sack of whole blood and platelets, grew quiet and began to slip back into darkness as the darkness of winter evening fell over the city.

Then, as their duty ended in other parts of the hospital, nurses who had been Eric's friends through the years came running up to help. Instead of going home, they went through the tedious dressing and masking and added their calls to ours.

"Eric! Can you hear me?"

"Eric! Come on, love!"

Barbara. Maureen. Little Cathy, after eight-hour duty on another floor in Memorial. This was not nursing, it was something way beyond. A human being was going over the edge; other human beings were trying to pull him back. With all its ugliness, I felt the beauty of life that night, the beauty of people working together. Everything suddenly seemed part of the whole. Help was forever on the way. For a moment it was as if all the good in the world were known to me and held inside my head. I saw firemen racing to help people they did not know, miners risking their lives to help a buried comrade, hundreds of people hunting for a lost child.

The moment passed. By eleven o'clock that night I didn't care who lived or died, especially me. Dying, in fact, began to seem a comfortable alternative to going on, like sinking down in the snow. I was wrapped in fatigue like padded clothing. Let the expedition go on without me. Somebody got me on my feet. We all went home.

It was astonishing to wake the next morning and realize there was still more to come. When we got to the hospital, we found Eric looking, if possible, worse. His fever was still over 105. But there was one small change which gave us hope. Although still unable to see out of his black, swollen eyes, he now seemed able to hear.

Two technicians came in with a portable X-ray machine and then recruited Sidney's help in propping Eric upright for a chest picture. (With a fever like that, and with such low white counts, pneumonia was a constant threat.) Now, at the sound of male voices close to him, Eric began turning his head, this way and that, trying to locate the person who was speaking.

"Dr. Dowling? Dr. D.? Is that you?" he said again and again. It was his first real effort to communicate sensibly.

It was also my first realization of how supportive Dr. Dowling's presence was to Eric. I, too, began to long for his return. That morning, however, we were taken to see Dr. Timothy Gee, one of Memorial's top oncologists. The journey from Ewing Eight to Dr. Gee's office took nearly fifteen minutes. We were led by a nurse through many sets of dark double doors in the labyrinth of the old hospital. At last, after two elevator rides, we emerged into another world. Deep carpets. Handsome desks. Modern chairs and sofas upholstered in luxurious blue, green, or red wool. It was our first glimpse of the new Memorial. We had never before met Dr. Gee, but as he came toward us across the spacious lobby, I recognized him right away from one of Eric's cartoons which featured Dr. Gee ironing shirts in a Chinese laundry. While his office was remote from Eric's room, it was immediately obvious from talking with him that Dr. Gee had been in close touch with the situation all along. Finally Sidney asked the question which I hadn't dared put in words, even in my own mind.

"If you can bring Eric back, will he be permanently brain damaged?" He had been clearly deranged for over four days.

Dr. Gee thought not. The pattern was usually this, he explained: Either the patient survived the crisis and recovered his senses, or his disintegration was total. In other words, death followed.

"We haven't given him up yet," said Dr. Gee. "But both Dr. Maresh and I agree that the sooner we can get him some family platelets from one of you, the better. We've been getting about forty to fifty volunteers a day showing up to give blood just for Eric, but no matter how much we manage to give him, he's still got a platelet count of zero."

Dr. Maresh sent us to the Donor Room, where Margaret and Jeanne took down all the family medical histories. Following that, we were escorted to Dr. Reich's laboratory over in the Sloan-Kettering building across the street, where more elaborate blood typing and analysis was to be done. We were back and forth, in and out of these places, all that afternoon, and during that time we were amazed to learn from the nurses about the massive Blood Donor program that had been under way for almost four days to try to save Eric. Friends at home had organized other friends. Housewives, businessmen, fathers of Little League players from Eric's team of years ago, football players from the local league in which Eric had played, church members, club members, YMCA members were all recruited. Car pools had been arranged, appointments made and kept at the Donor Room. All this had been happening while we were home fighting the flu or standing by Eric's bedside, without anyone bothering us with a single unnecessary phone call. It was as if the whole town gathered silently behind us.

Much of the credit for the fact that the operation ran so smoothly belonged to our friend, Frank Fay, Jr. His front-page story in our town paper, headlined "Soccer Star Battles Leukemia," gave all the details that were needed to dramatize the problem and to help people find their way to the right place at the right time to give blood for Eric. His follow-up stories kept donors coming through the weeks that followed. Papers in neighboring towns picked up the story, too. And soon Soccer Coach Joe Morrone of the University of Connecticut launched an effort of his own to help Eric. Soccer players, the entire lacrosse team, and friends from all over the campus made the three-hour bus trip down from Storrs to the Memorial Donor Room. Coach Morrone also circulated a letter among 800 Connecticut alumni living in the New York area telling them of Eric's plight. We were overwhelmed to learn of all this going on. There would never be any way to seek out all the people who came and give them our thanks.

The Donor Room was nearly swamped. The girls there had a hard time keeping up with the tide, and several nurses, Margaret among them, worked overtime or all through their days off. It was not an easy matter to schedule and process whole busloads of donors. Each person who showed up had to be carefully checked in a dozen ways. A few always had to be turned down.

Memorial's doctors have no doubt that blood donations from Eric's many friends saved his life by getting him through the dangerous time between his first hemorrhage and the moment when family platelets could be used.

"We needed all the platelets we could get for Eric," they told me later, "and we had no hesitation in calling for them. With Eric's friends coming in in such droves, we knew we weren't depriving any other patient in the hospital. We aren't always this fortunate. Usually we might give five or six units when a patient needs platelets. Eric got thirty-two units in one hour! That means donations from thirty-two people! And when he needed more that same day, he got them, too."

Of the many who gave, some of the hardy soccer players failed to pay any attention to the requirement that "you do not ride in an elevator for an hour after giving blood." That Saturday afternoon five or six of Eric's best friends on the team went right from the ground-floor Donor Room to the eighth floor to see for themselves how Eric was doing.

A senior nurse who'd had many years of experience on Ewing Eight told me later this was the worst day she ever lived through in any hospital. Eric's delirium was so wild that it took two nurses at all times just to keep him in bed. Yet even in his semi-consciousness, he was somehow aware that his friends were there in the doorway. He could not see them but he kept shouting, "Who's out there? Tell me their names."

The nurses told him. The boys could not speak. Several fainted, whether from the forbidden ride in the elevator or the sight of Eric, no one could say for sure.

"They stood there with tears pouring down their cheeks," the nurse said. "I've never seen young men weep like that. And every once in a while Eric would pull himself together and try to smile and call out their names and thank them for coming. Then he'd go right out of his mind again."

• • •

It was Mark who turned out to be the perfect donor for Eric; until he'd turned eighteen, he hadn't been eligible. That Sunday afternoon Mark gave double platelets for his brother. Sidney, the next best donor, would be used the following day after he'd had a little more time to recover from the effects of his flu. Eric didn't need flu germs on top of his other problems. No one could understand why Sidney had been rejected as a blood donor years before. "I think they told me my veins were too small," he said. "Anyway, they couldn't get anything out of me."

"Probably somebody didn't get the needle in right," said the technician who was testing him. "You've got good big veins. And very high hemoglobin."

Meredith's blood was supposedly not entirely compatible with Eric's. But Dr. Maresh, who'd been desperately using every creative measure he could think of to keep Eric alive, decided to use her anyway.

"It won't hurt," he said, "and it might help. We don't know all there is to know about blood compatibility factors anyway. Maybe we know enough to look for four very important things and thirty or forty fairly important things. But there may be two thousand other things that we don't understand yet but that are involved. Meredith is Eric's sister. Siblings are usually the ideal donors. She may help in some way that we couldn't even suspect. I want to use her."

I was once again, positively and forever, ruled out as a blood donor. I'd had labyrinthitis, an inner ear balance disturbance, off and on for years. Twice it had been severe for periods of nearly a year. The doctor in the Donor Room at the time I was examined said there had been some cases where people with this condition tried to give blood and sustained permanent damage. He would not take this risk.

The next day the battle began to turn. When Dr. Maresh came around that morning to take a look at Eric's chart, the fever was down to 103. The bleeding had slowed. Platelet count, following donations from brother and sister, was no longer zero and was coming up noticeably.

"Now we're getting somewhere," said Maresh with satisfaction. "That Eric is a tough cookie!"

We heard later that the top doctors had told the floor nurses that Eric Lund would surely die that weekend. One of them said, "There's just no way he can survive." The nurses had sadly agreed. They had never given up fighting for his life, however. And Dr. Maresh had fought for it minute by minute. Now he had his reward.

More impressive even than all the good signs on the chart was the fact that the patient himself was now making an active effort to rejoin the world. He still could not see. But he could talk and he could feel us.

"Mommy? Is that you?"

"I'm right here, Eric."

"Are you sterile? I'm not supposed to let you in here if you're not sterile. Where's your hat?"

I bent down and put his fingers on it.

"I can feel your gloves, too," he said, smiling a little drunkenly. "But where are your boots? I can't see them."

"I don't have them on, I—"

"Listen, Mommy." He sounded petulant, like a tired small boy. "You've got to be sterile, all the way. I can't let you in here if you're not."

"They decided boots were too much trouble, Eric." In the emergencies of the past few days, the need for perfect sterility had given way to the practical need of keeping the patient alive—and in bed—from moment to moment. Our standards had been officially lowered from "sterile" to "clean."

"I don't know about that," Eric said, trying to look out of his swollen eyes. "They told me boots! You gotta have boots, Mommy!"

He was finally somewhat reassured by his nurse. But he gave each of us the third degree about our outfits every time we went in or out of his chamber. He also had many ideas about his own medical treatment and tried to give us messages that he wanted smuggled out to Dr. Dowling. For some reason, although we told him repeatedly that Dr. Dowling was on vacation, on that particular day he had the delusion that the hospital was in a conspiracy to keep him from seeing Dr. Dowling. We tried to comfort him. We tacked up Dr. Dowling's office number and even his home phone number, at Eric's determined insistence, where he could feel them, even if he couldn't see them.

"Mommy?"

"Yes."

"Here's what I want you to do. You get hold of Dr. Dowling and you tell him that—that—"

"Yes?"

Eric laughed a small embarrassed laugh. "I forget," he said. "Now wait a minute—I *know* I have to tell him something. I'll think of it. . . ."

"I'm waiting. I'm not going anywhere, I promise you."

He's not put together yet, I thought. But good Jesus, just to hear him talking half sense was so great!

Then, as he got more tired, he got more suspicious. "Go away—you're not sterile," he said that evening to a nurse he couldn't see. "I'm in this important room. *I'm* sterile—so don't you touch me!"

"Take me home," I said to Sidney. "Just put me in boiling water for fifty minutes and let the germs fall where they may." We were both so tired, we were staggering as we walked to the car. Yet underneath, there was this small singing feeling. I explored it, sleepily, all the way home. Amazingly, it was joy.

CHAPTER 17

IT TOOK ERIC A DAY or so to get his brains unscrambled. In the meantime, he was often confused and deluded, but very insistent. He was certainly hard to care for. It was at this difficult moment that Fortune smiled on us and sent us a new private-duty nurse. Her name was MaryLou.

We met over bloody shit. I arrived on the scene one morning to find Eric, nearly naked, lying in a bed of black excrement, shouting elaborate orders to a nurse I hadn't seen before. She was laughing (yes, laughing!) behind her mask as she tried to clean him up. She had the tiny waist of a teen-ager. My God, she looks so young and pretty, I thought in that first glimpse. I wonder if she's up to coping with this?

"You don't touch that!" Eric was saying vehemently. "That's my brother's bowel movement. Not mine! You're not allowed to touch it."

"Now, Eric—" The pretty nurse had a good strong grip on one leg. "You know I've got to clean you up. C'mon, now." She was still laughing. "Try to help me, Eric."

For answer, Eric put a leg out of bed.

Not sure if I could really help her, but wanting to, I hurriedly gowned up and went on in.

"I'm his mother. Can I help you?"

"Grab his other leg, would you? Hold him still just a minute—"

In an amazingly short time she had him cleaned up, in a fresh, clean gown, lying in a freshly made bed. During this time he was groggily aware of me but more interested in pursuing his battle with MaryLou.

"MaryLou?"

"Yes, Eric. What is it?"

"I've got to go again."

"Oh, no!" She laughed as if this were the funniest joke of the week. What amazing blue eyes she had over her mask! Black lashes that long. And light blue eyes. "All right. I'll get the pan."

"No! No! No! Listen, MaryLou—here's what I want you to do. I need two sterile bowls. Hate that old pan. Pans are no good. Just bring me two sterile bowls. One for the front. And one for the back. You understand?"

"Yes, Eric." MaryLou sighed.

"How long has this been going on?" I asked her.

"All morning. All night, too, I guess. He threw his urinal at the night nurse."

"That's right," said Eric, sounding pleased with himself. "Old Joan doesn't get the idea. Got to get rid of old Joan."

"Joan is a very good nurse," MaryLou explained to me, "but she doesn't understand that Eric can only urinate facing east."

"Can't piss west," affirmed Eric. "Only can piss facing east. *That* way—" He showed us with a violent wave of his hand.

"Mecca!" I said, astonished. The bed was against the east wall of the room. Probably, in his confused way, Eric was preserving some last trace of modesty by turning away from the door. But it

232

was much easier for a nurse to care for him on the open side of the bed—or west.

It went on like this all morning. A doctor came by and told me they thought Eric might have a prostate infection which gave him constant pressure, a feeling he had to go every minute. They were treating it with a broad-spectrum antibiotic.

"Are you sure he isn't bleeding from the bowel? I thought blackness always came from blood."

"It does. But we're pretty sure this is from the nose and mouth hemorrhages. He's swallowed an awful lot of blood. But he's not bleeding now. This will clear up."

MaryLou brought Eric the sterile bowls many times. She never fought his delusions, she worked with them. But Eric could never get organized to use the bowls. He began to be very distraught.

"Look, Eric," said MaryLou. "Just let go in bed if you have to. It's okay."

I helped her as best I could for about an hour and a half. Then I began to feel dizzy. With sterile clothes over regular clothes, rubber gloves strangling my wrists, the heat in the room seemed terrific. Finally I gave up and sank down on a chair just outside the door of Eric's room. MaryLou came out and gave me an appraising look.

"I'll get you some apple juice."

"Oh, no, please don't bother. I'll be all right. You're the one who must be tired."

Private-duty nurses worked a twelve-hour stretch in the laminar air-flow room. It was tough duty. I couldn't see how they stayed on their feet. As for MaryLou, she had to be the finest nurse I'd ever seen. And she made it seem a lark. Now she was coming back, flying down the hall with two little glasses.

"This is marvelous! Just what I needed."

"Me, too."

Without our masks, we were really seeing each other for the first time. But she's lovely, I thought, with that rich, dark curly hair, those startling blue eyes.

I spent the rest of the day with Eric and MaryLou, and that afternoon was one of the happiest of my life. Eric began to feel much better. He relaxed, and then he grew very loving.

"Mary Lou? I want to be alone with my mom for a minute—"

"Sure, Eric. I'll be right outside."

"Mommy, you're sterile, aren't you?"

"I've got everything on I'm s'posed to have."

"I can't see you but, Mommy, I want to hug you."

We hugged long and gently.

"I'm sorry we didn't get along—sorry we had that fight."

"It's all right."

"No, I want you to know I'm really sorry. I want to hug you every day."

"I like hugging. We haven't done enough of it, maybe."

"And listen, Mommy—I want to thank you for all you've done." Suddenly he began to cry. "I didn't mean to get so sick and scare everybody. Please tell everybody I'm perfectly all right, will you?"

"Sure, I will. You're going to be fine now."

"Okay." He drew a long breath, the breath of a child after crying; then he lay still. "MaryLou can come in now."

When MaryLou came in she had six pills for Eric to take, each one big enough for a horse. She started to give him the first one but he waved her away. "I want my mom to give me those pills, MaryLou."

Oh, no, I thought, what if he chokes? His mouth was still

234

cracked, his tongue swollen. He could only take water from a spoon. But we did it slowly, carefully; he helped me as best he could and then lay back pleased.

"Well," said MaryLou, "I guess you won't be needing me around here tomorrow."

"Listen, Eric," I said, ignoring her mock sarcasm, "you've got to get those eyes open tomorrow so you can see MaryLou. She's the prettiest nurse you ever saw."

"I don't have to see her," said Eric. "I've been with her all day and I know she's beautiful."

That night Sidney gowned up and went in to see him.

"Daddy, are you sterile? Are you sure?"

"I'm sure I'm fine, Eric."

"Then come closer. I can't see you but I want to feel your body. I want to hold onto you."

Sidney bent down. Eric put his arms around him. I was standing in the doorway, and I could see tears in Sidney's eyes above the mask.

"Do you remember when I was a little boy and you let me hold onto your shoulders and then we'd swim out to the float together?"

"I remember."

"It was way over my head and scary. It was so dark in the deep water down below. But that was a good feeling—holding onto your body."

I stood in the doorway, listening, watching them through my own tears.

"I want to hug you now, Daddy. I want to thank you for all you've done."

• • •

Eric got out of bed for ten seconds the following morning. He stood there, unself-consciously, with a boyish smile, and he said, "That's happiness—being able to piss straight down!"

Then he got back in bed, exhausted, and just lay there savoring the glory of this moment. He was also beginning to see out of the slits of his black eyes—just barely, but he could see. This was such an improvement that soon he demanded to have his bed cranked up and his door opened so he could wave to the world once again.

The world of Ewing Eight was impressed. No one had expected Eric to survive. Yet here he was, propped up, wearing Mark's pancake hat, wearing his triumph somewhat askew, with his eyes x'd out like some drunk in a comic strip (like Jiggs after Maggie'd hit him with a rolling pin!), his nose still lopsided, his mouth still black—but he was smiling. It was enough to make you weep, yet everyone who saw him began to laugh. He was so full of joy, it was catching.

Dr. Gee came to see this miracle for himself. Eric was delighted to recognize his friend.

"Dr. Gee, old buddy! Where have you been?"

Poor Dr. Gee, who'd been holding the fort during the long holiday weekend, managed a smile. "Ask your mother where I've been, Eric."

"But I missed you," Eric said innocently. "Where's *everybody* been? I mean, what's been going on? Everybody's acting as if something funny had happened."

Then he caught sight of the poster I'd taped up to cover his washbasin mirror the day before. I'd been afraid he'd scare himself the first time he got a look.

"Let me see—I want to see myself."

We pulled down the poster and Eric stared in the mirror at the battered, ghastly stranger.

"Oh, boy!" He crowed with joy. "Look at those black eyes! They're really something, aren't they? How'd I ever get those? Was I in a fight?"

Dr. Gee smiled at me and then just shook his head. "Yeah, you were in some fight, Eric," he said.

Eric was on a jag of affection all that week. It was exactly as if he'd been dead and now, reborn, could not believe his marvelous good fortune in being alive. He was astonished at the beauty of the world. He was overwhelmed at the remarkable qualities of every human being around him. He hugged us all repeatedly. The nurses had to put sterile clothes on over their winter coats and hoods, or else take them off, when they stopped by on their way home to say good-bye, because just a simple good-bye was not enough. Eric insisted they come all the way in for hugs, too.

"I'm so glad to see you!" he cried. "Oh, it's so good to be here!"

"I've been a nurse for many years," one of them told me later, "but that's the first time I ever got in bed with a patient. And let me tell you, I wasn't the only one."

The only real fault Eric could find with life was that he seemed to be missing four days. He had almost no memory at all of what happened, and he was at great pains to reconstruct every minute of those four days.

"But why were you all so upset?" he kept wanting to know.

Miss Somerville, one of the head nurses, told it to him calm and straight. "Eric, you had zero platelets for about four days.

And hardly any white cells either. That was a pretty serious situation. Your family and your friends had to give you a great deal of blood."

Gradually he began to take it in. For one thing, he was now getting dozens and dozens of get-well cards every day, especially from the girls he knew. There were telegrams. One girl called him three times from France. "How will I ever repay everybody?" he kept asking.

The answer was obvious and we told it to him. "By getting well. By being you."

This was something he understood. He was impatient, eager to try everything. Then one afternoon while I was visiting him (it was Saturday, February 20, almost three weeks since he'd been placed in the laminar air-flow room), disaster hit us again. An intern visiting from another floor came in to take a look at the unusual survivor, Eric Lund. Memorial is a teaching hospital, after all. He wanted a look at Eric's nose. He poked around with a light and a probe, and within seconds after he departed Eric began to hemorrhage once again.

MaryLou flew to get help. Eric sat there in bed holding his nose with both hands, while the red blood splashed over his shirt, the white covers. Sidney, Meredith, and Jim were expected to come in later in the day. We needed family platelets immediately! But I was the only "family" there—and I could not help him.

"Mommy," Eric said. "Go down to the Donor Room and see if they've got any donors around who are a close match to me." He had no time to waste in panic or anger at what had happened. He wanted to survive, and his control could help him.

I ran to the elevator, ran to the Donor Room on the first floor.

I didn't entirely understand the message but I relayed it exactly. Soon I learned that Jeanne and Margaret, on their own, had been making up a separate file, trying to match some of the regular donors with the patients, for blood types, white cell types, and a dozen other things. It was a fairly new idea to try such a thing, but already it had begun to help.

They both went to work on the problem. As luck would have it, two Memorial employees who were regular donors were nearly compatible with Eric. Some others were found. In all, it took ten outside platelet donors, plus four donations of platelets (spread over three days) from Sidney, and one platelet donation from Meredith (who was on the edge of being anemic and could not give more) before the new nosebleed was brought under control. Fortunately, it in no way approached the violence of the earlier episode.

From then on, anyone who examined Eric did so with a gingerly respect. He, himself, was not allowed to brush his teeth, shave, or even cut his fingernails or toenails. He was hardly a pretty sight. He looked, in fact, with his straggly red beard and blue eyes, emerging at last, surrounded by solid red where they should have been white, as if he had been on a two weeks' drunk with very bad gin. Nevertheless, on February 24, it is recorded that Eric got out of bed, with the I.V. drip needle still in his arm and still taped to a board, and jogged in place for five minutes on three different occasions during the day. He was determined to get himself in shape, perhaps more grimly determined than he had ever been, for he had been unsuccessful in trying to badger his good friend Dr. Dowling into guaranteeing him a remission. Dr. Dowling played straight with Eric. "I can't guarantee it, but I'll do my best," was all he would say.

Eric's reply had been, "All right, Dr. D. I don't need you then. I'll do it myself."

"Do you think I can make it on my own?" he asked me.

"Of course," I said. "You can do anything you want if you try hard enough." It was a cop-out, a pat and positive response. But it was what he wanted to hear. And I was impressed with his will. I didn't really know what factors were at work. It was difficult enough to measure the aftereffects of drugs, used in combination, at a previous time, without adding the unknown value of a surge of determination, a strong desire. Every fiber in Eric's body was bent on surviving. Three days after he'd announced that he'd do it himself, he was in good remission.

That day, February 26, he was allowed to leave the laminar air-flow room for the first time in twenty-three days. In celebration he and his father walked the length of the long hall on Ewing Eight. The other patients in the hall stared at him.

"Hey, Eric!" one of them called out. "How'd you do it? How did you get out?"

"The governor phoned. Just in time," said Eric, smiling.

They kept on walking until at last they were standing in front of the big window that faces south overlooking the city. It was a beautiful day. Eric stood there looking. "Wow! The sun!" he said.

CHAPTER 18

ERIC COULDN'T STAY on that high peak of ecstasy and gratitude indefinitely. He had to come down. For one thing, he knew what was facing him. More and still more weeks in the laminar air-flow room. No one could say how many. He was going to be "consolidated."

"Did he hug you today?" Lisa demanded one evening when I came home from the hospital. (Being only thirteen, she'd not been allowed to visit.)

"Not today."

"I knew it!" she wailed. "Oh why couldn't he have come home and hugged *me* before it wore off?"

I put my arms around her, hoping it would help. None of us was ready for the steep ascent so soon again. Before the struggle began, however, Memorial's doctors granted Eric a brief afternoon pass to go out and take another look at the world. He'd been working out rather grimly in his tiny chamber as best he could. Jogging in place three or four times a day. Even managing to do a few cramped pushups half under the bed. He'd begun doing his own housekeeping again, too. It'd been some time since he'd needed a private-duty nurse. MaryLou had departed. And with her gone, the laminar air-flow room seemed more than ever a cell. Eric needed to get out.

I often thought how wise they were, those doctors. It was their responsibility to pick the terrible moment when consolidation must start once again. They faced it bravely, looking at all the facts, looking at their patient's needs. But first they always tried to add a few drops of life to the prescription. "Find a friend to go out with you and take a walk, Eric," they said this time. It was March 1, 1971.

Eric picked his father for the outing. Sidney and I drove in to town together. I was really on my way to Bloomingdale's and had no intention of spoiling the fun. But I did want one glimpse of Eric, out of his glass box at last, standing on the sidewalk just like anyone else, enjoying the early spring sunshine.

When Eric saw me follow Sidney out of the car, however, he began to dance with rage. He literally jumped up and down.

"Why did you come? I didn't ask for you!"

His red eyes blazed furiously. He was a terrifying sight, whirling around on the sidewalk, his thin face and beak nose sharp as a bird's under Mark's pancake hat, the huge winter jacket and heavy muffler making him look twice as frail as he was.

"I only wanted to say hello. I'm going shopping."

"The hell you are! You came to take care of me, to make sure I wouldn't overdo. This is my first day out of this place in over a month, and you've ruined it!"

I lurched away from them both and ran half a block in the wrong direction just to get as far as I could from that accusing voice. I stood by a traffic light unable to see it, blind with pain, and then I nearly stepped right in front of a truck. I heard the screech, the driver's snarl, and I came back to earth. This wasn't the end of the world. I hadn't ruined his day. He was unreasonable, unfair, but maybe he was entitled to be, considering where he'd been. And if I let him ruin my day now, that was my problem. I walked around the city for an hour or so, feeling the waves of pain subsiding. By evening I was almost back together. I decided to spend the night in town with a friend, having dinner, forgetting the hospital world, being good to myself.

As for Eric, I'm told he shrugged off the whole incident as soon as he'd chased me away. He and Sidney walked over to the East River. Eric's nose began to bleed slowly. They sat on a bulkhead for half an hour waiting for it to stop. Then they walked three miles up the river and back to Memorial. Before going up to the eighth floor, Eric wanted to stop in the Donor Room and thank them for all their recent efforts. Most of the nurses had been up to see him once or twice and knew him. But a new nurse, recently assigned to the room, happened to be behind the desk that afternoon. According to Sidney, she took one look at this frightful apparition with the wild red eyes, scruffy beard, and frail blue wrists and nearly screamed.

"My God!" she told her companion nurses later. "He looked like a drunk who'd probably wandered in hoping to sell his blood so he could buy some more booze. All I could think of was 'How will I ever get rid of him?'"

The following day Eric's nose had quieted down. His doctors were pleased that he'd survived such a long first outing. A few wished he'd been more conservative. But Dr. Dowling granted him one more pass. This time Eric asked Susan, a young research assistant on Ewing Eight, to accompany him. Susan was a small dark-eyed girl, not more than a hundred pounds. She was a bit terrified by the responsibility and decided to call Dr. Dowling.

"Look," she said, "I've got a date to go out with Eric in a few minutes. What'll I do if he wants to run?"

"Sit down on a bench and wait for him," came back the reply.

Cytosine. Thioguanine. Asparaginase. The names of hope and fear. Once again, on March 4, we began carrying them in our heads and hearts as Eric began carrying them in his bloodstream. The consolidation was under way.

It was an ugly time. A time of nausea and dry heaves. The dry heaves led to nosebleeds which again led to more nausea. There were nightmares—or rather, *the* nightmare, for he had the same one over and over. He was in total blackness. Lost. He did not know if he had gone blind or if it was just that blackness was all there was in his whole world. He kept looking for the way out, trying not to panic, trying to find a crack of light somewhere. He never found it and he woke up, time after time, shouting. The ultimate nightmare—death.

"Oh, I'm so scared," he whispered to his nurses. "I'm really scared." They comforted him, held him, gave him what strength they could.

By March 17, Eric's platelet count was down to 12. (Doctors and nurses commonly said "Twelve" when they meant 12,000—a dangerously low platelet count when you consider that 150,000 to 250,000 is normal.) Mark and Sidney both rushed in to give double platelets on two different occasions. We all went to see him often, hoping it would help. Yet he hardly wanted to see anyone. He sat, knees drawn up, huddling against the back far corner of his bed, as a bird huddles on a rocky ledge, too hurt to fly, yet starving. Even his legs were bird legs now. His calves were gone, the round muscles of his arms gone, too. Seeing him like this, a broken bird in a glass cage, I walked to the end of the hall one afternoon and leaned my head against the cold windowpane. Below was the rushing world of the city, people streaming home, a thousand lights beginning to twinkle in the towers, but looking through the glass I saw only Eric. He had caged me out. He was caging us all out. The light in his eyes seemed to be slowly withdrawing, like a camera slowly closing its lens. The light was his life, fading away to a pinpoint. How much more could he stand?

Mark, seeing my distress, said, "His chest is still okay. He's fine in the chest, Mom."

But Eric's listlessness was more frightening to me than all the flailing around of the earlier days in the laminar air-flow room. I walked back down the hall to see him once more. He hadn't wanted me to put on the sterile clothes and come in when I'd first arrived.

"I'd like to come in, Eric, and give you a good-bye hug."

"I don't need it."

"Maybe I do."

"You'll be okay," he said, without expression. The pupils of his eyes looked so small. He wasn't really seeing. I went on standing there. I couldn't reach him but I couldn't leave.

At last he said, "If you're in here, you're in here. That's all. I know nothing of life out there." He waved his arm, such a tired wave, dismissing the rest of the world.

"Good-bye, Eric."

I know now that even as withdrawn as he seemed, he was trying to survive the only way he knew. His strength was so little that he conserved it by making no effort, reducing his desires to the smallest, simplest things. A smooth bed. Quiet. A few drops of water. Sleep without dreams. And breathing. Just breathing, for one more day.

But I could not see it then. His rejection seemed as cold as death itself. Hours later, standing by my window in Connecticut, I looked out into the wet black night. Beyond the streetlight a furious wind was whipping the bare willow branches into golden tangles. But again, by a trick of reflection or shadow, I saw only Eric beyond the glass. Broken bird on his ledge. I began to weep. I wept for a long time. There was no comforting.

CHAPTER 19

TIDES TURN GENTLY while we are not watching. Just when life seemed to be ebbing away from Eric, slowly, ever so slowly, it began to flow back. He was able to eat a little bit. He got out of bed for a few minutes every day. Soon he was struggling to make his own bed again.

Perhaps an even greater indication that Eric was becoming himself again was that his creative drive returned. He had begun the fifth edition of "The Adventures of Ewing 8" during his first joyful week of convalescence as soon as he got his eyes really open. But the illness of consolidation had forced him to put it aside. Now, although still in the laminar air-flow room, he picked up his felt marker and his pad and resumed work on the "Adventures." This edition, entitled "The Great Race," was a gripping thirty-three-page cartoon drama starring Dr. Dowling and featuring those other Memorial notables, Dr. Burchenal, Mrs. Livingston, Bruno the newspaperman, Ralph the Camel, and others. The plot was based on an imaginary letter from the National Cancer Institute in Washington challenging Memorial to compete in a race. N.C.I.'s competitor was to be none other than the famous Dr. Delano Merriwether, in real life a Fellow at the Cancer Institute and a track star who had recently appeared on the cover of *Sports Illustrated*.

In response to the challenge, Eric's story shows Dr. Clarkson calling an immediate meeting of the Memorial brass. It is finally determined that the hopes of Ewing Eight rest with "the Harvard flash," Monroe Dowling. Since Dr. Dowling is "a bit on the soft side," a crash program, including gut-protocol drugs, is begun to get him in shape. At the last moment, because of the drugs, he is stricken with diarrhea and unable to run. The crowds are assembled in the stands. Dr. Merriwether is ready and confident. The honor of Ewing Eight is at stake. Ralph the Camel suddenly arrives on the scene and is called upon to substitute. There is a hurried search for size 19 track shoes, and Ralph, although nervous, manages to win the race—by an ear—and save the day.

About the time Eric finished this epic, his doctors decided to let him go home for a week. Two more weeks of intensive consolidation in the laminar air-flow room awaiting him after the break.

Sidney drove in alone to pick him up—I didn't want to draw the smallest fire—and he told me later that Eric had been stunned almost into panic by the outside world. Every taxi horn, every brake screech made him flinch. The wild traffic roaring up First Avenue—the same traffic he himself had negotiated casually just a few months before—terrified him. But the next day, on slightly wobbly legs, Eric walked the block to our beach with his father. Sidney skipped rocks while Eric bent over and began taking tiny steps along the water's edge.

"It took me a minute to realize he was *running*—trying to run, anyway," Sidney said afterward. "He looked like a little, very, very old man."

Three days later he was well enough to make the two-and-a-half-hour drive alone up to college to have dinner with his soccer coach and see his friends. On March 29 he went back into Memorial for consolidation. More CA and TG. More everything. He survived. On April 12 he was released. Finally and forever, I thought, released.

Did I really think "forever"? In my need I did. Eric had paid his dues. From a persistent, naïve, leftover belief in Justice, I felt, more than thought, he's safe. My "logic" came from years of public school and parental teaching. Virtue, Rightness, and Fairness eventually triumph. There was also the mosaic logic of my black and gold Edmund Dulac fairy tale book where the handsome prince always overcame a thousand obstacles in story after story. In one he falls under a spell; then the princess (translate "nurse") snatches his heart from the witches' caldron and saves him at the last possible moment. In another I saw Eric, like the prince, descending to the very doorstep of hell, fighting his way past every dragon, finally wrestling Death himself and putting him down. It was a glorious four-color illustration inside my head. I had witnessed it all with my own eyes. It seemed a real and personal victory. I forgot that Death does not die.

And Eric helped me forget. Three days after he was released from Memorial he went up to the high school track to run a mile or so. Our local newspaper, which had carried the stories of his battle for life, sent a photographer over to the field. The next day Eric's picture appeared on the sports page captioned "Back in Stride." From then on the weight and strength returned rapidly. Within weeks he was running ten to fifteen miles a day.

In May Eric was offered the job of head counselor at the inner-city camp where he'd worked two summers before. Originally known as NEON, a local Economic Opportunity project partly supported by the U.S. Government, the camp now had a doubtful

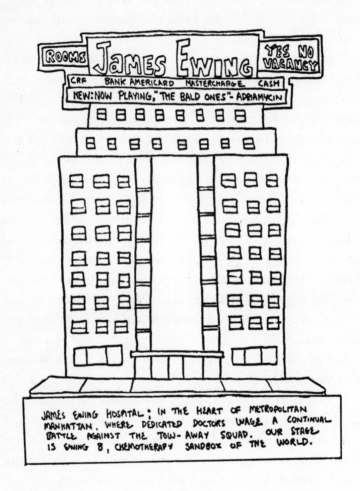

Page 1 of *The Adventures of Ewing 8,* "The Great Race"

Page 11 of "The Great Race"

WITHIN MINUTES THE ENTIRE CAST IS ASSEMBLED IN THE EWING 8 CONFERENCE ROOM. AFTER EVERYONE HAS SETTLED DOWN, DR. CLARKSON PROCEEDS TO READ THE MYSTERIOUS LETTER (AS FOLLOWS:)

TO: C.R.F. EWING 8 C/o DR. BAYARD CLARKSON
FROM: NATIONAL CANCER INSTITUTE

GENTLEMEN:

WE AT THE NATIONAL CANCER INSTITUTE HAVE ALWAYS ENJOYED A SENSE OF FRIENDLY COMPETITION WITH YOU, OUR ASSOCIATES IN NEW YORK. IN CONTINUING WITH THIS SPIRIT WE WISH TO MAKE A PROPOSAL: FOR THE HONOR OF OUR RESPECTIVE INSTITUTES, WE CHALLENGE YOUR TOP MAN TO MEET OUR TOP MAN [DR. DELANO MERRIWETHER] IN A RACE TO BE RUN ONE MONTH FROM TODAY. IF YOU SHOULD DECIDE TO ACCEPT WE WILL CONTACT YOU ABOUT SUCH DETAILS AS RULES, DISTANCE, ETC. WE HOPE YOU BOYS IN NEW YORK ARE CAPABLE OF MAKING A RESPECTABLE SHOWING.

SINCERELY,

THE NATIONAL CANCER INSTITUTE

Page 12 of "The Great Race"

Page 18 of "The Great Race"

Page 21 of "The Great Race"

Page 27 of "The Great Race"

future owing to a cutback in federal funds. But our town, feeling the need was still there, was going ahead and raising funds on its own. As it turned out, Eric and several others, using NEON guidelines for procedure, finally went out themselves and found the boys who wanted to come. By June he was making dozens of phone calls a day, lining up volunteers and paid workers to staff the camp. He talked to women in the neighborhood who might help with transportation and lunch programs, to other interested adults who could help with crafts, art projects, or coaching various sports. He talked to his own friends, who called often about the paying jobs.

"But I'm not picking just my friends," he told his father. "Some of them, yes, but not all. I'm not even picking my own brother this year. I'm just trying to get the guys who I think will be the very best for each spot."

We all took dozens of incoming calls from hopeful applicants, too.

"Hullo. Who dis? You tell Eric I coming, pliz?"

"Who's *this?*"

"Wilfredo García de la Rosa. You tell Eric?"

"Wilfredo, spell your name slowly, please. What's your phone number? Not so fast, Wilfredo. Once more, please. Now, how old are you?"

Eric sat at his battered old desk, keeping track of everything, doing his organizing. He had gained back all the weight he'd lost. He was busy, happy, full of purpose. Camp was to start on Tuesday, July 6, the day after the long traditional holiday.

Operation July Fourth was launched that Sunday. Eric had sent out an announcement to forty or fifty of his friends which read, in part: "*The Fourth of July Gala Bash*—The same people who brought you the 3rd Annual New Year's Eve Gala Bash cordially invite you to participate in all-night festivities to be held on Fish Island, commencing at 12 noon, July 4th, and ending in time for the 4th Annual New Year's Eve Gala Bash."

Eric's New Year's Eve parties had become famous. He'd never let anything stand in their way in the past few years, and each year they'd grown bigger. He might be just out of the hospital or on his way back. He might have low hemoglobin, a dubious white count, and a few side effects from drugs. But he loved to entertain his friends, and he got "psyched up," as he put it, at the thought of a party, much as he did at the prospect of a big soccer contest. The "3rd Annual," six months ago, had put over a hundred guests and a six-piece band—the band arriving in a truck with their own organ and a full set of drums—in our house for the better part of two days. Sidney and I usually tried to be somewhere else, preferably a thousand miles away, at the time. So far, the police had never been called, and all the guests had lived through each event. I always arrived home expecting to find the place looking like a saloon in the movies after there's been a shoot-out between the bad guys and the sheriff. But everything would be immaculate. Once Eric confessed he'd had to take a quick course in antique restoring before I got home. "But look around, Mom," he boasted. "See if you can tell what got broken." I never could find it.

The Fourth of July invitations listed a minute-by-minute schedule of events and concluded with this note: "This will be an all-night, all-weather party. Sign out for an all-nighter and don't come if you're not psyched. Remember, only you can prevent mediocrity. Awards will be given for outstanding individual and group performances."

The Fourth dawned hot and beautiful. I went down to our beach around noon and sat on a rock to watch the start of things from afar. The expedition seemed to be involving at least as many boats as were used during the evacuation from Dunkirk. Anything that could float, sail, or be towed by Eddie Kline's Boston Whaler was immediately loaded to the gunwales with kegs of beer, bottles of wine, and the dozens of former half-gallon milk cartons which had been making blocks of ice in our freezer for days. There were hampers and picnic baskets, sleeping bags and rolled blankets, pretty girls and teddy bears. Many of Eric's friends were the soccer players who'd given blood and sweated out his long recovery in the laminar air-flow room last winter. Now Eric ran among them, as brown and strong and glowing as the rest. What could there be in the bones of one that differed from the others? Watching him, I relaxed. He must be safe at last. This was a day to celebrate.

The following afternoon the happy, sunburned survivors of the bash staggered ashore, bringing back all their trash neatly segregated in plastic bags and cartons. Immediately they ran afoul of our local association's beach director, who tried to refuse them permission to bring outside refuse to our sacred trash cans. Eric pointed out that they could just have dumped it overboard and let it float up on the beach, where it would then qualify. Those kids are ahead of their time, I thought. They realize that your trash is my trash is our trash. I was pleased to see them outtalk the authorities at last and stack their rubbish where it belonged, alongside our own garbage.

Eric got the day camp started off on the right foot the next morning. He told his assistant, Jay, to take over at noon for he had to keep an appointment at Memorial's outpatient clinic. The July evening was still warm and bright when he returned. We were having supper out on the porch. I heard the car door slam and soon Eric appeared in the dining room doorway, standing tall and straight, looking right at me.

"I'm sorry to have to tell you this—" His voice was husky but he kept going. "I know how hard it is for you when I'm sick. They want me back in the hospital as soon as they've got a bed. I'm out of remission. They knew it last week when they did the bone marrow. But they didn't tell me. They didn't want to spoil my Fourth of July party."

Tears glinted in his eyes but did not fall. I watched his dignity, his sweetness, his courtesy throughout that evening as he called the adults in charge of the camp to tell them he must resign, called the young men he'd hired to tell them how to take over. Several times I saw him struggle for control.

Later that night I went into the back of my bedroom closet. I can still feel the heavy towel I stuffed against my mouth and bit with my teeth, so he wouldn't hear me. I hadn't known I could make sounds like that.

We had progressed along the drug trail. Now we were ready for something called adriamycin and something else called 5-HP.

"A Greek goddess and an insect spray," I said to Sidney. "Well, that ought to do it. The goddess adriamycin can work the miracle first. And then 5-HP can kill all the little bastards dead." But not all. Never all. That was the trouble. How brilliant and sneaky were those last leukemic cells, hiding out in some remote spot in the body like guerrillas, just waiting for a letup in the battle to strike again. I lost my hope that summer.

And Eric lost his hair. In one afternoon. The goddess adriamycin took it as a sacrifice. I was there the day it began to happen. Eric sat with me out in the lobby, which was unusually deserted. His tan had already turned sallow, his eyes were gray-shadowed with drugs. He pulled a tuft from his head, then another, and stared at the red-dish-gold clumps in the palm of his hand.

"It's all going," he said. His mouth trembled slightly. He touched it with two fingers to make it stop.

"Maybe not," I said stupidly.

"Of course it is."

He was right. I had seen too many hairless souls walking these halls with their I.V. hat racks to dispute him. Soon he would be one of them.

"I've been thinking, uh—" He stopped.

"Yes?"

"If it doesn't work this time, uh—maybe . . . well, maybe I just want to come home."

I waited. Was he telling me he wanted to come now? Asking me if I could take it? Dying at home is better in some ways for some patients. But it is always hard on a family. You don't know what's coming. And you can't walk away—not for a single minute.

I said at last, "Do you want to come home now? If you do, I'm ready. It's all right with me." I didn't like the way I'd said that. The words had come out wrong.

Eric flashed me a look of anger. It thrilled me! He looked so much more alive than he had just a moment before.

"You think I'm through fighting? Well, you're wrong! God, you make me angry!"

"I'm sorry." I wasn't, though.

"I'm not ready to give up. I know that now. I'm glad you said that." He gave me another scathing look.

"All right." He got up, suddenly full of energy from somewhere. "Maybe that's what I needed. Don't count me out!" he said. "The fight's not over yet. Remember that."

He turned on his heel and walked away without saying good-bye. He was pushing his I.V. stand so angrily and vigorously I could hear it clattering all the way down the hall.

The next day one of Eric's oldest friends, a warm, lovely, com-forting girl named Barbara, visited him at the hospital and helped him shave his head.

"I'm not walking around with a few foolish wisps," he said. "All or nothing."

I'd had wild thoughts of different ways to salvage his vanity. Hats? Hairpieces? But he was right. Baldness had honest style. I'd been afraid of the skull. Now it seemed to me to have a purity and beauty. And his features appeared more defined, sharp yet sensitive. His eyes told more. When he came home on infrequent passes, however, he ran into some neighborhood flak. I suppose it was to be expected. An older man, a friend who might have been expected to know better, asked him if he'd shaved his head because he'd become a religious nut. Then I heard a couple of little children, maybe six- or seven-year-olds, turn to Lisa one day as Eric appeared and say, "Hey, is that your brother? He looks funny with no hair. How come? Is it because he has leukemia?"

Lisa looked upset. But Eric just said lightly, "That's right, that's the story, men," and tossed a basketball at them. "Here—catch!"

But one day he came home from the high school track where he'd been trying to work out (for he still kept on trying), and he was both elated and furious.

"I nearly dropped two guys just now," he said. "They got on

me about my bald head. 'Hey, Baldie! Watcha tryin' to prove?' Man, I was ready to flatten somebody. There were two of them, but I could have taken them both."

"So what happened?"

"Mr. King stuck his head out of the gym. That ended that."

(Mr. King was Eric's former high school coach, a man he loved and respected. "I'd jump off a bridge for Mr. King," he said once.)

He was never out of the hospital long that summer, and his friends, worried about him, tried to visit him more often. They were shocked by his thinness, his baldness. One day a couple of them hailed the wrong guy in the hall, thinking it was Eric. He was a man of about fifty, gaunt, bald, leukemic. I'd nearly made the same mistake myself. From the back they looked too much alike, these prisoners of the disease, victims of the drugs they had to endure. Eric, coming out of the ward just then, caught his friends in their error. They were embarrassed. To relieve them, he launched into a comic takeoff on Coach Morrone's probable reaction to having a totally bald captain show up for the fall soccer season. It was well known that Morrone gave no quarter in the short vs. long hair controversy. Either you cut off your locks or you didn't make the team.

"All right, Lund," drawled Eric in Coach Morrone's voice. "You're putting me on and now you've gone too far. When I said I wanted it cut off, I didn't mean *all* off. Lund, I want you to grow that hair!"

Days blurred, that summer. The swings were too violent. Sudden ups followed by sudden downs. He seemed to be making it. He seemed to be dying. Perhaps because they knew his time was running out, the doctors began to be more lenient, gave him frequent short passes.

Since the afternoon he'd turned on me in fury when I asked if he'd like to come home, Eric stayed out of my way and rarely told me his plans. One morning, about eleven o'clock, I went upstairs thinking the house was empty, and suddenly he appeared around a corner, naked, dripping, a towel half round his middle. His eyes burned me. He might have been an Apache savage, with a feather at the back of his bald skull, looking for someone to scalp.

I screamed.

He looked grimly pleased. "Didn't know I was home, did you?"

"No. I'm sorry."

"Don't be. I planned it that way. My life is my affair, remember?"

And your death? I thought. Can you shut me out of that, too? Tell me it's none of my concern? His comings and goings exhausted me. Hardest of all was organizing my own feelings. Was this the end? Or the beginning of another round? How long did I have to hold on? Appropriately, I dreamed that I was hanging from a window ledge, terrified of the drop below, feeling my arms aching, growing weaker. They still ached when I woke, especially my elbows. I couldn't pour coffee, I couldn't open windows most of that summer.

Sidney and I spelled each other visiting, as usual. We weren't always welcome, but we found we couldn't let too many days go by without going in to see how he was.

One day when Sidney went in, he and Eric began discussing the construction work on the new Memorial Hospital which dominated the view from Eric's window in Room 830. Its steel skeleton was complete and the structural floors were in. But up through this transparent lattice ran a huge vertical stack.

"What do you think that is?" Eric asked.

Sidney said he thought it was the chimney for a boiler or some kind of incinerator.

"No," Eric said. "It's a rocket launcher. They can't get money for hospitals any more except through the Pentagon budget. And the generals only okay the ones where they can conceal missile installations. Every hospital being built in this country has to have a secret rocket launcher because the Pentagon insists."

Sidney, a bit shaken, looked at Eric. Eric didn't smile. It was one of the few instances where some bitterness came through. I recall one other, during the second year of his illness when his first good friends had died on Ewing Eight. He was reading the *New York Times* one day at home. A big headline, upper right, told of billions just appropriated by Congress for a new experimental fighter-bomber. A smaller headline, lower left, told of cutbacks in funds for cancer research and also basic research in metabolic studies. "How can they do that?" he cried. "Don't they know what's going on? I feel like writing the president."

How indeed? I thought. The war is on the eighth floor, all the eighth floors. Here is the enemy who can cross any border, pick any lock, crack any defense. I felt sad, helpless. There was nothing I could say to him.

Not long after that, Eric went out on pass with two friends in the city. They walked about twenty blocks up to Carl Shurz Park. On the way back his nose began to bleed. He sat down on a curbstone and held his nose while his friends watched for a downtown bus. (Why not a taxi, for God's sake? I thought, hearing the story later.) Finally the bus came. The three of them made it back to Memorial just before the whole thing got out of control. Blood all over the hall.

Yet a week later he'd pulled out of trouble and he came home and went water-skiing off our beach. Water-skiing! I watched him come in, thin, wet, hollow-eyed but still strong, and walk by me without a word. He went upstairs to take a shower and suddenly I thought, "Goddammit, why are you walking around when you are dead?" It was the lowest point I ever reached. I understood all the thousand reasons why he had to seem to reject me. Hell, say it—he *did* reject me. But understanding it was one thing; anger was another. Finally I was able to look my anger in the eye. He was already destroyed, and by living on, he was destroying us. Or so it seemed.

Overnight he became gravely ill. His temperature rose to 105, then 106, and stayed there. They brought refrigerating machinery into the ward and laid him on a mattress pad of ice coils. His face grew gray, his teeth chattered. My anger vanished as swiftly as it had come. His defenses disappeared as if they'd never been.

"Hold my hand," he whispered, eyes closed.

This was love, sitting here through the blazing afternoons of early August, holding Eric's cool fingers in mine. This was peace, to be needed in this small way, at last. I was ready to sit forever.

CHAPTER 20

THE DOCTORS DID NOT think he could last. His marrow was full of all the wrong cells. But they pushed on. And Eric held on, even got a little better, to their surprise. There were many days of this simple hand holding, sitting beside the bed. Sometimes he wanted another pillow under his head; he was able to look around, talk a little.

Across the ward, in the opposite bed, a friendly bald man in his early forties tried to cheer Eric on. He'd survived the same drug course, adriamycin, 5-HP; now the doctors were giving him a rest. At the moment he was feeling pretty good.

"You've just got to ride it out, Eric. You'll make it."

"I know." Eric managed an exhausted smile. "Jerry—do something for me?"

"Sure, Eric, what?"

"See if Dr. Dowling is cooking out. I want to know how his steak is coming along."

"Lemme see—" Jerry stood up on his bed and peered out the big window. It was possible to look down on the terraces of some apartments across the way. The ward liked to think they could keep track of Dr. Dowling's barbecue activities.

"Yeah, he's cooking out. But I think he's overdoing it." This was pure speculation, part of the game.

Eric groaned. "What a waste! Imagine being up for a steak and pulling a bummer."

"I like it rare myself." Jerry looked as if he could use a steak. He was still standing on his bed, his pajamas almost falling off his thin body.

"Jump around a little, Jerry, while you're up. Somebody around here ought to be working out."

Jerry obligingly did a few jumps on his mattress. At that moment, a tiny gray-haired lady with a bandaged throat paused in the doorway of the ward to admire him. Seeing Eric with his head raised, she held up two fingers in a V and blew him a kiss. He smiled, gave her a victory sign back.

"Who's that?" I'd seen this little person walking vigorously up and down the hall.

"Mrs. Hardy. She's a wonderful woman. We've had some great conversations. She's got thirteen grandchildren. Go talk to her, why don't you?" Eric was tired. He pushed away the extra pillow. I took it and his eyes closed immediately.

I walked down the hall and found the tiny lady by the window. "Mrs. Hardy? I'm Eric's mother."

Her smile was radiant and quick. She whipped out a pad, one of those magic erasable ones with a plastic sheet on top, and began to write.

My God, he didn't tell me she'd had her larynx removed! He just said, "We've had some great conversations." Well. I was a bit staggered. I should have known from the bandage.

Now she was showing me what she'd written. "He looks a little better today. That's good! He's such a wonderful boy, friendly, personable."

It took me a moment to get organized to "talk" this way. My

first impulse was to shout. But there was nothing wrong with her ears. She just didn't have a voice.

"He says you've got thirteen grandchildren."

Mrs. Hardy started to laugh. It turned into a choke which frightened us both. She had to be careful how she breathed. And she didn't have anything left to laugh with really—just spirit. When she recovered she began to write again.

"He exaggerates. I've got eight. But maybe I can hope for thirteen."

We discussed her children. Three married. Two still at home in New Jersey.

"I've got two at home, too."

"All this must be very hard for you."

She was sympathizing with me!

"Well—sometimes. Eric wants so much to be in charge of his destiny. Sometimes he confuses me with the enemy."

"Because he's afraid of his own emotions," she scribbled.

"Yes, of course. Part of him wants to put his head in my lap and howl for help."

"You understand!" she wrote.

"I think he's quite a man," I said. We were looking down at people crossing the street eight floors below. "Even lying in bed in here, he's more of a man than many who are walking down there below."

"You have said it now!" Her face was bright as she wrote. What is beauty? I could see that her lips were beginning to swell as the cancer spread on. Her cheeks were slightly swollen. Yet she was beautiful to me.

"Have to do my lengths—up and down." She put the pad away.

"Good for you!" We held hands hard a moment; then she set

off almost gaily down the hall. We never spoke of *her* problems, I thought, walking back to the ward.

That night on my way out I was stopped by a tall, pretty black girl. Thin. Bouncy. She had on a short Memorial smock over her miniskirt. On the collar there was a name pin with some sort of title underneath.

"Hi! You Eric's mother?"

"Yes."

"I'm Jackie."

"Hello, Jackie. I can't read your title from here but I see you've got one."

"I'm the Recreation Director."

"What's the recreation for tonight?"

"I'm passin' out halves of jigsaw puzzles." She gave me an impish smile. "That's all there is tonight, folks." She giggled.

"That's all there is most nights," I said. "Who ever puts the whole picture together anyhow?"

"You've got it!" Jackie began doing a little dance step as she waited for the elevator. It was crowded when it came, but we managed to squeeze in and ride down together.

You're getting the hang of it, I thought the next afternoon, riding up once again, getting out once more on Ewing Eight. You can get used to anything. I remembered the very earliest days when I seemed to move through this floor in a protective veil, not seeing the wreckage around me, seeing only Eric, and seeing, too, with some pride, that he was not like the others. It was W. Murphy who had first helped me pierce the veil. Mrs. Hardy and others had followed. As I became involved with their lives, and some of their deaths, as I began to accept that Eric was really here, there was no turning back. And now there is no way *not* to see. It's as if I had no eyelids.

Here's the lady with the gigantic arm, like a burst sausage, that she carries tenderly around on a pillow. Here's the frail black man who always sits painfully half off his chair. (Wonder what's *his* problem?) And here's the hairless girl. Ah. Have I really, will I ever become used to her?

When I first saw her I could not tell who or what this might be. A creature in a wheelchair. Almost a skeleton and yet so active. (Many of the dying are restless. If they can move at all, they keep moving. It's as if to sit or lie down might be to fall out of the procession, never to rise again. If they can do nothing else, they may just stand in a doorway.) She—it *was* a she, tiny, shrunken, hairless, missing one leg from the knee down—was a teen-ager. Zipping around in her chair, her little claw hands pushing the wheels frantically, her bare stump protruding from a short, stiff hospital gown that sat like a tent on her bony frame. I was there the afternoon she asked an intern for change. She wanted to telephone. I was there while she dialed, straining out of her chair to reach the numbers. I was listening when she began to cry and said, "You've got to come. Somebody's got to! I'm dying! And I'm not hanging up, I'm not getting off this phone until one of you says you'll come—"

But there she is sitting next to the lady with the arm, across from the black man. They are still here today, and I raise my hand in greeting to them all as I go by on my way to Eric's ward. The striped curtains are pulled around his bed. Two pairs of white trousered legs showing. Doctors doing something. Back out to the lobby to wait. Not many visitors today. A lovely summer afternoon.

Ten minutes later I got up and headed for the ward again. An aide stopped me. Her face was serious.

"You got something on your pants."

I shrugged. But she was insistent. I twisted around to see. Dark brown all down the back of one beige leg. Chocolate, I thought? Then almost laughed out loud. What a puritan the mind is, taken by surprise, grabbing at the first euphemistic explanation! That's shit, honey. Eric told you, remember? This is "the floor of the deep shit."

"Uh—is there somewhere I can go?"

"I'll show you. The nurses' bathroom."

Someone was there ahead of me. A stout lady puffing and fuming, scrubbing at the backside of her printed jersey dress as best she could.

"Oh, my! You, too!" she gasped. "Isn't this the most terrible thing? I'm so embarrassed. Oh, what if my son saw me! I hope he didn't see me!"

Her prissiness annoyed me. *Shit*, lady, I wanted to say. This isn't the worst. Some poor bastard whose guts were riddled with drugs couldn't make it to the john. He let go in the lobby. You and I haven't got his problems. We're in clover. I pulled off my slacks and looked at them. Then I ran warm water in the basin next to the open window. Standing there in bikini underpants, feeling the afternoon sun warm on my stomach as I washed my slacks, I felt drowsy, almost happy. I might have been at a beach. Outside people were walking around free under the blue sky. I could see the flashes of summer dresses, the bright dots of children scampering on the sidewalk. It seemed astonishing that life was going on out there while I stood here, a million miles away, in the nurses' bathroom on Ewing Eight. How lucky was I that I hadn't worn my white linen skirt today! Happiness is putting on 100-percent Dacron slacks the day you're going to sit in shit. Another lucky thing—the fine hot weather. My wet slacks felt cool when I finally put them back on. Everything turns out for the best in this best of all possible worlds. I went back to the ward where Eric lay with eyes closed, shivering on the ice blanket. He gave me his hand once again. By six o'clock my slacks had stopped feeling clammy. Again, what luck! They'd dried just in time, for the moment had come to go out and get something to eat.

The next day, driving on a road only three or four miles from home, a road I've driven many, many times over the last fifteen years, I suddenly didn't know where I was. I looked around nervously but I was completely lost. The houses, the trees, looked totally unfamiliar. I might have been in Massachusetts or Ohio instead of Connecticut. I was, in fact, in still another state—that of complete fatigue. Emotionally and physically I was going over the edge. The car, like a faithful horse, seemed to know all the turns and got me home all right. I stopped at stop signs, waited for little children to cross, did all the right things. But I knew I couldn't go on much longer when the same thing happened again several days later. There had to be some change, some break in the long strain.

One afternoon, soon after I'd been lost twice several miles from home, I walked into the ward on Ewing Eight and found Eric sitting up in bed looking 100 percent better. A nurse with dark curly hair and a deep tan was twirling around beside his bed, laughing and talking to him.

"Look who's here!" said Eric, obviously pleased.

I didn't recognize her.

"Don't you know me?" She laughed.

"MaryLou!" Those light blue eyes, suddenly seemed to jump out of her beautiful tan face. "It's just that I've never seen you with a tan before, that's all."

She'd been on vacation. She was working in another hospital now, but occasionally she still did private duty at Memorial. She'd heard Eric was back in and decided to stop by and say hello.

During the next few weeks Eric let it be known that he didn't need—didn't want—visitors. We were a bit slow to get the message. His father went in twice and found him out on pass. He was improving nearly every day, and no one knew exactly why. It was beyond reason and beyond the odds. In the bed directly across from Eric, the bed where he'd once jumped around and tried to watch Dr. Dowling's cookout, Jerry Parker lay dying. He had been on almost exactly the same drugs as Eric. He had seemed to respond to them well for a while. Suddenly they were failing him. He did not have long to live. Yet Eric was out running around the city some-where.

I remember thinking, vaguely, well, maybe he's going to par-ties. Maybe MaryLou's introduced him to someone nice. She was a few years older than he, I knew, so I imagined she herself was out of reach, too sophisticated, too sought after.

A day or so after her visit, Eric was having more or less the same thoughts. (All of this I learned much later, of course.) He went to see his friend Susan, the chemotherapy research assistant on Ewing Eight. Susan had, some time ago, appointed herself Eric's fairy godmother. To prove it she'd even bought him a pair of pink bed socks (they were really shoe bags, for no store carries man-size pink bed socks) because, as she said, "Everybody knows a fairy godchild has to have pink feet." Most of Eric's and Susan's friendship had developed in the Ewing Eight laundry room. They would tack up a sign, "Please Knock Before Entering" (written with black marker on a Chux disposable bed pad), and then sit down on the floor—Eric in his pajamas, Susan in her Memorial smock over a miniskirt—and talk about life and death and friendship and what mattered and what didn't. The nurses' aide coming to get clean sheets would knock respectfully, then open the door. "May I come in?" Eric and Susan would look up, say, "That's all right," and stop talking. The nurses' aide would hurry to take what she needed and get out. Then the conversation would resume.

Now Eric, in the laundry room, said to Susan. "Look—do you think an older woman could like me? She's not a lot older. I mean, do you think she might like to go out for a walk with me, for instance?"

Susan, who is not at all slow and who had been watching the approach of this question on the horizon for several days, regarded him with wry friendliness through her dark-rimmed glasses. "Why don't you ask MaryLou and find out, Eric?"

But that afternoon Susan, like a true fairy godmother, decided to take matters in her own hands and speed things along. She went upstairs to Ewing Nine where MaryLou just happened to be working a private-duty shift. They had never met, but Mary-Lou was not too hard to find; Eric had been describing her in some detail for days. Susan introduced herself. Then she said, "You know, we're all out of pajama bottoms down on Eight, and Eric needs some. Have you got any up here?"

"I don't know," MaryLou said innocently, "but I'll see. If I find some I'll bring them down."

• • •

There was a walk in Central Park. There was a lot of laughing. There was talking for hours, sitting by the fountains in front of the Plaza. And there was the moment at last when MaryLou leaned forward and kissed Eric.

"Oh," he said shyly. "I was just going to do that myself."

"Eric!" said MaryLou, suddenly having a second thought. "What's your white count?"

"Nine hundred," said Eric.

"Oh, my goodness! I shouldn't even be touching you, much less kissing you!" MaryLou drew back, alarmed: 5,000 to 10,000 is the normal white count; below 1,000 there is always danger of infection from something.

"Don't worry, MaryLou," said Eric. "I'm sure I won't get sick from kissing you." Then he sighed peacefully. "It's such a relief, though, to be with someone who understands the situation."

They never had much time, but they used it well. There was no looking back, and not too much looking ahead. "Tomorrow is a long way off, MaryLou," Eric often said to her. And so they lived out the hours gently, tenderly. With a great deal of laughing, too—so much, in fact, that Eric remarked wryly, "The trouble with this girl is she never smiles." They knew how good it was. Perhaps they knew, too, but never said, it could not last.

One night—it was about the middle of September—they were about to order dinner when Eric suddenly began to feel very dizzy. They left the restaurant and went straight back to the hospital. It was a foretaste of what was to come.

275

A few days later Eric asked for another pass. By now his doctors knew, even if we didn't, that he was dating a certain pretty nurse. And a very good nurse at that. So it was easier to grant him passes than if he'd been going out with a librarian. (MaryLou by this time had given up all work at Memorial and gone to another hospital. A professional who falls in love with a patient finds it wise to put some distance between her working life and private life.)

Eric arrived at MaryLou's apartment before she'd gotten home. Her roommate, Judy, who'd just begun her own training to be a nurse, let him in. Eric had only time enough to say, "Judy! Hold me!" Then he fell unconscious, his back arching, limbs flailing, to the floor. The terrified Judy did her best. It wasn't easy. Eric was her first patient. He was very strong. The brain seizure was violent.

Describing it to us when we visited him the next day, Eric downplayed the whole thing. "Had a little incident yesterday," he said. "Just something to break up the old routine. I went out on pass waving good-bye to everybody. Twenty minutes later I came back in on the ambulance stretcher waving hello."

I wasn't satisfied with this. "Eric, what exactly happened? Where were you, anyway? And who were you with?" It was the first time I'd really put it to him.

"Well—" He had a very small smile, shy and proud. "You see, I've been seeing a lot of someone—"

"Yes?"

"It's MaryLou." He told me all about everything. And he couldn't stop smiling. "It's so great," he said. "It just gets better and better—"

"Oh, God, that's wonderful!" I cried. "But why didn't you tell us before!"

"MaryLou was afraid you'd disapprove."

"Disapprove! Good heavens, why? I think she's a lovely girl."

"I know. I told her that the problem with you was that you'd overreact."

"Hmm. I see."

We smiled together at this.

"Would you like to bring her out to the house sometime? I mean, I'll try to fix it up a little—"

"I want to bring her out on my next pass if she can get off," said Eric. "I'd really like that."

"Get well, then," I said as I left.

Our upstairs was a terrible shambles from three years of little money and no decorating. I'd recently heard Lisa, showing a friend around, saying, "—and this is our dog's bedroom," as she came to our so-called guest room.

"It looks like a dog's bedroom," remarked the friend.

I bought a remnant of gold shag carpet. I found a black and gold Spanish bedspread for half price. It was marked "Defective" but I never found the defect. I moved a little antique table upstairs from the living room to make a dressing table. A friend gave me two lamps, and I found an old mirror in the attic. We were in business; we had a guest room. But the bathroom still looked pretty depressing. So I unscrewed the rusty knobs and began painting the towel cabinets and doors a deep Bristol Blue. I was mixing in witchcraft and magic with that paint. Penelope, not at the loom but over her paint pots. I felt that as long as I went on painting it meant Eric would surely come home. And some day soon he'd bring MaryLou with him.

There was a little magic going on in Eric's own room, too. A brand-new vermilion ten-speed Schwinn racing bicycle stood by his bed. He'd never seen it. He'd ordered it with almost his last savings. "I'm going to get the hell out of here," he said once on Ewing Eight in August. "I'm going home to ride my bicycle to get back in shape."

The irony of his recent troubles with seizures was that a recent bone marrow showed that Eric was once again almost in remission. His doctors were pleased, astonished. But the leukemic cells in his brain were still a concern to them. They were treating him with methotrexate, which sometimes proved helpful in these cases. But Eric's former long months on this drug had possibly left him too resistant to benefit from it. The doctors were watching.

Almost before their eyes he had a second seizure. It happened right in the hall in Ewing Eight while the other patients, many of them his friends, watched in horror. He saw it coming. He tried to lift his hand, say something, warn somebody. There was no way. It was more terrible than the first. He fell writhing, twisting, foaming at the mouth, banging and rolling against the walls and floor. When he came to he was back in bed in the ward. A young doctor, the resident on the floor, was bending over him.

"Eric," he said, "I know how you feel now. Pretty scared. But I'm going to give you some Dilantin to try to make sure this doesn't happen again. I think it will help you. I take it myself. I'm an epileptic, Eric. For a few days we'll give you twice the dose I take. Then we'll taper you down. Okay? Take it easy now."

I thought later how kind, how generous it was of that young doctor to share his own problem with a patient. Look at me, he was saying, I'm going on with my work, my life. You can too.

It was not easy to go on. For the first time, Eric's confidence was deeply shaken. Here was something way beyond his control.

No matter how strong his will, here was something which could strike out of the blue at any time and turn him into a completely helpless victim. Despite the Dilantin, the doctors knew they still had a problem on their hands. Methotrexate had failed. No one knew how effective Dilantin might be over a long period of time. Something new and more drastic had to be tried. They called us to come in that afternoon. Sidney couldn't go, so I took the train.

The ward seemed to be full of agony. Curtains were drawn. People were gasping, retching. I went up to Eric's curtain apprehensively. All was still. After a moment I peered around—then stopped. It was quite a scene. MaryLou sat on Eric's bed kissing him, stroking his bald head, while Eric's right arm, strapped to a board and with I.V. needle in place, patted her tenderly. I'd never seen them together before, except as nurse and patient. All at once they realized I was there. MaryLou jumped up, kissed me, then ran away.

Eric looked pretty flat out, black and blue in places. Still, he also looked happy.

"You better go get MaryLou," he said at last. "She's probably scared."

"She still thinks I'll disapprove?"

"Yes."

I went out and found her. She was blushing, she looked very young, but she had on her nurse's whites, she'd probably just worked an eight-hour stretch in some other hospital, and she was nobody's helpless ingenue.

"I'm trying hard not to overreact, send up sky rockets or Roman candles," I told her. "Eric likes me to be cool. But I don't feel cool. I think it's great."

We hugged each other, then went back to Eric and sat

together for a while. MaryLou started stroking Eric's head again.

"What are those subdivisions they've got staked out on his head?"

Eric's bald head looked like the plot plan of a new real estate development, all marked out with red lines and squares.

"They're going to radiate his brain tomorrow to try to stop the seizures from coming back. Those lines show the radiologists where to shoot."

"MaryLou," Eric said, somewhat groggily, "if they radiate me I'll lose my hair."

"That would be awful," MaryLou said. "Then I wouldn't love you any more."

"How would we ever stand it if you lost your hair?" I said. Then we all looked at each other and began to laugh. For a while we didn't even hear the terrible sounds other people were making around us in that place. We were laughing and happy and brave.

On my way out I met Mrs. Hardy in the hall, still walking up and down, still trying to stay with it. Her legs looked as if they might break. Her nose now had a tube dangling from it. Her lips were huge, rolled back, distorted. But her eyes were bright as ever, and she was right there, alive and eager behind her eyes. She began to write vigorously the minute she saw me.

"We all get so upset when Eric is worse. We saw it coming. Right here this morning. He tried to ask for help. But it was too late. Then afterward he was so scared."

"I know," I said. "They're going to try something new tomorrow. I hope it works."

"If anyone deserves to make it, he does," she wrote. "We're all rooting for him."

What a woman, I thought. I'm rooting for you. A doctor came

up then and got my attention. We moved away. He told me what was planned.

"Will his brain be damaged?"

"Not likely. Almost certainly not," said the doctor. "He may be confused for a while. And the radiation may make him pretty sick."

I saw Eric the next evening after the radiologists had done their work. He looked half out of this world. Blurry. As if he'd had a massive blow. MaryLou was there, sitting on his bed, arm around his neck supporting his head, trying to feed him small bites from a largely untouched dinner tray. She was still in her uniform from a long day's work at the other hospital.

"Want a little of this, honey?"

Eric's eyes rolled away. He brought them back with some effort. "MaryLou? You still here?"

"I'm still here."

The next day I painted the bathroom all day long. It seemed crazy. How was he ever going to get out of that bed? Yet the blue paint kept on flowing. And I kept on thinking, come home, Eric, and see what I've done.

Once I went into his room and stared at that gleaming red bicycle. I thought of little children having their presents in September because they weren't going to live until Christmas. The mad thought occurred to me that maybe we should take the red bicycle in and put it beside his bed in the ward. Would that encourage him, pull him out of this slump? Or would it tell him it's all over?

Instead I took a small jade plant in to MaryLou at the hospital that night. It was an offspring of our grandfather jade tree in the playroom. I also gave her a small sunny snapshot of Eric. "With hair!" she said, pleased. "I've never seen him look like that!"

"Let me see," Eric mumbled, waking up.

She gave it to him.

"That was taken in my youth," he groaned and fell back into half-consciousness.

"He's heavily sedated." MaryLou looked worried. "It isn't good for him, really. But his stomach muscles and his whole chest are still torn and terribly painful from the seizure. The trouble is, he doesn't really want to make the effort to come back."

MaryLou got mad at the patient the next day. She accused him of giving up, deserting her. She let him know how upset and angry she was. And she reached him through his blurriness. That day for the first time he didn't ask for sedatives. He tried to feed himself. He began to look at the fact that he'd been afraid, that he'd been sinking down, running away from the possibility of another seizure. By nighttime he was ready to test himself. He got out of bed and walked slowly to the doorway. He stared out in the hall at the place he'd fallen. Then he walked slowly back and climbed into bed exhausted. But he was all right, he was on his way.

CHAPTER 21

ON OCTOBER FOURTEENTH we learned that Eric had finally achieved and nailed down his sixth remission. He went out on his first pass in a long time. MaryLou was probably as scared as he was. Eric wasn't really put together yet.

"But," he said, "either you live in a box or you take your chances out in the world. I may end up lying in the street, but I'm going."

They went to visit Susan, who was herself recovering from surgery in another hospital. Susan's aunt and uncle were there, and Eric was introduced. He went up to the aunt and said, "Nice to meet you, Uncle Max." Then he turned to the uncle. "How do you do, Aunt Elsie." No, he wasn't all together. He laughed when they laughed, but he didn't know until later what he'd done.

On October 16 Eric was released from the hospital. Dr. Clarkson invited him to attend a Yale-Columbia game that day at Columbia's Baker Field in upper Manhattan. Eric was pleased and honored. He was also frightened at the prospect. Noises, crowded places, people still overwhelmed him. But he accepted the invitation at once.

"How's he going to get home from Baker Field?" I asked Sidney.

"He'll manage. He can take care of himself. He'll just go back down to Grand Central and take a train."

"No," I said. No subway, no buses, no trains. Not yet.

Sidney shrugged. He was always sure Eric could take care of himself. This time I couldn't go along with his view.

"Enough is enough," I said. "Mark, will you take the car in and go get him?" At that very minute Mark had arrived home from Yale for the weekend.

"How's Mark going to find Eric in a place like Baker Field?" Sidney interrupted

"I'll find him. Don't worry, Mom," Mark said. "I'd like to see that game anyway. When it's over I'll bring Eric home."

That evening the front door pushed open—and there they were. Mark, at six feet five inches, with his full head of curls, looked huge and shaggy like a St. Bernard who'd gone out on a rescue mission and come back with a frail, lost traveler. I'd never seen Eric look so small. His eyes were enormous and dark in his pale ivory skull. He looked like a young priest who'd been fasting for days on a wintry mountaintop. But his smile had the sweetness we all knew well.

For a few days he just slept, ate, and walked around our yard looking at things as if he'd never seen them before. "It's so beautiful here," he kept saying.

Looking through his eyes, my own vision improved. Instead of weeds choking the brick path and paint peeling off the carport, I saw the water lily floating like a perfect star in Mark's fishpond. Golden fish darted under the lily pads in clear, still water. I remembered the day Mark, Eric, and Sidney together had dug that pond. What a wreck they'd made of the yard—wheelbarrows and planks, shovels and trowels, cement sacks and gravel. That had been beautiful, too.

Eric was pleased by my efforts to spruce up the place inside.

"You've staged a fourth-quarter rally in this house, Mom."

From him that was praise. Suddenly everything was looking better to me. There might be dents in every door in the upstairs hall (the time Meredith chased Eric with a broom—*slam!* The time Eric chased Mark with a paddle—*slam!*) but there was life on all the walls, life coming in every window. The first rosebush we'd ever planted had climbed to Eric's sill and was clambering over the side of the house to Mark's; the yellow birch was flickering in the sunlight beyond Lisa's curtains. When Meredith lived in that room, the birch had been a baby, four feet tall, tossed aside by a bulldozer over near the beach. Sidney had rescued it, carried it home, and planted it.

We spent those first evenings at home with Eric—for he was just content to be there—enjoying, savoring the house his father had built. Every board was Sidney's work. Our builder had put up only the outside shell. We'd moved in sixteen years ago almost to the day. But then we didn't have any walls inside. We'd found a silvery gray barn on a hill thirty miles away to use for paneling. I remember lying in tall grass and Queen Anne's lace, waving off the bumblebees and watching Sidney high on a ladder taking down the barn nail by nail.

We lived for a long time with the barn boards stacked in the living room, staring at the insulation which said "Gold Bond Rock Wool" over and over on every wall. Sidney worked evenings and every weekend to try to put it all together. When we used to put the children to bed (their rooms had no sides at first), we'd tuck them in and shut the doors, and they'd come right out through the studs. "Hello!" they said. "Good night," we said firmly. "Hello!" they said, laughing.

Now, sometimes, we talked of these things. Sometimes we didn't have to. The silvery gray barn boards were all in place. Outside, the world was holding its breath in the reprieve of October. Reprieve for Eric, too, I thought. He was waiting for MaryLou to finish her week's duty and come out to join him. Yet he was not impatient. I'd never seen him so gentle, so loving, so at peace with the world. It was as if he had entered another time span where minutes, even seconds, could be enjoyed for the quality that each one held.

When Dr. Dowling had called me on October 16 to tell me of Eric's remission, I'd shouted, "Oh, joy. Hallelujah!"

He'd immediately pulled me back to reality. "I'm not sure how long we can keep him there." This was one of the fine things about Dr. Dowling. He could say it hard and true, yet somehow it never seemed cold or cruel to me. I knew very well he was not indifferent.

I'd just said, "I know. I'm not confused. I think I know where we are. I don't expect any real miracles any more. This is miracle enough for now."

And somehow it was true. A conditional miracle. Life for now. ("Tomorrow is a long way off.") I don't mean that Eric or any of us gave up planning altogether. One day he went out shopping and came back with long winter underwear, heavy socks, wool hats. A dashing new denim jacket lined with sheepskin, too. "I'm a two-time loser in the battle of February," he said. "I need to be warm to stay in that ring."

He began riding his red bicycle. Two miles, five miles, ten

miles. "I'm getting there," he said. "I feel stronger." Yet more often than not these days he was happy just to ride around the streets close to home while little boys of all sizes trailed after him on their bikes.

John Bair, Tom Bair, Steve Bair. Peter Ahl and George and Jeff. Billy Wubbenhorst and others. These were his close companions now. The youngest not more than six. The oldest not more than thirteen. On Saturdays he organized them into "hoboes." Each little boy took a peanut butter and jelly sandwich wrapped in a bandanna or a rag and tied on a stick. Eric had his lunch tied on a stick, too. Then they all got on their bikes, with the sticks over their shoulders, and rode off to a secret place in the woods to eat lunch together. Sometimes they had races from the ice cream store to home—about ten blocks. They all had handicaps. John Bair got to go first because he was the smallest. Eric had to go last because he was biggest. Eric couldn't take any shortcuts, either. Then there were the soccer games. If Mark was home, he and Eric would stand all the little boys in the neighborhood. If Eric was alone with them, he picked John or maybe Peter, who was six and was just getting over a broken leg, and took on all the others. "It's not winning that counts," he told them. "It's that we all get to play. Of course," he went on, "I want you all to hang in there and do your best."

Was Eric still hanging in there himself? His quietness was different from his fighting hustle. His gentleness had in it some acceptance, some letting go that I'd never seen before. He was no longer the carefree jock, but he was free of care somehow. I looked at him and saw old paintings of saints.

One afternoon we drove out in the country together looking for a Halloween pumpkin. The days had been warm and windless. Even in late October all the trees were still on fire. Now and then a few leaves drifted down like yellow sparks to lie on the black pavement.

"You know," Eric said quietly, "I may be dead in four months. Or then again maybe they'll come up with something and I'll be cured. But that's not the point. What counts is right now. I've got this day. Look at it—it's so great!" He shook his head in awe and wonder.

I couldn't speak. His quiet happiness and love for the world overflowed and filled me, too. His acceptance gave me my own. I've got this day, I thought. And it's quite a lot.

The moment we'd all waited for came at last. MaryLou was on her way.

"Is she really coming out?" Lisa couldn't believe it. She'd been left out of too many things these past few years, had to hear about them third-hand. True, she had finally paid Eric a few visits in Memorial for the first time that summer. (Her fourteenth birthday in May made her eligible to visit.) When Eric had become ill again in July she'd been determined to go in. I'd wondered if she could take the sights, the smells.

"Mommy, I'm ready! Don't protect me."

She was right. Rising to occasions, Lisa grew stronger. She wanted to become more involved on the eighth floor than I could have guessed.

"Why didn't you introduce me to Mrs. Hardy today? You were talking to her—I saw you—and I was right there," she said one night.

"Well, I wasn't sure—you were ready." I was somewhat used to Mrs. Hardy's no voice and nose tube by now, though I found each new deterioration hard to bear.

Lisa gave me a scornful look. "I'm ready. I'm strong enough. And I know she hasn't any voice. You told me she was a wonderful woman. I want to meet her."

"All right. Next time."

Lisa had met MaryLou just once. "She's like a sister!" she'd said right away. Now she said, "It's like an extra Christmas, having her in our own house." The problem for Lisa and for me was to stand back and let Eric do it all. For he wanted to make all the preparations himself. "When you make a bed for a nurse, it's quite a challenge," he said, pulling the new gold and yellow striped sheets so taut they might have been nailed to the floor. He found the only decent extra blanket in the house, arranged two towels and a washcloth in perfect symmetry on a stand by her bed, then drove off twenty minutes early to meet her train.

Lisa and I, going down later to get some last minute groceries, passed them coming back. Eric was trying to concentrate on his driving. MaryLou was sitting as close to him as she could possibly get, peering into his face, talking excitedly. "I hope they get through the center of town without hitting anything," I said to Lisa.

When we got back MaryLou was established in the biggest chair in the living room, feet up on a hassock, one foot bare. The nurse had vanished. In her place was a teen-ager in striped skinny sweater and blue hiphuggers with butterflies on the knees. Dr. Eric was examining the teen-ager's sore toe.

"This must hurt," he said gently, indicating the new blister.

"Oh, it isn't too bad." She smiled

"Listen, we've got to take care of this. I'll go get the Band-Aids and something to put on it, too.

"She has new shoes," he explained to us as he disappeared upstairs.

"Well, I see who's in charge. Quite a switch!" I said to MaryLou.

She giggled. On her lap was a huge textbook with the title *Intensive Care Nursing*. "My homework," she said, patting it.

Eric came back with gauze pads, scissors, Band-Aids, and bottle of antiseptic. "Now let me have that foot," he said.

The good weather held through most of that fall. Eric took MaryLou out walking through his world. "Here's the tree we always climbed to get mulberries. . . . Here's where I always climbed through the hole in the fence to get to the Little League field. . . . This is the field Danny Rose and I set on fire by accident when we were running down the street with torches. . . . And here's the bridge where Mark had to hang underneath by his hands while the cops were chasing me and Buster for trespassing. Mark couldn't run fast enough to escape with us."

One Friday he took her up to Storrs to the university to meet his friends. It was a proud day and a painful one, too. Eric had never been able to play on the soccer team he'd been elected to lead. Despite his severe illness of the summer, there had been no thought of replacing him, however. "He was our captain," said Mark Kurimai. "That's all there was to it. There wasn't anybody else for the job. What we did was just choose an acting captain for each different game we played."

Even in his hospital bed, Eric had felt a strong responsibility for the team. In August, when he'd seen he wouldn't be able to get in shape in time for the season, he wrote a letter to his coach and another to the team.

This last letter was not only read by the soccer team; coaches of other sports at the university read it to their teams, too, and later it was widely reprinted in a number of New England newspapers. The letter reads, in part:

Dear Everybody,

I've never really had the opportunity to address you as a team. I guess that's one of the things a captain should do. . . . Each of us is affected by what happens to the other. Just as our movements interract on the field, so our lives interract to a certain degree. This is what is so great about being a member of a team. Some organizations present the facade of being a team yet never reach a point where each individual contributes equally to his own personal success and the success of his teammates.

Right now all of you will have to fill in and assume just a little bit more leadership. . . . The sophomores will have to work extra hard not only at learning the game but at learning to work with and accept each other. You should all establish an attitude early in camp . . . of using suggestions instead of criticism, being constructive in what you can offer someone else. These are the things I would be striving to establish if I were in camp now. I've been fortunate in my own athletic career . . . in receiving help and encouragement instead of ridicule and contempt. . . .

I hope all of you have a great pre-season. Believe me, I would give anything to be there with you. I'll be back as soon as possible, so whoever winds up playing center back better work on another position, just to be safe.

It had been a hard letter to write. In spite of the last sentence, he knew it was the end of his sports career, the end, too, of his dream of making All-American—something, the sports writers wrote later, that he surely would have managed in one more season.

Eric had also wanted to enter the Boston Marathon wearing the greens of Memorial Sloan-Kettering Cancer Center with MSKCC on his back. Not as foolish a goal as it might have sounded. During his good times in remissions earlier, he had run from ten to twenty miles a day.

"Do something for me, Eric," I said when I heard about this last hope. "When you enter the Boston Marathon, be sure to beat Erich Segal."

But Eric didn't go in for either putdowns or delusions of grandeur. "Segal's a serious runner," he said. "He works at it a lot. I'm not out to win over anybody. I just want to finish. Then maybe people would notice what goes on in a place like Memorial."

The marathon was out, but there was now. Eric had come home to the campus he loved with a very pretty girl on his arm. He had also been invited to play with his old team in an intersquad game set for the following morning. Mark Kurimai, his teammate and long-time friend, gave Eric and MaryLou his own room to stay in. There was quite a party that night to celebrate his return. The following morning Captain Eric was in no condition to hear the alarm. When he finally looked at the clock, he saw to his horror it said ten—the hour he should have been suited up and already on the playing field. Leaping out of bed, he gathered up some clothes and fled down the stairs, trying to dress as he went. In true vaudeville style, there was one item that began to give him trouble—

MaryLou's bra. Back up the stairs. He tossed it to her, shouting, "I don't need this!" Then, dressing and swearing, he raced all the way to the field house.

Coach Morrone was walking up and down in classic coach fashion. Everyone else was suited up, ready to go. Eric arrived, breathing hard, and all he could say was, "Do you remember when you used to say soccer and women don't mix, Coach? You were right!"

A few moments later MaryLou arrived to see him play. She was terrified. Eric was ten or fifteen pounds below his normal weight. He was still on Dilantin and other drugs. He'd been bicycling, but he hadn't been on a playing field for nearly a year. What if he banged that newly radiated brain against some hardheaded player on the enemy team?

Eric tried a few runs, a few kicks, but the mainstream of the action swept past him. It was a symbolic performance more than anything else. Many in the huge throng of spectators crowding the stands knew what it had cost. Some of them had given blood at Memorial. When he left the field after only ten minutes of play, he was given an ovation.

He said simply, "It felt so good to be out there again." Mary-Lou was glad it was over.

I'd gotten into printmaking that fall and taken a small studio about five minutes from home where I had room to leave my stuff spread out. The rollers and tools, the etching ink, palette knife, and benzene were soothing, serious toys to me. I forgot everything in this different world. Two hours could go by in a flash and I'd never know. Surprisingly, I'd begun to sell some things. Then in November when I sold a children's story I'd written some time ago, I was able to sell twelve pages of illustrations to the art editor to go along with it. The job was somewhat over my head, which was fun and challenging. It took me much longer than it should have. Sometimes I had to dash home in the early evening, my hands still black with etching ink, to rush a chicken into the oven so we'd have something to eat for supper. While I was racing around the kitchen it was reassuring to hear the beat of music pounding down from Eric's room above. (He was on outpatient status now, going in only once a week for tests.)

"What's that Eric's playing? I like it."

Lisa was humming along with it as she poured milk. "'The Beginning.' It's a Chicago record. Eric always plays that one first when he gets in remission and comes home from the hospital."

The Beginning. Forget what you've just been through, start all over. If only it *could* be the beginning. . . .

One evening in early December I was trying to get things cleaned up in the studio, wiping the plate with benzene so I'd be ready to go to work the next day, when there was a knock at my door.

"Mom? Can I come in?"

"Eric!" He'd never come to the studio before on the spur of the moment. He'd been up once and admired it, but it was my working place and he left me alone. "Of course you can come in. I'm so glad to see you."

Inside, in the light, I took another look at him.

He sat down on the piano bench, a slim almost-twenty-two-year-old, in the new sheepskin jacket that was going to help him get through the winter.

He'd been to Memorial that afternoon, he told me. His remission was at an end. MaryLou had decided to quit her job. They wanted to go away together for a Christmas vacation in the sun before his return to the hospital. The doctors had told him he had to be back in by January 3. "Will you help us?" he asked.

Then he leaned his head against me and cried. I hadn't seen him break down like this in all the years of his illness.

Now we both knew he was going to die very soon. There were no more doors to open, no more effective drugs left in chemotherapy's cupboard (well, none that were very good, and we both knew that, too). I held him in my arms and rocked him. His head against my cheek felt like the new baby head I'd held so long ago—warm, with a faint, soft covering of hair, hair just now growing back from the baldness of adriamycin.

Heartbreak. I'd always thought it a tarnished word from the tabloids or old-time movie mags. ("What's the real truth behind Lana's—or Liz's—or Debbie's heartbreak?") But in that moment, holding Eric, I felt the break, literally. The crack was so real it seemed to be something I could see. God help me, I thought. One more moment and we might both be lost if I couldn't hold, if I couldn't find some way to help him go on.

Words Eric had said another time, another place, came back to me. He'd been talking to some nurses about whether or not they should tell leukemia patients what their chances of survival really were. "No matter what you know, or think you know," he'd said to the nurses, "never take away their hope. They need it all the way."

"Eric," I said. "I know you're going to make it. You've got so much to live for. Of course we'll help you. And it's going to be all right. Once you get away with MaryLou, once you get out on that beach and start running again—"

"I know it, I'm sure of it," he said quickly, raising his head. There were tears on his cheeks, but his voice was stronger. "Once I start running, I know I can come back."

He was happy that week getting ready. (MaryLou wouldn't leave her job until a replacement could be found.) He went Christmas shopping. He rode his red bicycle every day. He ran with Sancho along the beach.

One night after midnight, when I went upstairs, a light from Eric's room drew me to the end of the hall. I started to speak, then stopped. He was deep in concentration, beautifully serene, working on a large drawing. When I draw well I always think of ice-skating. Eric was skating now, light, swift, happy strokes. The felt marker, flying along in his left hand, flowed swift and black as if the images in his brain poured from his fingers. Suddenly aware of me, he stopped and looked up.

I said quietly, "May I see it?"

"Okay."

"But it's beautiful!" I was astonished. I knew he loved to draw cartoons, caricatures. But this was something else. An interior landscape, a fantasy of arches, stones, passageways opening into other passageways, intricate and complex as a spider's web. Was there a path leading out? I couldn't find it. Was he looking for the door to escape?

"Would you like to have it?"

"Yes." I was afraid to say more.

296

"When it's finished then." He went back to filling the space in the bottom corner as if he knew exactly what to put there.

"Can I drive you to the train?" I asked on the last day. (Sidney was in Pennsylvania that evening.) There was a midnight party planned that night in the city for Eric and MaryLou. They were to fly from Kennedy the next morning.

"No, thanks. I'll call a taxi."

That's crazy, doesn't make sense, I thought. But it was the old pattern. Independence. Don't take care of me. No good-byes. I hung around all afternoon, hoping Eric would change his mind. I cleaned house a bit, fussed around the kitchen. It was getting dark, almost five, when I finally decided to drive up to my studio to try to work for an hour. Little boys were playing soccer in the nearby vacant lot, laughing and tumbling in the dry winter grass. I recognized John. Tom. Steve. Then I stopped the car to watch a moment, for one was not a little boy. One was Eric.

"Hey, Mom!" he called out, running over. "You still want to take me to the train? About nine?"

"Sure I do. I'll be back in plenty of time."

We left at twenty to nine. But not before he'd shown me the little pile of carefully wrapped presents he was leaving for all of us. (Christmas. The first one without him. Practice for Christmases to come.) He was dressed up. Dark blazer with gold buttons. Shirt and tie I'd never seen before. Not a duffel bag this time, a real suitcase. And a shopping bag bursting with Christmas packages. "Fifteen!" he said, holding it up. "I'm going to give MaryLou a good Christmas for once."

Then just before we left the house he said, "Look at this!" He showed me an envelope with $22 in it. The card said, "Eric and MaryLou—for LIVING! And because you're going to be twenty-two, Eric. Love, Lisa."

"Think of Lisa doing that!" Eric's voice was husky with tears. "That's her money from baby-sitting. She probably had to sit twenty-two hours to do that." He shook his head.

"We'd better go."

Driving to the station, his excitement returned. He was full of plans. He was going to teach MaryLou to swim and jump the waves. She was a little scared of the ocean because she was so near-sighted, but he'd hold onto her and get her over that. We got there just ahead of the train. He swung his bags up on the platform. He looked young, fresh, and happy.

"Don't worry, I'll make it. I'll be ready for them when I come back." He hugged me, bounded up the train steps, and was gone.

He looked so much like the bridegroom, I thought, dazed. I walked slowly back to the car, got in, shut the door. Then I screamed, "No!"

Eric and MaryLou returned December 30. Before he went back to the hospital on January 3, Gala Bash Number 4 took place—a combination New Year's Eve and twenty-second birthday party which lasted four days and which, at its peak, filled our house with nearly a hundred and fifty guests. First there was the party-to-plan-the-party, which began spontaneously the night before New Year's Eve. About fifteen or twenty friends dropped in and made their battle plans. Among other events, they hastily organized a four-town soccer tournament which was scheduled to start the next morning and last all day. Eric, looking a bit wan after the planners left, confided to MaryLou that he wasn't sure he could play very well or very long. Yet next morning he went off with his buddies and we didn't see him again until five o'clock. In the meantime a corps of pretty girls arrived at our house carrying their own pails, brooms, rags, and vacuum cleaners. When they'd finished cleaning the house, they began taking down pictures and mirrors, removing antique lamps and delicate chairs. Shortly after that, other volunteers began arriving with food, drink, ice, records, paper plates, cups, and so forth.

"You know," I said to Sidney, "somehow I don't think they need us." We fled.

It was the "bash of the century," we learned later. By dawn some thirty to forty revelers had decided to sleep right there on couches, benches, outdoor chaise pads, old blankets, new bathroom rugs, and other people's fur coats. When we came back about 2 P.M. on New Year's Day, the survivors were just staggering out into the open for more sports events. More soccer. Basketball, touch football, plain wrestling, and a Frisbee-throwing tournament in which Sancho was declared the winner. For those unable to move there was continuous, never-ending, big-time football on the TV screen in the house. By nightfall we were down to six or eight guests who planned to stay in position to help Eric celebrate his twenty-second birthday the following morning. He was served birthday cake in bed for breakfast. By the evening of January 2 we were back down to just family.

For four days not a moment had passed without someone scrambling eggs, someone pouring a new beer or finishing an old one, someone loading or unloading the dishwasher, making another pot of coffee, putting on another record while someone else turned up—or down—the TV. If Eric had not needed hospitalization before, it is likely he would have required it just to recover from the festivities.

None of the guests except MaryLou, and by this time she was family, suspected that their host was throwing his last epic party. On the morning of January 3 he put on the white turtleneck sweater MaryLou had given him for Christmas, his sheepskin jacket, and a floppy suede hat, and went by me without a glance. It was his custom in such moments. "If you gotta go, go in style."

CHAPTER 22

IT WAS JANUARY BUT THEY called it the "Summer Camp." It was Room 830, the same six-bed ward Eric had been in and out of for three years, but someone had nicknamed it the Summer Camp now because all the occupants were under twenty-five, although some of them looked like tired old men, and almost all of them were far from home and very homesick.

There was a Greek in the bed where Eric had lain shivering last summer. He had only a few wisps of black hair left, and he spent all his time wandering out to the front desk asking about the mail. He never had any visitors.

Next to the Greek, in the middle bed, was Luigi, a cheerful, round Italian who had a young wife and several talkative sisters who visited often. On Luigi, baldness was rather becoming. He looked like a prosperous vegetable merchant. Luigi ordered a full dinner tray every night, but his wife and sisters ate most of it. When you looked closely you saw that Luigi's roundness was the swelling of cortisone. He was nearly as homesick for the Bronx as the Greek was for Greece. Still, he was an optimist and always talked about the future.

"Whatcha gonna do when you get outa this place, Eric?"

"Going into something steady—like aluminum siding. No ups and downs."

On the other side of Luigi lay Ricardo. Little Ricardo, the Puerto Rican who had once played the horses from the Ewing Eight telephone. I hadn't realized he'd survived the winter of 1970. But I wouldn't have recognized him. Ricardo, someone told me, had gotten so lonesome for Spanish Harlem that one day he'd just put on his clothes, walked out of the hospital in the middle of his treatments, and taken a subway home. It hadn't worked out. After a week, Ricardo grew frightened and turned himself in. Now he was too ill to talk.

Across the ward from Ricardo was a Korean boy who couldn't speak a word of English. When the doctors or nurses tried to communicate with him, he just turned his head away and groaned. At least he had a brother who came to see him every other day and brought many little packages. The brother was very flashy, with nail-studded leather jacket and the widest bell-bottoms I'd ever seen. The sick one always improved immediately, sat up, and stopped groaning when he saw his brother appear. Then the two of them would open the packages together and talk in rapid Korean.

In the corner by the door was a beautiful boy named Michael. All the others were young without their youth. Michael still had thick black curls, strong arms, large dark eyes unshadowed by drugs—but the eyes were full of fear. He had never been in the ward before. He tried not to see the terrible things around him, but there was nowhere to look. His girl came often to comfort him and then he seemed happier, staring at her long, shining brown hair, touching it gently with his fingers. His mother and father were often there, too, and the father gave Michael a little silver medallion, the Jewish symbol of life, to wear on a chain around his neck. He gave one to Eric as well, for Eric was Michael's friend and now Eric was vomiting away his life from the poison of cytidine. The last resort, cytidine. Doctors don't give up easily; they keep trying things as long as there's the slightest chance. In any case, no one could have stood by and simply watched Eric die. He was the long-time survivor of the eighth floor. All the patients were watching his desperate struggle. "If Eric dies, what hope can there be for me?" Michael said to his mother.

In addition to cytidine, the doctors were giving Eric cannabis to try to control the nausea. It was well known among the patients that smoking marijuana often helped you through a bad time. Eric had used it on the outside sometimes, and it had given him some relief. He had also smoked for pleasure now and then—not too often, for he was an athlete at heart and, besides that, he usually was pretty high on everyday life without having to turn on. I know he thought pot far less harmful than alcohol. But swallowing thirty-two cannabis capsules a day—while you're trying not to vomit—turned out to be a major ordeal in itself. Perhaps a few puffs on a joint might have helped. But cannabis capsules didn't help. Nothing helped.

After five weeks the doctors stopped the cytidine. The patient could take no more. He had lost forty pounds. Perhaps they would resume it later, they said. But at the moment Eric needed a rest.

One day when I went into the hospital, I found Eric sitting up in bed for the first time in weeks, wearing his brother's Christmas present—the blue and white satin windbreaker of the Yale University soccer team. The jacket was bulky and hid the fact that he'd lost all that weight. Still, from the collar up, the boy was gone. In his place, a man twenty years older, with hair recently grown back (barely an inch long and almost gray), looked out with hard, steady eyes and the mouth of a skeptic.

He was just sitting there, arms folded, confronting a doctor who seemed to be making a pitch. The bed table was in place over the bed for lunch, but instead of dishes of food there was a small paper cup full of mushy-looking orange liquid in front of Eric.

"I'm sorry if I'm interrupting," I said. "Should I disappear for a minute?"

"No, stay. I want you to hear this," Eric said. Then he said, a bit coldly, "I'd introduce you to my mother, doctor, if I knew your name."

The doctor introduced himself. He looked anxious, a bit flustered. "I've just been telling the boys here about our idea. We've been looking for ways to help them fight infection. Now the hope is that if they could go on this low-bulk diet for two weeks, it would reduce the body's chances of poisoning itself with its own wastes. Somewhat the same idea our astronauts employ in space flights."

"That's *lunch!*" Eric said, indicating the little cup of orange mush.

"How does it taste?" I asked.

"Not bad. Not good. I want a club sandwich. I'm hungry, goddammit, for the first time in five weeks I'm hungry."

The doctor looked sad. He was a good man trying to help, offering straws in a situation where straws were all that could be grasped. "I'm sorry about the taste," he said. "I know how unappealing this must seem to you, Eric, but—"

"Don't apologize, doctor," Eric cut in. "Just give me the facts, and then I'll decide if I want to go on with it."

"Do you have any previous trials?" I asked. "Do you have any idea if it really helps?"

"Well"—the doctor tried to look cheerful—"we think it does. Not too many people will stick with it. We've just had a small sample, but there seemed to be definite improvement. Maybe in fifty percent."

After a few more words, he had to leave. Michael's mother came over. "Are you going to do it, Eric? I think maybe Michael ought to try—"

"I don't know," said Eric. "I'm going to think about it."

About an hour later I got up to leave. I had an appointment with an editor to ride out on the train together and discuss some work I was doing. As I got up, Eric said, "Mom, would you go get me a club sandwich with the whole works? Everything? There's a good deli three blocks down First Avenue."

I hesitated a fraction of a second, calculating the time. There's no way to tell somebody you've planned to meet on a train that you're not going to show.

He saw my thought. "Never mind. You've got something you have to do. That's okay. Never mind."

Now I was determined to get him the club sandwich. The hell with the editor, the hell with everything.

"No," he said. "I'm not going to cop out on this without talking it over with Dr. Dowling. He wanted me to try it. If I don't go through with it, I ought to tell him first."

I feel wretched to this day about the club sandwich Eric never got. As it was, he handled the problem in his usual style. He made badges, big badges five inches across so you could read the lettering on them, for every member of the Summer Camp. He managed to get out of bed and pin one on everybody's pajama top. The Greek and the Korean didn't know what the badges said, but they smiled and went along. When the doctors walked in later that day everybody was sitting up or lying down wearing the "Dr. Monroe Dowling Official Junior Space Cadet" badge on his front. The motto around the badge read, "One small step for obesity, one giant leap for malnutrition." In the center was each man's name. On Eric's it said, "Airman Lund may eat." That was the end of the space diet for him. The end of all his attempts at fun and games, too. After that, it was downhill all the way.

Sidney's business diary for that February reads, day after day:

> Went to hospital.
> Gave double platelets.
> No billable time.

> We all went in.
> Mark gave double platelets.
> No billable time.

> Worked two hrs. power plant booklet.
> Paid bills.
> Hospital later.

> Gave platelets again.
> Tried to work afternoon, but no billable time.

Then there was another afternoon when I went in alone. A strange afternoon: the sky was bright yet it was snowing, big, fluffy, lazy flakes. Eric watched them drifting slowly by his window. His eyes closed now and then. When they opened it seemed to be with enormous effort. Even breathing seemed to tire him. His fingers lay still on the covers.

"Snow was fun," he said at last. And then, as if looking back from a great distance, "I remember making a snowman. . . ."

After a while he said, "Running—that was the best. Just running on a beach for miles and miles."

He's talking in the past tense, I thought. Telling me, without telling me, be strong. He talked of the wild things he'd done with Mark, the wonderful fun they'd had. "You never knew we did that, did you?

"Meredith is the brilliant one," he said suddenly. "And Lisa is going to be so great. . . .

"Mom," he said quietly, "have you talked at all to Lisa? Do you think—she's ready?"

"We've talked. Quite a lot. She's going to be all right, Eric."

"It's MaryLou I'm worried about really," he said. "She should never have gotten mixed up with me."

"No one who gets mixed up with you loses, Eric."

"No." He waved this away. "She's been through a lot. I just wish I could help her. I want to so much. I gave her this book to read."

On Death and Dying by Elisabeth Kübler-Ross. For MaryLou, the expert on death. With love from Eric, I thought. Now that it had come to this, he was not saying take care of me, he was trying to take care of her.

"I gave it a helluva try, you know," he said suddenly. "But there comes a time when you're ready to rest. You say, well, that's the ball game—" Then he smiled a little. "Sure, it's frustrating. There are so many things I'd like to do. But then I might have just spent fifty years punching the time clock down at the boiler factory waiting to get my gold watch. As it is, I've seen so much . . . so much."

He looks happy, I thought, astonished. He slept, then, and I watched him. When he awoke, I thought maybe the light was hurting his eyes. I started to lower the window blind.

"No, no!" He stopped me. "I want all the sky!"

He couldn't move (too many tubes), but he looked at that bright blue square with such love. The snow had stopped and in its place we now had blazing, brilliant sunshine. "The sun," he said. "It was so good—"

The February afternoon grew dark. He grew more tired. After a while he whispered, "Do something for me? Leave a little early. Walk a few blocks and look at the sky. Walk in the world for me. . . ."

I walked through the blue, luminous city night which suddenly had the look of spring. I walked lightly, carefully, cherishing his gift. He is dying—yet he is giving me life. Look at the sky! For all the days you may live, look at the sky and never lose it. It is there. It will always be there, if only you can see.

The world shrank to the few feet on either side of his bed. He saw no one but us. We saw no one but him. Around us were dozens of others. They existed as blurs. He slept through the long afternoons, often with his head in MaryLou's arms. I felt her pain as separate, distinct from my own, and awareness of her coming loss, added to mine, was too much. Sometimes I had to walk away.

There was an afternoon when Mrs. Hardy was pushed in her wheelchair down the hall and into Room 830, up to the bed where Eric lay curled on his side. She had not been out of her own bed for days. Now she'd just been given two transfusions to help her get stronger. She was using that strength to visit Eric.

He opened his eyes and saw her. "Oh, Mrs. Hardy," he whispered. "You're the one person I wanted to see."

She leaned out of her wheelchair to hug him as best she could. He smiled, tried to raise one arm clumsily to hug her back. Her tears fell on him but she was smiling, too. A beautiful woman with a tube dangling from her nose, her neck swollen grotesquely around the hole in her throat where they'd taken out her voice, her eyes being squeezed tighter by swelling every day as the cancer pushed upward and on toward her brain.

("You're the one person I wanted to see. . . . Ewing Eight is both a heaven and a hell.")

This is hell. But heaven is here, too, I thought. This is a holy place. For I have seen love here.

On February 18, Eric's fever soared. The doctors sent for Sidney. He spent the better part of the day hooked up to the white cell separator in Sloan-Kettering Institute across the street. The separator, invented, I am told, by an engineer father who lost his own son, was designed to skim off white cells, as well as platelets, from a suitable donor to help a patient in deep crisis when his own body is failing to produce what is needed. Until this development there had been no way, beyond the use of antibiotics, to help a person with a dangerously low white count fight off massive infection. The separator had been in use for only about a year and a half when Sidney was put on it. It was already credited with saving over a dozen lives, not all from leukemia, of course. The first donor ever to go on the separator had been the father of one of Eric's first friends on the eighth floor. The son, a young man in his thirties, a leukemia victim who had contracted hepatitis from transfusions, had rallied noticeably when he'd been given his father's white cells. But eventually the hepatitis had overpowered him.

Now Sidney lay in that father's place in what looked like a strange dentist's chair. He was surrounded on three sides by gray boxes of machinery, each one like a giant refrigerator on its side, and each equipped with a battery of instrument panels, lights, tubes, buzzers. Overhead a small television set jutting out on an arm from the wall aimed blasts of various laundry detergent commercials and quiz shows at Sidney's head. Since both his arms were strapped down with I.V.s in place, he was helpless to change channels. Looking at this science-fiction setup, I wondered vaguely if the show he was looking at might affect the quality of his blood. What was the chemical effect on the cells of anger, disgust, mild annoyance, or prolonged boredom? Dr. Reich and her attendants went on monitoring the instrument panels and checking the patient from time to time as routinely and casually as gas station attendants might check a car's oil and battery. I learned from them that Sidney's entire blood supply would be circulated through the machine four times. With each circulation, centrifuges would keep on removing white cells and platelets from Sidney's blood and packaging them in the sterile plastic bags that were an integral part of the I.V. withdrawal unit. By the end of the day, Sidney had given 12 units of platelets and 14 units of white cells for Eric—amounts about equivalent to what you could extract from fourteen pints of whole blood.

The next day those cells did their job. Eric's fever fell from 105 to 100.8. The following day it was down to 99.6. Yet anyone could see he was growing weaker.

"Can I rest now?" he whispered to MaryLou. "I'm so tired. Is it all right to rest now?"

CHAPTER 23

SIDNEY AND I made a mistake in judgment then. We kept looking for the massive bruises and the purple dots of petechiae which come all over the skin with platelet failure. We expected Eric to look as he had in the laminar air-flow room the year before. How could this be the end when his skin was still clear? There must be another day or two, another week to go. Each night we went home to Connecticut.

And so it was, after four and a half years' warning, we were all in the wrong places the morning it began to happen.

Mark had sprained his ankle badly the week before. He'd been hobbling around on crutches, but the ankle was still giving him plenty of pain, so on Monday morning, February 21, he decided to make a quick trip back to New Haven by train and get it looked at again in the Yale infirmary.

Our street had been flooded with several feet of tidal water brought in by a northeast storm during the night, and Sidney had rushed his car up on a nearby hill to protect it. On the morning of February 21, he'd made three tries to start it and failed. The ignition was sluggish after all the rain, and the battery was beginning to make ominous sounds from all the attempts and false starts. Nevertheless, he went off to try again.

I'd left my car parked at the studio for safety, gotten a ride up with a friend to get it, and just driven it home again and found the house empty when the phone began to ring. It was Mary-Lou. She was gasping. "Come in as fast as you can—all of you. Eric is very bad. He's septic."

So there was Mark on a train heading for New Haven, Sidney on some hilltop—I didn't know exactly which one—Lisa off somewhere in the neighborhood (it was school vacation), and Meredith and Jim in Illinois.

The next thirty-three hours ran together. There was no morning, no afternoon, no day or night. There was *now.* In days and weeks past I had often stood by Eric's bed, swaying with exhaustion. Now I felt I could stand there forever. Only a few times before in my life had I felt such a concentration of will and energy—when giving birth. Whatever came, I would be ready.

I was dimly conscious of light. Dark. People coming and going.

Michael's girl, a delicate, shy creature, coming up bravely, whispering, "Can I get you some coffee?"

Meredith and Jim in the doorway with suitcases. Looking scared. When I'd called them earlier, Jim had asked, "How bad is it?"

"They've just put a catheter in his heart, Jim. They're keeping track of changes from minute to minute."

"We'll come right away."

Mark finally there, turned around and back from New Haven, in such a hurry he is hobbling on his bad ankle, dragging both crutches along behind him with one hand.

• • •

Sidney never still, walking in and out of the ward, up and down the hall.

MaryLou never moving. She's hardly left Eric for days.

"Mouth hurts—MaryLou."

She sponges it with wet gauze. Repeatedly, gently. All her movements are sure.

He struggles awake, sees me. "Mommy—my mouth. Can you fix it? Fix it for me?"

"I'll try, honey. . . . Would ice help him, MaryLou?"

"Not really. He's so dried out. His kidneys aren't functioning the way they should. What he really needs is another I.V." MaryLou is restless. She knows how to do this with one hand tied behind her. But she is not in charge, has no authority here. There are no orders for another I.V.

Someone else is coming. A big black woman with reddish hair, blue uniform. Handsome strong face. An expression of powerful concern. She comes right up to me, grasps my arm.

"How is he?"

"Not good. Look for yourself."

"Ah, God, it makes me mad. So many of 'em out running around the streets, tearing things up, gettin' into trouble—and here *he* is! Such a good kid."

Who is she? I wonder. Doesn't matter. Eric's friend.

"We had some good times," she goes on, sighing, then smiling. "You know what he said to me once? He patted me on the head—

he was so tall, you know—and he said, 'Mildred, us redheads have got to stick together!"'

Now they want Mark for the white cell separator. He goes across the street.

Darker now.

MaryLou still there by the bed. I've been watching everything she does.

"You have to go home, MaryLou. It's just a few blocks—"

"No."

"You've been here for three days. I know what to do. I've been watching. Just go for two hours? Sleep—please, sleep."

"Well—but call me right away if—"

"Of course. I promise."

Now I moisten the gauze, wet the lips, help him move. No position is right.

MaryLou is back five minutes early.

"Did you eat?"

"I can't—"

Mark is laid out, hooked up to the separator. He has as many tubes in him as Eric. There will be more hours of this. He can't move, mustn't move. His eyes are wide.

Going back, I see Mildred in the hall. (Someone has told me she works in the chemotherapy lab.) Again she comes up, takes my arm.

"I know what this day is to you. Twenty-three years I've been on this floor. And I lost my daughter to cancer, too. Right here on this floor. Ten years ago. She was seventeen. It's like yesterday to me." She looks at me with deep, sad eyes. "I know, I know," she says.

In this minute we are sisters, sharing more than many sisters can in a lifetime. I'm awed by the strength of this marvelous woman.

"I'm glad there are some who can stay. Like you," I say to her at last. "It can't be easy on this floor. But Eric needed you. And so do all the others. I'm just glad you can stay."

Sidney has found something to do. He waits by Mark, then runs across the street with the precious cells as fast as they come off the separator. (Gift from brother to brother.)

It is not enough.

Oxygen. Eric fights off the mask. He wants to breathe for himself, the way he always has. This thing over his face is in the way. "No!" he gasps.

They are going to move him. An orderly comes to push the bed. And suddenly here is a man with a pile of newspapers. Short, dark, heavy-browed. It has to be Bruno. I recognize him right away from "The Adventures of Ewing 8." Eric always drew Bruno as a grizzled Romeo who ran panting after pretty nurses.

"How is he?"

Bruno's face is full of worry. He is not a hospital aide, but just the same he puts down his pile of papers and takes hold of the other end of the bed to help push it.

"Watch it! Careful—" he growls as if he were in charge. "Don't bump him."

Eric is leaving the Summer Camp, but he cannot wake to say good-bye. Michael's eyes are frightened as the bed rolls past his own. His dark-haired girl leans across him, holding him, helping him not to look.

Down the hall. . . .

Dr. Dowling came up to us. "I'd like to talk to all of you—in here." A small lab across the hall from the single room where they're putting Eric.

Seeing Dr. Dowling standing there, calm as always, in charge of destiny as always, we snapped out of our various trances and began to focus.

"We have a decision to make," he said, "and I want to know how each of you feels about it. Eric has kidney failure. He will die very soon if we don't do something right away. We're considering a peritoneal dialysis."

He explained the procedure—installing tubes in the abdomen to carry off wastes which the kidneys no longer could handle. It wasn't a kidney machine. They weren't usually successful in cases like this, he told us. But the dialysis would help the patient somewhat in the same way as the machine. He wanted to know if we were in favor of the operation.

"I don't want you to worry about influencing the decision. Whatever you say, I will have to make that on my own."

There must have been other doctors involved, I thought. But it was Dr. Dowling who'd loved Eric, who'd fought to save him, who was losing him now, who stood there.

Jimmy was the first to speak. He was sure Eric would never want to give up. Eric was a fighter all the way. We must play the hand out and have the operation.

I spoke next. "I want to know how MaryLou feels."

316

"Let him go," MaryLou said softly.

Then I saw Dr. Burchenal, Eric's first and oldest friend at Memorial, standing in the doorway.

"If you bring Eric back, what do you have for him?" I asked Dr. Burchenal.

"Well," said Dr. Burchenal. "We have VP-Sixteen. It's quite effective with mice, and we've also had some interesting results with several humans—"

I heard MaryLou say "Jesus!" under her breath. We had already proved many times that Eric was not a mouse. And "interesting results," if they involved one more day of nausea, were not enough. Eric had come to the end of his will. I had seen the look on his face a few days ago when he whispered, "Is it all right to rest now?" His body was broken. His spirit was not; it was simply, finally, at peace.

"—after all, he's fooled us so many times before," Dr. Burchenal was saying.

I said, "A year ago when Eric was in the laminar air-flow room, I saw how he was suffering and I didn't want him to live then. I just didn't see the point. But I was wrong. He came back and he had a good life. He had a good love, too, which he'd never had before."

MaryLou began to cry quietly.

"It was a tremendous thing," I went on. "It gave all that struggle a meaning, it fulfilled him. And I don't think he would have made it last summer if MaryLou hadn't fought for his life and pulled him through. But now—even though nobody wants to play God, I think we've come to the end. Eric wants to rest. He's ready. I say let him go, too."

"He's got to have the operation! If he doesn't—"

I turned around, startled. Meredith's eyes looked into mine. She was the sister who'd patted new baby Eric lying in his bassinet. She was the four-year-old who'd buckled a holster onto two-year-old Eric so they could be cowboys together. She wasn't ready. How could she be?

"Please—" said Dr. Dowling. "I've told you I'd make the decision. But I do want to hear what each of you has to say."

Then Sidney said, "I think we should recognize that we all feel differently. I feel differently from the way Doris feels. I don't know what the medical chances are, but I think we should keep trying."

The doctors left the room. Soon after that MaryLou went out for a few minutes. When she came back, she said, "They're going to do the operation."

"Dear God, no!" So they might keep him "alive" for days, maybe weeks, with their machinery, their oxygen tanks, and all the rest of it? My anger was for no one, not the doctors, not those who had spoken for the operation, but it was there, blazing helplessly.

"Someone should tell Mark." Mark was still staked down like a captive on the white cell separator.

"I'm going over to see him right now." Sidney got up. "Maybe they've got more cells for Eric by now."

The rest of us just stayed there crowded in the little lab room. It was as close as we could get to Eric.

The operation was under way. People coming and going in the room across the hall. Doctors. Nurses. Technicians with more oxygen tanks. A nurse with a tray on wheels. Instruments, jars, tubes.

I sat on the black Formica countertop leaning against tall cupboards. Suddenly I was back in the pantry of my old house in Bronxville where I lived as a little girl. My mother used to put me up on the counter so she could put on my rubbers. How could I ever have been a little girl in small brown rubbers scuffing through brown, wet leaves, pushing my doll—he was a boy doll—in a wicker doll carriage around the yard?

MaryLou sat on a low stool, leaning her head against a cupboard door. Judy, her roommate, stood behind her, rhythmically patting her shoulder. Susan, Eric's friend and fairy godmother, had left her desk to come and be with us, too. She sat on a high stool so she could watch what went on across the hall. Another doctor went into Eric's room. Another nurse.

"If anybody else goes in there, somebody will have to go out the window," said Susan. "It's like that act in the circus where dozens of clowns keep climbing out of a broken-down car."

"It *is* a circus act," I said.

MaryLou sat up, alert. "Are there any head and neck men going in there?"

"No head and neck men," Susan said.

"What do you mean head and neck men?"

"The little men with paddles and knives. If the patient arrests—cardiac arrest, I mean—then a Code Alert goes out. All the interns come running to pound on his chest to get his heart started again. They beat him with paddles. Or they do a tracheostomy and cut a hole in his throat for a tube so he can breathe better," said Mary Lou.

"I don't want that," I said violently.

"I don't either."

"Let's stand in the doorway and stop it. Do we have to have it?"

"No Code," said Susan. "We'll fight them off. We'll all stand in the doorway."

"Let him die with dignity," MaryLou said softly. "I promised him it would be peaceful."

She used my own words. This had been my own hope. I felt very close to her at that moment.

Mark was there all at once in his huge, dirty winter jacket. The woolly hat on the back of his curls brushed the top of the doorframe. His blue and white muffler trailed from one arm. With the other he was still dragging his crutches. I got up to give him room. He hobbled in and immediately lay down flat on the countertop and put his feet in the sink.

"How's Eric?"

"Not good. They're doing the operation."

"I know. Dad told me."

"How are *you?*"

"Okay. Tired."

I looked at his feet in the thick, muddy work boots he'd bought last summer when he landed a job in the icehouse. Somebody ought to tell him to get his feet out of that sink. That's the sink where they mix things to save people. The hell with it. Let his feet stay there.

"Do you want an open casket, Doris?" MaryLou is looking right at me, her blue eyes wide open.

"God, no!"

She sighed with relief. "That's good. I was so afraid you might. I couldn't stand it."

I saw Sidney in the hall and went out. He looked gray, shaken.

"I just talked to Dr. Clarkson over in Sloan-Kettering. I was waiting to bring Mark's last cells back here. Dr. Clarkson said, 'Well, it looks as if we've come to the end of the line.' I said to him, 'Oh, no!' . . . How is Eric, anyway?" Sidney asked me.

"No change. They're still in there busy with him."

• • •

Eric survived the operation. We took turns going in to see him. But there was no change. He lay unconscious on his side, breathing oxygen in short, deep gasps. They had run out of obvious places to put tubes in him long ago. Now they were putting tubes in his feet. Blood and drugs and the clear fluid of I.V. solution and the cells from Mark's body were all still pouring into Eric. Our love was still pouring into him, too. It was not enough. He was slipping away. His shoulder was growing cold to my touch.

By nightfall we were all half mad. My winter boots felt like buckets of concrete. I'll burn all the clothes I'm wearing if I ever get the chance, I thought.

"Take me out of here," I said suddenly to Sidney. "Buy me a drink and a terrible hamburger." The plywood slab of hamburger eaten on a cotton bun, standard menu of the soon-to-be bereaved. The neighborhood around Memorial swarms with quick-eat spots, dark, noisy bars, and keen-eyed traffic police. Business in whiskey and traffic tickets is always brisk. Anxious relatives can be counted on to drink well and park carelessly.

We checked the car parked on a nearby side street. Still okay. No ticket. Sidney started to guide me into a place we'd been to several times before. "Not there. Not tonight," I said. "That loud music will hurt." So we bent into the February wind up one block, then another, till we found a refuge with a yellow awning which garishly shouted its name—The Recovery Room.

Forty minutes later I was in a panic to get back. Why had we stayed so long? For over four years I'd sworn to *be there* when it happened.

Sidney tried to comfort me. "You've been there," he said. "You've been there a thousand times. Missing the exact moment won't—"

"Don't talk!" I groaned. "It doesn't help." The drink, the hamburger weighed heavy as stones as we half stumbled, half raced along First Avenue. I thought miserably of MaryLou, who hadn't been able to eat all week. "Oh!"

A brightly lit delicatessen caught my eye. "Let's take MaryLou some ice cream. Get chocolate—that's her favorite. But hurry!"

I danced around on the sidewalk, unable to be still, while Sidney went in and quickly came out with a small brown bag. Then we ran across the street, through the heavy double doors of Memorial, through the busy lobby of the elevator that was just closing, that was just able to hold two more. We went up. The eighth floor was quiet. Something had changed. At the end of the corridor our little band sat quietly outside Eric's door on folding chairs. They were very still.

When she saw us, MaryLou jumped up and ran toward us. "Dr. Dowling says Eric will die soon."

She was almost sparkling. Was it because her mission was almost accomplished? Because the one she'd cared for so tenderly was almost safe from harm at last?

"I'm sorry," I said stupidly, "but I brought you some ice cream—" Ice cream, the stuff of birthdays and celebrations! It suddenly seemed monstrous. How could I have done such a thing?

"Oh, ice cream! I love ice cream. What flavor?" MaryLou grabbed the bag happily.

"Chocolate."

"My favorite!" MaryLou already had the top off the container and she began to eat greedily with the little wooden spoon.

CHAPTER 24

I WENT IN to see him alone. There was a hush in the room. A nurse and an intern were quietly checking dials, needles, charts. But I saw only the figure on the bed. I had been frightened at the thought of watching Eric die. The actual moment when he would cease to exist. Wouldn't it be more than I could bear? Wouldn't my heart stop, too? Yet here, close to the end, there was no fear.

In the hour of his death, I searched Eric's face with wonder and awe, much as I'd searched it the day he was born. A son! From darkness he had come, the mystery of who he was still hidden behind the small brow, the closed eyes. Into darkness he was going (not fighting off the oxygen mask any longer . . . going . . . accepting), eyes closed once again, taking with him still too much of the mystery of who he was, yet leaving me unbelievably rich.

Pain waited for me when this hour was over. I had no time for it now. All the life force in my body was focused on knowing what little there was left to know. No tears, for I wanted to see. No faintness, for I wanted to be *there* in case he came back once more from the blackness. Only sixteen or so hours ago—was it afternoon, was it morning?—he'd opened his eyes for a moment, after hours of unconsciousness, and struggled to speak through broken lips.

"Come closer. Mom? Come closer—

"Have to get to Westport," he gasped. "Can't find the way. Please, Mom—help me? Westport?"

"You'll get there," I whispered back, not knowing what he meant, thinking he was delirious but wanting to comfort him. "You'll find the way, Eric. I know you will."

He hadn't roused again. And it was half an hour since Dr. Dowling had said he was dying. I took his hand. The cool, translucent fingers lay very still in mine, not responding, not curling in the fierce life grip of the baby. Strange, strange, I never thought you'd grow old before I did, Eric, that you'd die while I held your hand—

MaryLou darted in at that moment and came up to me. Urgently she whispered, "Talk to him! I just remembered, hearing is the last sense to go. Say something to him quickly." She left us.

Now! Now it must happen. I put my hand on his shoulder and bent close to the pale curved ear, the delicate microphone waiting for its last message. What could I tell him for the journey?

"I love you," I said. "I'm here with you, Eric, and you're almost there."

Suddenly I thought I understood. Westport! Scene of hard-won victories on the playing field, where he and his soccer companions became county champions long ago. There was one more game to be played, and he wanted to play it well. Death is an act to be well performed. It seemed to me he was out on the field again, lone player running through the darkness, trying to head off the enemy, trying to score just one more time before he went down forever.

"You're beautiful, Eric. You were beautiful all the way. You did it just right. You're almost there. I love you!"

• • •

He died in MaryLou's arms a few minutes later. Her head was on the pillow next to his. It was a good and gentle death, the death she'd promised him with peace and dignity. Her last great gift.

Most of us had spoken to him by then, given him our messages for the journey. The words were not remarkable in any way.

"I told him, 'You're a good brother,'" said Mark.

"I told him, 'Eric, it's good to be with you. I love you,'" said his father.

Love is the only message, after all.

We stood together in the doorway just outside his room to stop them if they tried to have a Code Alert.

A nurse came out and started to run.

"No Code," we said.

She stopped, surprised. No paddles for the heart, no holes or tubes for the throat, no machinery for the lungs?

"But—" she said.

Sidney looked at her hard. "No Code," he said again.

Afterward. I'd forgotten there would be an "afterward." We stood in the hallway, crying, hugging, once in a while laughing. We had suddenly lost our balance. The center of our world, on which we'd all been focused for so long, had suddenly been taken away. We were swaying dizzily around the edges, holding on to each other, feeling tears on each other's cheeks, not knowing yet how to let go.

I held MaryLou and said, "You've lost your lover and your best friend. But you haven't lost us as a family. We'll be yours as long as you need us and want us."

Then I remembered Mrs. Hardy. Let her not hear it from anyone but me. I walked quickly down the hall to her ward. She was sitting by her bed, little frail bird of a woman with sandpiper legs, a foolish ruffled shower cap covering her bald head, reading *McCall's* magazine. I saw the headline: Fashions for Spring.

She looked up as I came nearer, and her eyes were frightened.

"I'm sorry I have to tell you this. Eric lost his fight."

She cried, then, and I was afraid she might drown because she didn't have a whole face left to cry with. I put my arms around her and kissed her cheek; it was burning. She pulled away, signaling me to wait while she found her pad and began to write feverishly. Her handwriting was getting harder and harder to read. But I made out, "God bless you and give you peace. You were a wonderful mother."

We hugged once more. "I'll try to come and see you," I said. "I really will."

There were others to tell, others to comfort. I remembered what Eric had told me about the night Abby died. "Her husband tried to comfort *us*—he didn't want us to give up or be afraid because Abby died."

I remembered, and now I understood. I tried to think of what to say to the ones I knew.

There was the autopsy form. "Sign here, please." There was the Eye Bank form. "Sign here—below." Eric had already signed it himself. And there were two brown shopping bags with the possessions of Eric Lund. The nurse who handed them to us said,

"We're sorry it turned out this way." Then she turned to me. "Do you want a tranquilizer?"

"No, thank you." I know all the stops from Librium to Miltown, from the hills of Dexamil to the Valium of tranquillity, and there isn't a pill in the world that can put things right now. I'll take my pain straight, undulled, and with it the glory of knowing how much he was, the sense of his strength shoring up my life. Even though all seems to be lost, much will be found again. I want it all—as Eric wanted it all. I can wait. And trust. Life will begin again.

"Let's go home," I said.

Lisa had lived out the hours in the home of one of our oldest friends. It was a beautiful house. From nearly every window you can look out on a great pond, willows bending down, swans sailing grandly beyond the yellow marsh grass. Lisa told me later she walked from room to room that day looking at the calm, gray winter world outside, the serene, rich world inside—paintings, watercolors, etchings, jade figures, porcelain, crystal. Why is nothing shattering? Why am I not crying?

Around three in the afternoon she began to write. "Oh, I am shaking. Today is the day Eric dies. . . ." She wrote a sort of poem as she sat there in the peaceful library looking at the pond, a fourteen-year-old girl struggling with mortality. She wrote, ". . . yet I will endure."

It was ten o'clock that night before she heard our car in the driveway. We hadn't called. I'd wanted to be there when she learned about it. Nothing had to be said. She saw us. She ran to my arms in a burst of tears.

It was close to midnight when she found herself in her own room again after a vigil of thirty-three hours. She went to her desk and sat down. She unfolded the paper on which she'd written her poem. At the bottom of the page she wrote in very small letters, "He is dead."

In our room, lying in the dark, Sidney kept saying, "I never thought Eric would die. I never thought Eric would die."

Dr. Dowling called me the next morning. "What are you going to do about disposing of Eric's body?"

"Can we give him to a medical school—or something like that?"

"It's not easy," said Dr. Dowling thoughtfully. "*We* can't take him because we'd be accused of body-snatching. I think maybe I can help you, though. Let me give you the name of a doctor across the street at Cornell. Tell him I said to call."

"First, tell me how *you* feel about it," I said, knowing how much Dr. Dowling had cared about Eric.

His answer was quick. "The bodies you get in medical school are pretty bad. I'd have been honored to work on a beautiful body like Eric's."

All right. Let's go. Sidney had been listening. He agreed.

The next morning I sat up in bed next to the telephone and tried to give away my son's body. I looked first for signs of revulsion or horror in myself. There were none. He had given himself to science long ago, that part of him that was becoming less and less important. As his athlete's body finally failed, Eric—the essential Eric—had retreated to his skull. His eyes held all his life those last few days. His face had a purity and stark beauty that constantly reminded me of someone else. But who?

Later, when I went to Spain and saw Goya's etchings, and the face of El Greco's Christ on the cross, I saw the Eric of those last days. Still later, among photographs of the survivors of the Andes air crash who had cannibalized to survive, I saw—in the face of a young, near-starved youth—again, Eric. When we are reduced to the last essence of what is valuable in man, do we become more and more alike, as the newborn are alike? In the hospital where Eric was born, a nurse had brought out a tiny infant to demonstrate "The Bath" to a class of new mothers. "Whose baby is this?" she asked, before unwrapping it and putting it in the soapy little tub. There were about eleven of us sitting around in our wrappers or flannel bathrobes. Six hands went up! Mine almost did. I am ashamed and amused about that moment to this day. The baby was a girl! Now I think that the very old or the dying may be like the very new—less personalized, less stylish and defined. They are vessels that hold the deeply common experience.

It is not easy to give away a body. I called the number Dr. Dowling had given me. Four times. The doctor's secretary seemed embarrassed. Finally I was put through to the doctor himself. He was cautiously grateful. But the problems seemed to be legion. Forms. Red tape. And we would have to hire a hearse to take the body over to Cornell.

"But it's just across the street!"

•　•　•

I have since heard of other instances where people were successful in donating a body to scientific research in some hospitals in
New York. But at that time and that place there seemed to be no
legal way to transport a body several hundred yards across York
Avenue between 68th and 69th streets. I was too tired to go into
all the reasons why, but I did protest. "I thought all you medical
schools needed bodies." (I'd just read an article in the *New York
Times* the week before entitled "The Grave Shortage of Bodies.")

"That's true," said the doctor seriously. "But of course we can't
look too interested. In any case, you'd have to claim the body
again after we'd used it and have a funeral home furnish a casket
and—"

"Casket!" Ye gods! What for? For what would be left of Eric
then? Odds and ends. What was left of Eric now but the beauty of
his spirit, the memory of his laugh, his wicked humor, his open-
eyed honesty? You can't tell me I have to put up with this. I thanked
the man for talking to me and said we'd have to think of something
else.

I decided to talk to Susan, who usually knows about things.
"You know," I said, "we've shot our savings these past few years.
Mark's going to have to drop out of Yale next year to earn money,
and he already owes them three thousand dollars for loans. And
Lisa needs a new piano. She's been trying to play Bach and Chopin
on that barroom upright in the basement that has half the keys
sticking. Now they tell me we've got to have a casket and the works
for Eric. Even with cremation. What's it going to cost?"

"No way you can get out for less than a thousand dollars,
Doris," Susan said.

So for a thousand dollars I could buy a casket to get Eric taken
to the crematorium; then eventually Eric's ashes would be deliv-

ered to my doorstep in a small wooden box with "Eric Lund" on the cover. "Sign here, please," the messenger would say. What if I wasn't home? What if Lisa answered the door?

I called Dr. Dowling. "I'm not getting very far." I explained the difficulties. "So it looks like no matter what we do, we've got to buy Eric a revolting, candy-box casket. Eric would absolutely hate that. It's phony, it's useless, it's wasteful!"

"You can let the city claim the body."

"Then what?"

"He goes to potter's field."

Suddenly it sounded beautiful. Potter's field! Where the poor, lost, bottom-of-the-ladder people go. Eric belonged with them. He would have cared for them if he had lived. He was no rich kid from the suburbs. He belonged to the city where he'd loved MaryLou, where they'd ridden their bicycles, walked the avenues holding hands—where he'd loved so many other people, too.

When we were all together I asked each member of the family what they thought of letting the city claim Eric's body, of sending him to potter's field, with love?

MaryLou said, "As long as I can go, too, what do I care?"

Susan thought Eric would have loved the joke of outwitting the system.

Sidney, struggling with tears, laughed and said, "Well, the human body is about ninety-seven percent water and twenty cents' worth of other ingredients—even with inflation. So why not?"

Meredith and Jim thought it was a good, practical idea.

Mark said, "I'll go along. I'll go to potter's field, too—only I'm not ready just yet."

"But how do you feel, Mommy?" Lisa asked.

"Oh, I guess the only thing I really would have wanted is a

funeral pyre with beautiful flames soaring seventy-five feet in the air. And maybe a parade with lots of music and flags and everybody in town, especially the little boys he played with—and maybe *Aida's* elephants and all the animals from Noah's Ark, too—marching down the main street right to Eric's bonfire."

"Pollution, Mommy!" said Lisa, my child of the seventies. "Bonfires make too much smoke. No. This is better. Give Eric back to the earth. We should send him to potter's field. Then he'll be recycled."

So it was settled. Eric went to potter's field. We're all going to potter's field, if we can manage it. It's the family plot. And now when somebody asks me where Eric is buried, I just say, "In the family plot."

There was a memorial service in the church by the river. It's the same church where Eric had started out to be head counselor in the boys' camp the summer before he died. Each of us wrote something for Eric, and the minister, who was Eric's friend, read our words. The pews were nearly full, and there were many small boys among the soccer teammates, college boys and girls, old family friends and relatives.

Afterward a great many people came back to the house. Then it was over. Hard to believe, but it was really over.

I've been in to the Donor Room several times. The last time was about a year and a half after Eric died. The place was unusually quiet, but then it was a very hot day and lots of people go away in August. Jeanne was off on vacation. But Margaret was there at the desk.

"Hullo!" she cried and jumped up to greet me. "What a coincidence! You know, I was just thinking about you yesterday."

"Really? What were you thinking?"

"Well, we've got this lovely boy in here now. Peter. He's just eighteen. Somehow he makes me think of Eric. He's got a younger brother, too, just two years younger like your Mark. So I was thinking about all of you. How *is* Mark, by the way?"

"He's coming along. He's going to be fine. It was very hard for a while. I think maybe it was harder on him than anybody. But he's making it. He dropped out for a year, you know, and he's been trying to save money from different jobs. And jobs weren't all that easy to find this year. But he's going back to Yale this fall."

"Oh, I'm so glad!"

Sidney came in then. As usual, he'd been trying to park.

"Here's my sacrificial lamb—Sidney," I said. "I brought him as an offering. Since I can't give blood, he's going to give double platelets for both of us." Sidney enjoys the Donor Room; it hadn't taken any persuading.

"Terrific!" said Margaret. "We can use them."

I visited a few more minutes, then went out to walk around the neighborhood. Double platelets takes something over an hour. All these hamburger joints, all these bars—how well I know them! Sometimes I drank to celebrate; he was better! Sometimes to dull pain. But always I'd been afraid of what was to come.

I couldn't imagine a world without Eric. I saw endless howling blackness whenever I tried, a world without sun or leaves or a single sound of joy. In my grief, imagining him gone, I was too centered on his actual physical person. I forgot that the things he gave me, gave all of us, would never be lost.

His irreverent humor; I can still see his skeptical eye cocked at the pompous and overserious. His ability to look at hard truth without blinking. His sense of time, which has rubbed off on all of us. He saw the marvelous opportunities in *minutes*. One whole good day was a feast. To begin with, there was always the sky. Sometimes I feel as if Eric had made me a personal present of the sky. He was always looking up, noticing the patterns of branches or boat masts or maybe some wild birds coming in to our marshes. He drew them, spoke of them.

When he wasn't looking up, he was looking straight out at those amazing creatures—Man and Woman. He drew them, too, and his cartoons were funny, sharp, perceptive, but not cruel. He saw the people struggling to be born in children, and he treated even the littlest ones with respect. Playing their games, he was like a little kid himself, yet he was always building them and teaching them, without being heavy.

In spite of the fact that much of his youth had been spent fighting to live, the world was beautiful with possibility for Eric. And now I find it is more so for me. Eric's death is not the end of joy. It's somehow a chance for another start. I hear his favorite Chicago record still playing, "The Beginning." . . .

When I got back, the needle was out and Sidney's coffee cup was empty. He was lying there with his punctured arm held up, while he pressed some gauze against the tiny wound with his free hand.

Margaret came over. "I'm putting your donation down for Peter, the boy I told you about," she said. "He's been needing lots of platelets."

She pulled out a roll of stretch adhesive tape and Sidney slipped his fingers away just as she wound the tape over the gauze and around his arm several times. "All right. Now you be sure to come back and see us. Good-bye, love!" she said to both of us.

We opened the door and went out.

"C'mon, love! C'mon!" I could hear the nurses calling to Eric once again back in the laminar air-flow room.

We walked down First Avenue. Eric no longer needed platelets or anything else from us. Yet our need to be needed, and part of it all, went on. Soon Sidney's blood would be flowing into Peter's veins, perhaps stopping a hemorrhage, perhaps making it possible for him to walk in the world again. And the day would surely come when Peter—or someone—was going to walk out of there cured, and not have to go back. We might not be around to see it. But we were connected just the same. And Eric would be part of that victory.

AFTERWORD

1989

IT HAS BEEN more than twenty years since the September day in 1967 when we learned that Eric had leukemia. Many things have changed on the medical front. The Memorial Hospital we knew has disappeared. In its place, on the same block of York Avenue between 67th and 68th streets in Manhattan, a gleaming new hospital was built slowly around the shell of the old. Inside this new Memorial the battle against leukemia continues, with an important difference. Today you are very likely to hear doctors using the word *cure*. Yes, cure! From 50 to 60 percent of today's young patients with acute lymphocytic leukemia (ALL) can look foward to being completely free of the disease if they are diagnosed in time and receive appropriate vigorous treatment.

My first hint that things might be improving for leukemia patients came in 1976, four years after Eric died. One winter afternoon I stopped by Memorial for a visit with Eric's old friend Dr. Monroe Dowling. "Why don't you writers ever talk about somebody who makes it?" he challenged me. "Give us some good news for a change."

"I'd love to," I told him. "Have you got good news?"

He handed me a snapshot of a happy family; proud father,

beautiful baby girl, radiant young mother. I stared at it puzzled. Suddenly something clicked. "The boy next door to Eric!" I cried. "Scott Helt! You mean he's alive? And that's his baby?"

Dr. Dowling beamed. "It sure is. That was taken four years ago. Scott and Pat have a second baby now—a little boy."

I remembered the desperately sick young man who'd arrived from Nebraska to begin his fight just as Eric was losing his own battle at twenty-two. Scott's mother had told me her son was twenty-three and that he had myelocytic leukemia, an adult form of the disease which often killed within weeks. My heart had gone out to her and to the pretty young wife who was carrying a baby that Scott might never live to see. Yet here they were all these years later! This was more than good news. This had to be a miracle, one of those spontaneous cures one hears of now and then.

Not so, Dr. Dowling told me. The timing of Scott Helt's arrival at Memorial couldn't have been better. After months of success treating patients with increasingly heavy doses of anti-leukemic drugs in various combinations, the hospital had just made a decision to step up the doses still further. It was risky, but there was good reason to believe the gamble would pay off. Scott was one of the first three patients to receive this intensive chemotherapy. I decided right away that I had to write his story. I began gathering the facts, and by the time I finished my article, "The Survival of Scott Helt" for *Good Housekeeping* (February 1977), I was able to include even more good news. Memorial had 25 patients who had been off all drugs for periods of one, two, and even three years. As Memorial's foremost leukemia expert, Dr. Joseph Burchenal told me at the time, "We aren't using the word *cure* yet but we think it's very possible that we are now in the first wave of a major breakthrough."

Now, twelve years after I wrote about the survival of Scott Helt, that first wave has become a rising tide. The cure rate for young patients in 1989 is currently an impressive 50 to 60 percent. When I first heard those figures I thought, "They must have some real wonder drugs at last. Maybe there's more exciting news here I can write about."

Most of my old friends at Memorial had retired or moved on. Dr. Dowling, after visiting Scott Helt and his remarkable family in Nebraska, had been inspired to move there and resume his practice in a Lincoln hospital. I decided to call Dr. Victor Grann, the local oncologist who had confirmed Eric's first diagnosis. Victor had been Eric's sailing partner and friend, as well as his doctor, and he was happy to talk to me. I was astonished when he told me that many of the drugs most commonly used today are the very same drugs that were tried on Eric. He rattled off some of the old familiar names—Methotrexate, Asparaginase, Vincristine, and others, as well as Prednisone. At first I couldn't believe it. "But how can doctors cure all these kids today when they couldn't before?" I asked him. There was a pause. "That's a good question," Victor said. "Let me pull some of the latest material from the files for you."

We talked three or four more times after I'd studied the files. Now I think I have the answer.

While many of the drugs that were used in the 1960s still play an important part in today's chemotherapy, doctors know a great deal more about how to use them effectively. "We are able to use much higher concentrations of the drugs," Victor told me. "We also use them in combination with new drugs such as VP 16. Then we have drugs like Norvantrone which is a first cousin to Adriamycin—one of the drugs Eric had—but is much less toxic."

"Eric, and the young patients of his generation, made a tremendous contribution," Victor assured me. "We were able to tap them for all sorts of information, study our successes or failures, and make careful judgments about what to try next time." I began to understand that today's breakthrough was not sudden. You couldn't point to a magic bottle and say, "That's it!" You might, however, point to a computer.

The most decisive weapon currently being used in today's fight against leukemia has to be the Physician's Data Query computer in the National Cancer Institute in Washington, D.C. With a simple touch of a button, oncologists all over the country can now reach PDQ and get the latest information on how to treat any child with any type of leukemia. When you're dealing with a disease where days or weeks may spell the difference between life and death, this service gives today's young patients an enormous edge.

Even so, I found it difficult to understand how children could survive the side effects produced by some of the drugs—rampant infections, hemorrhages, severe nausea. "We can control all these things much more successfully today," Victor told me. "We have better antibiotics, better platelet typing, we can reduce nausea." There are other important new procedures which help save today's patients, including routine radiation of the head and spinal column and bone marrow transplants. If no suitable bone marrow donor can be found, doctors may use the powerful new drug, Amsa, to induce high-level remission.

But whether a leukemic child is one of the lucky survivors or among the 40 percent who will lose the battle, the family still faces years of treatment and uncertainty. As we groped our way in that dark first year following Eric's diagnosis in 1967, I often felt as if our whole family had been stricken not only with cancer but with leprosy. Neither my family nor my husband's family was able to talk about it. Many of our friends were uncomfortable. Some wanted to pretend nothing had happened. We felt terribly alone, and I had no idea where to turn for help.

It would be the mid-1970s before the Candlelighters Childhood Cancer Foundation was born.* Beginning as a small gathering of parents who met in the basement of a Washington, D.C. hospital to share their problems, the Candlelighters now have more than three hundred groups in the United States and in fifty-nine countries around the world. Their two newsletters reach more than forty thousand people, and their meetings regularly schedule doctors, nutritionists, family counselors, and other experts to discuss every aspect of childhood cancer. But perhaps the most valuable gift the Candlelighters offer to frightened parents is reassurance of a different sort. Many are astonished to arrive at their first meeting and see people laughing together—laughing!—as they make plans for a Candlelighter pot-luck supper or summer picnic for all their children, both sick and well. The message is clear. Family life goes on. It's all right for us to relax and be happy when we can. In fact, we must if we are to survive.

My own introduction to the Candlelighters came years after our patient was gone. Following the publication of *Eric,* I was asked to speak at a Candlelighter gathering in Connecticut. At the end of the meeting I found myself lingering, talking to other parents as if they were old friends. Many were glowing with hope; their children had been on chemotherapy for two or three years and never lost their first remissions. There were others for

*For information on Candlelighters groups in your area, write Candlelighters Childhood Cancer Foundation, Suite 1001, 1901 Pennsylvania Avenue, N.W., Washington, D.C. 20006

whom the battle was not going well. There were one or two like myself who had lost a child. But despite the differences in our situations, we were drawn together, there was much we wanted to share. This surprised me. While I was driving home I suddenly realized I'd been secretly afraid some of the parents might shun me as one who had lost. And hidden under that fear was another, deeper and uglier, fear. Wouldn't I be jealous of them? As long as their children were still alive, they still had a chance to win! I thought I'd achieved peace when I finished the last chapter of *Eric.* The last word I'd written was "victory." Was I mistaken?

It was the Candlelighters who finally helped me understand there is no timetable for grief and there's nothing wrong with a family that remembers, cares, and cries, even years after the death of a child. But we do get stronger as we go along. And when you are strong you want to light a candle to help the next person along the way. This afterword is my candle for those who come after.

Doris Lund
January 6, 1989